Green Syndicalism

Space, Place, and Society
John Rennie Short, *Series Editor*

OTHER TITLES IN SPACE, PLACE, AND SOCIETY

Alabaster Cities: Urban U.S. since 1950
JOHN RENNIE SHORT

At Home: An Anthropology of Domestic Space
IRENE CIERAAD, ed.

*Frontiers of Femininity: A New Historical Geography
of the Nineteenth-Century American West*
KAREN M. MORIN

*Globalizing City: The Urban and Economic
Transformation of Accra, Ghana*
RICHARD GRANT

Imagined Country: Environment, Culture, and Society
JOHN RENNIE SHORT

Inventing Black-on-Black Violence: Discourse, Space, and Representation
DAVID WILSON

Migrants to the Metropolis: The Rise of Immigrant Gateway Cities
MARIE PRICE and LISA BENTON-SHORT, eds.

Riverscapes and National Identities
TRICIA CUSACK

Tel Aviv: Mythography of a City
MAOZ AZARYAHU

Women, Religion, and Space: Global Perspectives on Gender and Faith
KAREN M. MORIN and JEANNE KAY GUELKE, eds.

Green Syndicalism

An Alternative Red/Green Vision

Jeff Shantz

SYRACUSE UNIVERSITY PRESS

∞ The paper used in this publication meets the minimum requirements
of the American National Standard for Information Sciences—Permanence
of Paper for Printed Library Materials, ANSI Z39.48-1992.

For a listing of books published and distributed by Syracuse University Press,
visit our Web site at SyracuseUniversityPress.syr.edu.

ISBN: 978-0-8156-3307-5

Library of Congress Cataloging-in-Publication Data
Shantz, Jeff.
Green syndicalism : an alternative red/green vision / Jeff Shantz.
p. cm.
Includes bibliographical references and index.
ISBN 978-0-8156-3307-5 (cloth : alk. paper) 1. Ecology—Political aspects.
2. Radicalism.   3. Green movement—Citizen participation.   I. Title.
QH540.5.S53 2012
304.2—dc23   2012019259

Manufactured in the United States of America

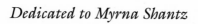

Dedicated to Myrna Shantz

Jeff Shantz has been a rank-and-file labor organizer since he was a teenager, in the auto plants of Windsor, Ontario. He has helped to form flying squads and workers committees in his own locals, as well as autonomous flying squads bringing together unemployed, unionized, and nonunionized workers to take direct solidarity actions. His book *Active Anarchy: Political Practice in Contemporary Movements* (2011) details tendencies toward mutual aid and solidarity that are present in everyday life, in order to develop a real world alternative both to capitalist and statist institutions and to social relations. He is the editor of a recent collection of essays against the repression of resistance in Western democracies entitled *Protest and Punishment* (2012). Dr. Shantz currently lives in Surrey, British Columbia, and teaches critical theory and community advocacy at Kwantlen Polytechnic University.

Contents

Preface   ⤊   ix

Acknowledgments   ⤊   xix

Introduction

Green Syndicalism, Ecology, and Labor   ⤊   xxi

1. Class Struggles

Marxism, New Social Movement Theories, and Ecology   ⤊   1

2. Radical Ecology and Class

From Fundamentalism to Green Syndicalism   ⤊   24

3. The Feminization of Earth First!

IWW/EF! Local 1 and the Convergence of Class, Gender, and Radical Environmentalism   ⤊   57

4. Green Syndicalism

An Alternative Radical Ecology   ⤊   102

5. Green Syndicalism and Mainstream Unions

Flying Squads and Rank-and-File Organizing   ⤊   130

Conclusion

Beyond Leftism: A Nonproductivist Radicalism   ⤊   164

References   ⤊   189

Index   ⤊   205

Preface

By now it is generally recognized that the burdens of ecological destruction are borne disproportionately by working class and poor people and their communities. These impacts include disease, illness, and personal health effects, as well as lost income because of sick days and the costs of family care. It is not only that the damaging effects of harms such as pollution, toxic contamination, habitat destruction, and waste dumping are felt most severely within working class and poor communities (including those of peasants and indigenous peoples). Even more, the destruction of nature tends to affect most negatively those who are most dependent on the land for sustenance—be they subsistence farmers or resource workers.

Despite being the ones overwhelmingly bearing the brunt of damage inflicted on the environment by industrial capitalist development (beyond nature itself, of course) working-class and poor people are the ones whose voices are the most marginalized, excluded, and silenced when it comes to discussions about how properly to address ecological concerns and protect nature from further harms. The concerns, fears, visions, and aspirations of the working classes and poor, and their strategies for positive change, are largely unheard—particularly within mainstream debates over ecology and environmentalism. Theirs are certainly not the perspectives that are shaping public discussions about ecological protection and the future directions or models of social development and human approaches to social and ecological care.

That working-class and poor people's perspectives on ecology and their activities to protect nature are ignored by major political parties and ruling governments in countries of the global North, particularly the United States and Canada, is fairly obvious at this point in time. Even more than this, though, it is also true that the perspectives and activities of the working classes and poor are largely absent from most of what passes for environmentalism or formal environmental movements, both radical and mainstream. Most recognized environmental groups have been composed of middle-strata or more privileged, often professional, sectors, rather than blue collar workers, the poor, or the unemployed. Much has been written about the "middle-class" character of mainstream environmentalism and its representation in groups such as Greenpeace, the Sierra Club, and the Suzuki Foundation. This middle-class character of formal environmental groups is reflected in the appeal to professional channels for environmental redress, particularly the formal venues of parliamentary democracy and political reform through legislation and policy change within established channels of political practice such as lobbying and media campaigns.

While some might expect mainstream environmental groups to have some difficulty engaging working-class concerns, it is perhaps more troubling that radical environmentalists, those with deep-green perspectives, have had as hard a time, or harder, engaging with working-class and poor people around environmental issues. Indeed, radical ecology movements have often taken an explicitly hostile approach to working-class, particularly blue-collar, workers. One might call to mind Sea Shepherd Society captain Paul Watson's vitriolic condemnation of resource workers as parasites or a rot whose demise would cause him not a single tear.

As a radical environmentalist and member of Earth First! and Greenpeace (back when it still preferred direct action to fund-raising), I was regularly shocked by the anti-working-class perspectives of movement comrades and the ease with which caricatures of working-class people were thrown around. Many saw working-class folks as the happy destroyers of the planet who loved their cars and big-box stores more than their planet. Often they were portrayed as mindless consumers who loved to work and shop and could not be freed from what was believed to be their "blissful ignorance." They certainly could not be expected to obtain the enlightened consciousness of the eco-activists (or eco-warriors). There was a tendency to dismiss without hearing what people's actual concerns, fears, and hopes were.

For many, talking with workers generally was considered a waste of time. For others, some workers, particularly industrial and resource workers, were actually the enemy. Indeed, blue-collar workers were presented as largely responsible for the destruction of the planet. They were held to be as culpable as the corporate bosses who dominated socioeconomic decision making. This perspective framed strategic and tactical approaches to movement building and educational work. The proper strategy, for many ecological activists, was to gain support from more privileged sectors who might bring pressure to bear on politicians or companies. Greenpeace canvassers typically preferred professional, more privileged neighborhoods and complained when sent to working-class "turf." Many simply felt uncomfortable talking with blue-collar workers.

As someone born into a working-class family and raised in a working-class community (even worse, an auto workers' community) who would develop into a person with a radical approach to ecological issues, I was regularly struck by how out of touch the environmentalists' constructed assumptions about working-class folks were from my own experiences growing up. The people I knew—family, friends, fellow workers of my parents—were generally people who were deeply concerned about nature. Many of them still felt very strong connections to the land, worked it directly, and/or spent as much time as possible in natural and wild spaces. At work they tried to make their workplaces less polluted, dirty, or wasteful. Many had some involvement with health and safety issues and worked with union representatives to try to address issues of industrial impacts on themselves, coworkers, and their communities. Some stood defiantly against their managers and union reps alike when health and safety issues were not being adequately addressed. For this they faced real punishment. Some were suspended or moved to harder jobs within the auto plant. Often they were harassed by management or the union.

Were any of them "radicals"? Perhaps one or two. Most, certainly not. But they were decidedly not the careless consumers of commodities that the deep greens made them out to be. Some might even have become radicalized had opportunities for such alternatives (and decent spaces for organizing) been available to them. At the very least they would have been open to and appreciated the conversation. Indeed, many were open to the ideas that I would later bring from radical ecological circles (even if they remained skeptical of some of the prospects for success).

Unfortunately that conversation was one that most of the deep-green activists that I knew and worked with did not want to have (or were uncomfortable with attempting). When I suggested that we environmental activists start attending labor council meetings in Vancouver, the response ranged from nervous laughter to outright derision. "Why would we waste our time with that?" "What could possibly be gained?" "Did I have a death wish?" "Was I trying to get people hurt?"

Yet labor council would have provided a fairly easy starting point for talking about issues with other activists, this time labor activists. It would also have allowed greens to become familiar to the labor council folks (and labor organizers to the environmentalists). Simply showing up and engaging in conversations would have provided some basis for trust and understanding.

Years later I saw, firsthand, the rewarding results of such interactions in the great efforts of the Windsor and District Labour Council, Environment Committee, and the Citizens Environment Alliance, a grassroots organization that brought together rank-and-file workers and environmentalists, also in Windsor (my hometown). These venues provided organizing spaces for ecological and labor activists to meet, discuss, strategize, and develop campaigns and other shared projects. Eventually, participants developed radical (participatory, democratic, deep-green, even anarchist) approaches out of their common work and through open confrontation with the limits of "their own" movements and movement organizations. This is an interesting process that I examine in detail in *Green Syndicalism*.

Unfortunately the greens often did not see or appreciate the irony of their own positions. During one Greenpeace campaign briefing session, the lead campaigner decided to open the meeting on an inspiring note with a list of ten things that could be done to help the environment right now. Somewhere around number three or four on the list was the call to "form a union in your workplace." The reasons were straightforward and compelling. If you want or expect people to work to defend nature on a day-to-day basis it will be difficult if they have greater and more regular opportunities to participate in decision making and implement decisions in the sphere of life in which they spend much (or most) of their day—at work. Even more, people are more likely to spend time defending nature where they feel they have greater security or support materially.

Urged on by this suggestion, a couple of us decided to take up the call presented, entirely unintentionally, by the campaigner, and we began talking to people in the office about organizing the canvassers within a union. Unfortunately the response was almost entirely negative. "Why do we need that?" "Aren't unions obsolete?" "The environment is too important to be distracted by such issues." "Aren't unions to blame for the industrial machine and ecological damage in the first place?" Worst of all, once the campaigner got wind of the union talk (which she herself had raised as a green action), threats were leveled against those of us identified as instigators or troublemakers.

These sentiments are not at all confined to the past of environmental politics. They find too common expression in modern movements, despite the evolution of ecological movements. I was reminded of this again while finishing the editing on this very book. In April of 2011, I helped to organize a blockade and occupation of a highway being built along the banks of the Fraser River in Metro Vancouver. Planned and designed solely to increase the flow of global trade into and out of British Columbia, the highway is part of a larger project, including oil pipelines across the northern and southern regions of the province. The highway itself will lead to increased pollution, contamination of land, destruction of wild areas, damaging of salmon streams, and loss of farmland, along with other harms. Even more, the highway represents a massive transfer of wealth upward as public funds are taken from social programs that benefit working-class and poor communities, such as health care, education, and housing, and directed toward a subsidy for multinational corporations and the oil industry. Unfortunately, some of the people who took part in the action showed little understanding of working people's concerns or the realities of living in a suburban area. Signs appeared suggesting that regular folks loved their cars more than the planet, even hated the planet, without any sense that people both were concerned about the environment and needed to drive to work in an area ill served by public transit. Many felt uncomfortable even canvassing the community to talk with neighbors about the issues. At the same time, some working-class folks expressed concerns about direct action and the decision to engage in an occupation of the road site. Clearly tensions remain.

This small example is not unique, and larger conflicts have appeared recently in the context of alternative globalization politics. The gap between mainstream unions and the direct action politics of ecological and social movements persists and provides still a major obstacle to broadened resistance to the social and ecological destruction caused by state capitalist development. And the antagonism is not all the responsibility of ecological activists. Much can be laid at the doorstep of the mainstream labor movement.

In events like the G20 protests in Toronto during the summer of 2010 and the state clampdown against protesters that occurred there emerge real opportunities for recognition and understanding that are not always so readily available behind the screen of "business as usual." The learning curve shifts and some things become much clearer. One of the interesting revelations of the G20 fallout is the extent to which many in the union leadership are governed by the morals, values, and prejudices of the dominant classes. This echoing of dominant perspectives has been expressed in the numerous calls for repression of the anarchist black bloc by would-be spokespeople of the labor movement in Canada. A rather stunning case in point has been the number of open statements of support for, indeed appeals for, the state capitalist rule of law. For some, the "rule of law" should have held against the black bloc. Others turn to the rule of law as a statist security blanket providing the basis for—the very conditions of—their "peaceful protests," which the black bloc supposedly infringed upon.

In expressing fidelity to the rule of law, what is really being affirmed is fidelity to the state and to the bosses. Any union that expresses fidelity to the rule of law must be responsive to questions. To do so is to negate the rich history of the working class and labor movements. For much of its history, right up to the present, the union movement has been "against the law," its actions criminalized, its organizers arrested, and worse. Anyone who's been on a picket line when it really mattered should know how to take the "rule of law."

It was within and from such a conflictual milieu that the work of Judi Bari and Industrial Workers of the World/Earth First! Local 1 sounded a clarion—a loud and lively wake-up call. Local 1 reminded us, workers and ecologists, that there had been alternative labor histories—expressions not of compromise and capitulation but of militance, action, and radical anticapitalism. Their work reminded us that the practices of sabotage, blockades, and direct action that greens thought they invented or had a monopoly on had already been used—and used effectively—generations before by industrial and resource workers against the bosses who were destroying their lives at the same time as they were destroying the planet. It was a revelation for many. Local 1 saw the very resource workers whom ecologists viewed as a threat as potential allies—as neighbors whose concerns about job loss were inextricable from concerns about the devastation of the environment in which they worked.

It is also necessary to recognize finally that properly addressing and overcoming ecological problems in a sustained and meaningful way will require the active involvement, and direction, of working-class and poor people—those humans who have the most to lose and the most to gain from the struggles over eco-social transformation. Radical environmentalists will also need to recognize that working-class and poor people are already making important contributions to ecological defense, even if their efforts take forms that are unfamiliar to ecological movement activists.

Some of my most memorable conversations on doorsteps were with working people who told me stories of their own clandestine activities in defense of the earth (their workplace or neighborhood). Whether blocking drains so toxic wastes could not be flushed out of factories or simply sabotaging equipment so that it could not produce waste matter, it was clear that working people, often on their own and without the support of a union, and often in opposition to their own economic interests, were taking drastic actions—in the face of possible job loss or legal penalty—to halt the abuse of the planet. Often the actions they took were more compelling, and placed them in greater immediate material danger, than the actions so trumpeted and mythologized by radical environmentalists who have simultaneously derided the passivity or ignorance of working people.

The critical challenges facing movements for positive social change involve the relationship between unions and community-based social movements. The form of alliances, coalitions, and organizations involving unions and community-based groups (antipoverty activists, no borders activists, and anarchists) will determine the scope of opposition to states and capital and the real potential of evolving opposition to neoliberal politics. Perhaps the key point on which this challenge pivots is the question of direct action and civil disobedience, the relationship of social movements to violations of law and property destruction. These are questions of strategy and tactics to be sure, but even more they are questions of how we understand the character of the state within capitalist societies like Canada. These questions have been ongoing, intensifying in the period of neoliberal globalization and the emergence of alternative globalization movements and demonstrations against institutions of global state-capital, such as the G8/G20.

These are issues that can be difficult to address honestly, tending to illicit strong emotional responses from participants on both labor and social movement sides. Criticism is often harshly received, and the critics can be too readily dismissed as "outsiders." If alliances, coalitions, and organizations are to develop and thrive on a more durable basis it is important not to paper over differences and divergences and instead to have honest, open, and critical analysis of challenges and obstacles to building movements that might be capable not of criticizing or complaining about neoliberal regimes, but of stopping them. Given my background and experiences as an environmental activist who has also been a union organizer, I am perhaps particularly well suited to address these issues.

The continued efforts of green syndicalism suggest a way out of the impasse. Green syndicalism suggests new (old) forms of organization for both green and labor politics—based not on hierarchical and formal structures (such as mainstream unions with their executives, board meetings, Robert's Rules, and contracts) but on the informal, egalitarian, affinity-based practices of which greens are so fond.

Green syndicalism can be found in a range of activities that take place every day in workplaces all around us. It is expressed in actions of informal work groups and neighborhood organizing. It is expressed in rank-and-file opposition to bosses and in criticism of union conservatism and passivity. It is found in health and safety committees and in efforts to stop dumping in poor and working-class neighborhoods, or in community efforts to clean up brownfields (and make the corporations responsible pay). It is expressed in the amazing efforts of environmental activists to organize their own workplaces (still a top-five thing that can be done for a green future after all). Green syndicalism has taken real form in groups, organizations, and alliances like the Citizens Environment Alliance, the Industrial Workers of the World, the Green Work Alliance, and various rank-and-file flying squads.

My own ecological perspective is deeply rooted in my childhood and youth experiences growing up in a working-class family and community. It is there that my first environmental concerns were expressed, nurtured, and supported—because I come from a blue-collar home, not in spite of it. In *Green Syndicalism* I draw upon these experiences as well as my organizing experiences within radical ecology, antipoverty, and labor movements to explore perspectives that express the commonality and mutuality between movements and broader struggles against the state capitalist structures and relations that destroy nature at the same time as they exploit people and harm their communities.

Acknowledgments

This work has developed over the course of years. It owes its development to conversations, debates, and discussions with a diversity of people who have generously taken the time to engage with the ideas have resulted in *Green Syndicalism*. Far from being a strictly academic project, it is a work rooted in real ongoing struggles, movements, and organizing efforts in defense of nature and working people. First and foremost I must thank all of the people involved in those movements and projects, particularly those who have challenged and encouraged my own thinking and writing on these issues. Among them are Jon Bekken, Rick Coronado, Peter Graham, and John Zerzan. I must also thank members of the Industrial Workers of the World and North Eastern Federation of Anarchist Communists who commented on earlier drafts of specific chapters.

On the academic side I must express deep gratitude to Barry D. Adam and Veronica Mogyorody of the University of Windsor and Alan Sears, now at Ryerson University. I benefited greatly from their support, commentary, guidance, and criticism while working on the earlier project in which this book is founded. Additional support was provided at various points by Jack Ferguson and Vito Signorile of the University of Windsor. Indeed the Sociology Department at the University of Windsor offered an amazingly lively and engaged environment in which to work, and I appreciate the wonderful opportunities I had to interact with an incredible range of interesting people during my time there.

In the early stages of this work, the most intense and helpful conversations were held with Sung Eun "Thomas" Kim. A true intellectual, in the best sense, his unwavering pursuit of knowledge and openness to new ideas were always appreciated.

Later stages of this work were supported in many ways by my crew. Thanks and love must go to Saoirse and Molly Shantz, my youngest comrades and pals. This work would not have seen the light of day without the remarkable work of P. J. Lilley, who put in a good deal of time to help it happen.

I must also thank Mary Selden Evans and Kelly Lynne Balenske at Syracuse University Press. Their ongoing commitment to this project has been much appreciated. Thanks as well to D. J. Whyte for rigorous and helpful editing. I would also like to thank the two anonymous reviewers of the manuscript for their time and commentary.

The work for this book was supported throughout by Myrna Shantz, my mom, who nurtured many of the values that are expressed here. It is dedicated to her.

Sections of the book are founded in the following earlier articles: "Judi Bari and 'The Feminization of Earth First!': The Convergence of Class, Gender, and Radical Environmentalism," *Feminist Review* 70 (2002): 105–22; "Green Syndicalism: An Alternative Red-Green Vision," *Environmental Politics* 11, no. 4 (2002): 21–41; "The Judi Bari and Darryl Cherney Lawsuit Against the FBI and Oakland Police: A Landmark Victory," *Feminist Review* 73 (2003): 166–71; "Scarcity and the Emergence of Fundamentalist Ecology," *Critique of Anthropology* 23, no. 2 (2003): 144–54; "Radical Ecology and Class Struggle: A Re-Consideration," *Critical Sociology* 30, no. 3 (2004): 691–710; "Anarchy at Work: Contemporary Anarchism and Unions," *WorkingUSA: The Journal of Labor and Society* 12, no. 3 (2009): 71–85.

Introduction

Green Syndicalism, Ecology, and Labor

Contemporary alternative globalization networks are not reflective of a coherent movement and are produced by and productive of a variety of social, political, cultural, and geographic fault lines and ruptures. These networks are at times overlapping, at times conflicted, often resonant, and sometimes competing (Williams 2010). The character of global capitalist expansion has convinced social movement activists and theorists alike of the strategic importance of alliances to counter the hegemony of capital. Countermovements against the superimposition of the capitalist market must now attend to the difficult tasks of developing their strength among disparate minorities of the population that when taken together form a majority increasingly excluded by the new global hegemony. Rob Walker (1994, 699) speaks of the crucial need for researchers to develop some insights regarding what he calls a "politics of connections." Walker is drawn to suggest as follows: "Exactly what a politics of connection would look like is not clear. Whatever the rhetorical and tactical appeal of a women's movement, or an environmental movement, in the singular, it is an appeal that cannot disguise the differences and even intolerances among such movements."

These concerns over connections and commonality across sectoral boundaries have become more pressing (with attempts still faltering) in the twenty-first century period of alternative globalization. At the same time divisions and divergences remain (Williams 2010). Particularly troubling and persistent have been tensions between more privileged actors, who operate globally (such as "middle-class" activists and of professionals in nongovernmental organizations or NGOs) and the economically rooted, less mobile rank-and-file members of the working classes who tend not to be directly connected globally. The professionals take part in mass mobilizations or "activist tourism," while blue-collar working-class members struggle to get their own unions involved in direct action campaigns organized outside of their local communities. Even getting buses to travel to demonstrations can be a point of struggle and conflict within working-class organizations (Shantz 2010).

Despite the great interest generated by the global justice movements within academic as well as various community circles, and the growth of research and writing on the new global movements, there remain substantial gaps in understanding the particular practices, ideas, and, especially, places and sites of movement development and interaction (Williams 2011). The growing resistance to neoliberal capitalism is not adequately reflected in popular academic notions of global civil society. As well, there have been relatively few works that examine the more durable institutions, what I prefer to call infrastructures of resistance, created and maintained within the movements that might sustain them in moving from ephemeral, reactive mobilization to longer-term struggle and social transformation (Shantz 2010).

Perhaps nowhere has the volatility of social movement relations erupted more explosively in recent years than in those interactions between labor movement and radical ecology activists. Rather than reflecting positions of disinterest regarding one another, certain forms of confrontation, such as the ramming of fishing vessels or driving logging trucks through demonstrations on timber roads, do represent serious acts of hostility. In the late 1980s and early 1990s the situation was so conflictual that Laurie Adkin (1992a, 145) could accurately state that many activists had become uncompromisingly aggressive toward their counterparts as "fixed stereotypes of both subject positions have developed, with environmentalists depicting workers as lumpen mercenaries, and workers depicting environmentalists as eco-nuts." At that time many prominent environmentalists argued that there exists a fundamental opposition of positions between radical ecology and workers' movements (see Bahro 1984; Bookchin 1980, 1987; Foreman 1991; Jensen 2006; Watson 1994, 2005; Zerzan 2005, 2008a, 2008b).

In the present period, one of the key issues facing social organizing, particularly within working class movements, is the relationship between direct action and mediated political action (Williams 2011). In the twenty-first century, in the context of alternative globalization movements, there has developed a serious, and potentially fatal, rift between advocates of direct action and proponents of representational approaches. This rift has been expressed debates over black blocs, property destruction, and militance during alternative globalization demonstrations in which union officials have sided with authorities in opposing direct action (Shantz 2010).

This sense of opposition has presented ongoing dilemmas for those seeking to find solidarity among environmental justice and social justice movements. It has effectively frustrated the ongoing efforts of environmental and labor activists alike to develop shared organizations, resources, and perspectives that might radically confront and challenge capitalist relations of production, property, and exchange through the early decades of the twenty-first century. For many (O'Connor 1998; Buss 2001; Foster 2002; Walker 2002; Jakopovich 2007; Williams 2009a, 2009b; Foster, Clark, and York, 2011) overcoming this frustration continues to pose the central challenge and task in building the movements necessary to adequately turn the tide of ecological harm.

> In this instance we witness the pressing need for a counter-hegemonic reframing of social visions, wherein labour activists and environmentalists can find common ground. On their own, the social visions that predominate in these movements are vulnerable to cooption and/or marginalization. Ecology can be reduced to little more than green consumerism and wilderness preservation, or it can be framed in such an anti-humanist and anti-modern way as to become sectarian. Labour's concern with economic justice

can be—and historically has been—diluted to little more than an accommodation with capital and the state in exchange for a share of productivity gains. It is only when these frames are juxtaposed that radical possibilities open up—that the dilemma between "jobs" and "trees" is refused in favour of a broader vision of ecological conversion. (Carroll and Ratner 1996, 429)

For many activists it is absolutely necessary to draw connections between the harm done to workers within capitalism social relations and the simultaneous harm done to nature (Jakopovich 2007; Williams 2009a, 2009b; Foster, Clark, and York 2011). Capitalism is not based on meeting the needs of the world's population but rather on profiting from the exploitation of labor and natural resources. Where for most of human history people have been engaged in the production of use values, in which humans produce to meet their own needs such as food, shelter, and culture, capitalism is centered upon the production of exchange values. Products are produced, resources controlled, and labor expended primarily toward the production of products for exchange. Workers do not produce for their needs, they produce for the needs of capital to exchange commodities for profit. This fundamental shift in the arrangement of human productive capacities was analyzed by Karl Marx 150 years ago. His writings follow the movement of the bourgeoisie across the globe constantly seeking to expand their markets and search for raw materials (Harter 2004; Foster, Clark, and York 2011). The results of this search include the ongoing expansion of industries based on for-profit production and exploitation, the destruction of vast ecosystems and the continued pursuit of cheaper labor markets (Harter 2004; Routledge and Cumbers 2010; Williams 2010). Environmental activists and workers can benefit from the understanding that neither workers nor the environment benefit from this process of globalization (Harter 2004; Carty 2008; Williams 2010). Harter suggests that one of the solutions to the current crisis rests in the communist slogan, "From each according to his ability, to each according to his needs." This idea is important because it challenges overproduction, commodity fetishism, and the exploitation of surplus value of labor and environment for personal profit that characterize social relations within capitalist societies (Harter 2004). Such a perspective properly situates the interests of the capitalists as directly opposed to the interests of the working class and the environment (Harter 2004; Walker 2002; Jakopovich 2007; Foster, Clark, and York 2011).

This is not simply a matter of social unity; it speaks to the real necessities of building a movement that can effect lasting environmental protections and halt the rampant destruction of nature at the heart of capitalist economies. For many, the protest power, the power to disagree, criticize, or dissent, of environmental movements is not enough to transform social relations fundamentally or radically, in a manner that would bring thoroughgoing and lasting change to protect nature. Such change requires the social power, the power to stop capitalist production, distribution, and exchange, that is represented by the collective power of working people. In the view of many commentators, directly confronting the corporate and government power holders who benefit from ecological destruction or indifference, requires the mobilization of this enormous collective power away from production for exchange and profit and toward sustainability and human and ecological need. According to labor organizer Charles Walker:

> That social power includes the working class's ability to choke off corporate profits, as demonstrated by the nation's anti-labor laws. It seems then that environmentalists would have a better chance of saving humanity from ecological disaster, if they appealed to worker's self-interest in living in a world free of ecological blight and social insecurity. (2002, 8)

Still, where is the evidence for such a possibly counterhegemonic movement in defense of nature? Too little attention has been given to real-world attempts by workers and environmentalists to develop such a radical movement. Few studies detail the work undertaken to make these connections on a day-to-day basis, examining the obstacles they face and the perspectives that inspire them to keep at it.

Almost all discussions of ecological alternatives and socioeconomic changes in response to environmental crises focus on the state. The emphasis is largely upon government initiated and managed projects and policies, particularly laws, regulations, and government-mandated industrial targets. The other main player is industry. Emphasis is placed on "green industries" or "green technology" and innovation led and implemented by corporations—typically using the promise of the market and expected growth in "green" products whether electric cars, alternative energy, or compostable chip bags. Here industry is asked to take a lead in regulating itself or transforming practices with the expectation that to do so will give the company a market advantage while helping the planet. Both of the dominant approaches are top-down, unequal, authoritarian, and hierarchical, relying on the initiative of state capitalist elites and placing decision making solely in the hands of economic and political authorities and reinforcing their hold on social power.

Recently there has been much discussion of so-called green jobs as a way to address working-class environmental issues (Llewellyn 2008; Cassio and Rush 2009; Deitche 2010). Yet "green jobs" leave untouched questions of control of production and workplace, and community, decision making. Green jobs also fail to address the fundamental issue—that of class relations and distribution of wealth and property regimes in capitalist economies. They also fail to address the structuring of society around ownership and control of resources and production within the context of capitalist market exchange for profit. They do not approach ecological or social justice but instead serve to reinforce relations of economic inequality and control (behind an ideological veneer).

Working-class solutions and organizational practices have been largely ignored or excluded. When working-class voices are introduced it is typically through official union channels—often as part of statist- or corporate-led projects as discussed within.

Perhaps understandably, given its philosophical hegemony within the radical Left, at least since the Russia Revolution, most studies of class, capitalist exploitation, and ecology uncritically put forward

Marxist perspectives. Indeed in terms of discussions of labor and ecology, the terrain is almost entirely occupied by Marxist analyses. In many ways the debate has been polarized largely between a "red" Marxist eco-socialism that has had little resonance in ecological circles, and a supposedly "post-political" or post-modern "green" radical ecology that has been incapable of addressing the concerns, daily realities, and organizing practices of industrial and resource workers. In some ways, as will be seen, this polarization reflects broader debates between Marxism, centered on class analysis, and new social movement theories that privilege supposedly new post-industrial values such as biocentrism or ecological ethics. This situation is largely unhelpful in understanding prospects for a radical articulation of ecology and labor. At the same time it has served to silence or erase alternative histories, practices, and perspectives on society and nature relations that might offer useful insights into other red/green visions. The present work attempts to break through the hegemony of Marxist approaches to labor and ecology and the dominance of Marxism within current red/green visions. At the same time it sketches the contours of an alternative radical ecology based not on conflicts with working-class people but through solidarity and mutual aid.

Recently, interesting convergences of radical union movements with ecology have been witnessed in Europe and North America. These developments have given voice to a radical "syndical ecology," or what I prefer to call "green syndicalism." The emergent greening of syndicalist discourses is perhaps most significant in the theoretical questions raised regarding anarcho-syndicalism and ecology, indeed questions about the possibilities for a radical convergence of social movements. Although most attempts to form labor and environmentalist alliances have pursued Marxian approaches, Adkin (1992a, 148) suggests that more compelling solutions might be expected from anarchists and libertarian socialists. Still others (see Pepper 1993; Purchase 1994, 1997a; Shantz and Adam 1999; Harter 2004; Jakopovich 2007; Williams 2009a) suggest that Greens should pay more attention to anarcho-syndicalist ideas. Pepper argues (1993, 198) that an infusion of anarcho-syndicalism might shake up the contemporary Green movement in North America just as syndicalism shook up the labor movement of the 1910s. Harter (2004) and Jakopovich (2007) argue that confronting "jobs versus environment" blackmail may require nothing less than militant labor-based organizations, arming workers with the necessary weapons to confront the power of capital and to strike over ecological concerns.

Significantly, it is precisely at the intersections of those battles between ecology and labor that one of the more intriguing of recent attempts to articulate social movement solidarity has emerged. It was at that intersection that we were introduced to Earth First! activist Judi Bari and her efforts to build alliances with workers in order to save old-growth forest "and replace the corporate timber companies with environmentally responsible worker-owned cooperatives" (Chase 1991, 23). Bari, who passed away in 1997, sought to learn from the organizing and practices of the Industrial Workers of the World (IWW), the revolutionary union that enjoyed great organizing successes in the first decades of the twentieth century, to see if a radical ecology movement might be built along anarcho-syndicalist lines. In so doing she tried to bring a radical working-class perspective to the agitational practices of Earth First! Looking at the emergent greening of syndicalist practices, reflected in the efforts of Judi Bari and the IWW/Earth First! alliance provides an opportunity to pursue a "phenomenology of alliance formation" that may aid improved understandings of the convergence of social movements in the global age.

The groundwork laid by IWW/Earth First Local 1 led to crucial ongoing alliances between environmentalists and union members on the West Coast. Almost a decade after Local 1's Redwood Summer initiative, a green syndicalist alliance that brought steelworkers together with Earth First! activists to support locked-out workers at Kaiser Aluminum, owned by Charles Hurwitz, who also owns Pacific Lumber, one of the main companies Local 1 confronted, would play a prominent role in the Teamsters and Turtles alliance that organized the Seattle protests against the World Trade Organization in 1999 (Early 2009). Thus green syndicalists played important parts in the emergence of alternative globalization movements in North America and beyond. Still their contributions, experiences, and stories have been largely absent from histories of the Seattle protests and alternative globalization movements that have emerged more broadly since.

Many critics have noted the lack of adequate or effective forms of organization among new movements within the current period of alternative globalization mobilization (Ghimire 2011). Yet the current generation of syndicalists have developed and experimented with a variety of new organizational forms drawing upon experiences of community and workplace organizing.

On the whole very little has been said about green syndicalism, the sociopolitical and environmental context of its emergence, its organizing practices and its specific red/green vision. Even particularly perceptive commentators, such as Steve Early, who are looking for examples of rank-and-file organizing and militancy have overlooked the activities of green syndicalists and the IWW. This book attempts to correct these oversights by offering a discussion of the varied perspectives, the different theoretical and practical strands, that make up a syndicalist ecology. In doing so it contributes to an understanding of ecological movements and environmental radicalism that is broader and deeper, examining a perspective that has been insufficiently engaged in discussions of ecological politics. At the same time it helps to enrich understandings of syndicalism and syndicalist theory, illustrating the real diversity of syndicalist theory and its continued relevance in addressing current issues. It also provides new insight into underreported and underappreciated practices of the Industrial Workers of the World, one of the most significant labor movements in North American history, focusing on a part of that union's history and practice that has been largely excluded from studies of that organization. Indeed the present work stands as the only full length study of contemporary IWW organizing.

Compromising on Nature?

The amplification of capitalist relations of production (enabled after 1945 through the mechanisms of Keynesian accommodation) has deepened that "great transformation" of the biosphere and its inhabitants into commodities for an ever-expanding market. "Such a 'commodification of social life' has destroyed a series of previous social relations and replaced them with commodity relations. This is what we know as the consumer society" (Mouffe 1988, 92). Underlying the politics of this paradigm has been a pervasive and largely unchallenged commitment to growth. Offe suggests that it was only through illusions of growth as unlimited and beneficent that the readiness of labor to reduce broad demands for social change to limited questions of income distribution, and the corresponding willingness by capital to concede some legitimacy to organized labor, could become possible. Economic growth on the side of capital was matched with an increased capacity to consume on the side of labor. Specifically, the possibilities for unimpeded (because of the truce called between sides), boundless growth made the limited concessions to labor acceptable to capital, while the perceived desirability of "getting a piece of the pie" provided ideological cover for the co-opting and circumscribing of unions (Offe 1985).

Significantly (and usually overlooked), this alliance, with consumption as its justificatory undergirding, enabled the displacement of class conflicts toward a mutual partnership in ecological conquest. The enlargement of consumerist relations into expanding social domains and the subordination of noncommodity relations to a logic of profit signaled a cultural displacement of militancy with profound consequences (Early 2009). Through the linkage of wages with productivity and a related diminishment of the autonomy and resistance of workers, the way was cleared for the discursive constitution of workers as mere consumers and all that that would entail. The ecological consequences of this dynamic have increasingly revealed the extent to which the relatively stable class compromise has been primarily "underwritten" by previously unimagined assaults upon nature (see Bookchin 1978, 1982, 1987; Devall and Sessions 1985; Devall 1988; Bookchin and Foreman 1991; Foreman 1991; Jensen 2006; Zerzan 2005, 2008a, 2008b).

The idea that growth benefits workers has been effectively challenged by numerous authors, including Richard Douthwaite (see also Harter 2004 and Foster, Clark, and York 2011). In his book *The Growth Illusion* (1999) Douthwaite incisively debunks myths about the benefits of growth, illustrating that as profits have gone up for capital, wages have gone down for workers (see also Harter 2004). At the same time, this same growth has been accompanied by the destruction of the environment that results inevitably from rampant industrialism (Harter 2004; Foster, Clark, and York 2011).

Recent developments, however, point to the collapse of what Laclau (1990) calls the "transformist capacity" of the system of social democracy and welfare state capitalism. The past three decades have ushered in the social transformations characterizing finance-driven capitalist globalism. The dominance of financial capital, and its accompanying eclipse of the industrial capitalist relations structuring the postwar formation, has brought a shift in the arrangement of power between business and state to overwhelmingly favor capital against the working class and poor—and against nature. Newly emboldened, capital has, with unwavering resolve, set about the project of dismantling the features of the postwar accommodation that most threaten to disrupt continued expansion of the market or to frustrate enclosure of any remaining autonomous spaces.

Labor and Ecology: Missed Connections?

The period of the late 1980s to the present—marked by a shift away from welfare state programs to neoliberal austerity measures—has been a difficult time for social movements throughout North America. For no movement has this been more true than for the labor movement. Organized labor, with an increasingly passive constituency (where it has any constituency remaining at all), isolated from social movements and forgetful of its own activist and militant histories, is suffering a serious decomposition as a force for change owing to a variety of convergent factors. These included shrinking or stagnant membership rates (see Lowe 2000), direction by bureaucrats with little appetite for politics beyond the polls (see Early 2009), and isolation from social movements and forgetfulness of its own activist histories (see Williams

2009a; Shantz 2010). In Canada, Lowe (2000, 164) reports that "the overall unionization rate has hovered around one-third of all paid employees for the past three decades." In the United States, the rate is below 20 percent. Much of this unionization is made up of workers in large industrial workplaces, the traditional union strongholds. Gains do not appear to have been made in smaller workplaces, which when taken together account for a major, and growing proportion of the workforce, and predominantly consist of younger workers. Unable to disrupt neoliberal legislative enactments, such as the North American Free Trade Agreement (NAFTA), that represented direct assaults upon its own social positions, the labor movement has seemed an unlikely candidate as a focus for any convergence of alternative rebellions (see Carr 1996; Clarke 2002; Day 2005; Early 2009).

Where attempts to build bridges were initiated, priority was given typically to building coalitions between mainstream environmental groups and unions. In the United States these efforts included the projects of Environmentalists for Full Employment and those of the Progressive Alliance (Adkin 1992a, 1992b). In Canada the most notable efforts involved the Labour and Environment Conference (Schrecker 1975), the Canadian Auto Workers (CAW) (Adkin and Alpaugh 1988), and the Windsor and District Labour Council (Adkin 1998). For the most part those efforts met with only limited success (see Sklair 1995).

Much hope for a labor and environmentalist alliance was generated in the wake of the protests against the World Trade Organization meetings in Seattle in 1999. Images of environmentalists, unionists, and a range of social justice activists standing together amid the billowing tear gas that filled Seattle's streets suggested to many the emergence of a new movement for positive social and environmental change. This new movement was famously dubbed the "Teamsters and Turtles." For over a year many believed that a new grand alliance, or counterhegemonic bloc, was taking hold, a national "blue-green" alliance bringing the union and environmental movements together. A good deal of excitement was created by the prospect of the AFL-CIO leadership coming together with major environmental groups to share support, resources, and ideas (Berg 2002; Loeb 2004; Engler 2008; Fellner 2008; Early 2009; Routledge and Cumbers 2010).

Unfortunately the hope began to fade sooner than many, including even hardened veterans of labor and environmental struggles, had imagined. By the time the events of September 11, 2001, brought much of alternative globalization movement organizing to a screeching halt, the Teamsters and Turtles movement was virtually finished. Among the issues that forced the collapse of the Teamsters and Turtles was the incredible and unexpected 2001 decision by AFL-CIO leadership, headed by supposed progressive president John Sweeney, to support President Bush's plan to despoil the Alaskan Wildlife Refuge (ANWAR) by opening it up to oil drilling. Even more major unions including the Teamsters, United Mine Workers, and several building trades unions openly endorsed Bush's overall energy policy, beyond the ANWAR drilling. Not surprisingly the endorsement was used by the Republican administration to provide progressive cover for its regressive policies. In response to the AFL-CIO endorsement, James Hansen, Republican chair of the House Resources Committee gloated: "This endorsement [by Sweeney] just underscores what we have been saying all along: This [Bush] energy bill is good for American workers, it's good for American jobs, it's good for America's economy" (quoted in Walker 2002, 1). Environmentalists, in moving away from the "Teamsters and Turtles" alliance, also cited the United Auto Workers' (UAW) ongoing support for the Big Three companies' fight against improved auto efficiency.

Much of the distress of such projects has usually related to the economistic priorities of traditional unionism (Early 2009; Shantz 2010). "In relation to environmental conflicts, they have tended to accept the logic of owners that profit is the only basis for economic growth and, hence, employment" (Adkin and Alpaugh 1988, 54). Corporatist unions still adopt a resource management vision of human relations with nature while favoring current legislative approaches to environmental protection. In accepting the domination of nature as the primary basis for "jobs" and through the continued equation of politics with the state, unions have resisted the more radical demands of ecology activists to forge "dark green" alliances that question the existing logic of production and consumption and the defining of nature within it.

The privileging of "legitimate" means through union-centered activism and statist reforms, helpful in forming relations with some workers, has stood diametrically opposed to the inclinations of activists raised on direct actions and decentered organizations. Conceptions of autonomy, participation, and cultural transformation that occupy the political ground of alternative movements have been only reluctantly engaged within strategies pursued within mainstream coalitions (Early 2009). At the same time rank-and-file workers, frustrated with declining conditions have begun to press for more (Shantz 2010).

Continuing stubbornly to pursue an "old politics" of broadened (or at least maintained) political consensus articulated via some form of welfare state, the Left refuses to see that there is no consensus to be had, no compromise to be made. Social democracy no longer occupies any vantage point from which to bargain with business. Perhaps that is just as well because ecological crises have already forced us to ask just who really wants these "bargains" anyway. Countermovements against the capitalist superimposing of the market must now attend to the difficult tasks of developing their strength among those disparate minorities of the population that together form a majority increasingly excluded by the new globalist hegemony.

This disparity encourages the widening of an already large gap between labor and newly emerging radical ecology activists. During the 1980s and 1990s, Earth First! co-founder Dave Foreman harshly criticized what he saw as a romanticization of workers by leftist ecologists. "It does not follow from the huge guilt of the capitalists that all workers are blameless for the destruction of the natural world" (Foreman quoted in Bookchin and Foreman 1991, 51). Foreman posited, ironically, a latter-day lack of "class consciousness" on behalf of workers as a major barrier to forming any relations of solidarity between ecological and workers' struggles. In his view "too many workers buy into the worldview of their masters that the Earth is a smorgasbord of resources for the taking" (51).

Ecology versus Labor?

Countermovements against the social and ecological dislocations characterizing recent global transformations must now attend to the difficult tasks of developing their strength through shared initiatives and a "common front" politics. This has been a very uneasy process, however, as broadened social visions are subverted by the interests and priorities of specific movements or even specific organizations (Carroll and Ratner 1996; Carty 2008; Williams 2010). As Carroll and Ratner argue, the sectoral defining of interests feeds a dynamic in which social movement organizations compete for resources and strategic advantage. This dynamic has the result that cross-movement coalitions, where they do emerge, tend to exhibit an opportunistic or instrumental character. In assessing the possibility for an alliance formation across movements, Carroll and Ratner conclude: "It is only by consciously promoting broadly resonant counter-hegemonic discourses and practices that the factional strife that issues from such competition can be significantly reduced if not overcome" (1996, 429).

However, this state of affairs has led many "postmodern" (Seidman, 1994) and new social movement (Cohen 1985; Melucci 1992; Hardt and Negri 2000; Smith 2001; Day 2005) commentators to conclude that there is no basis for a counterhegemony based on cross-movement solidarity. They reject leftist concerns for systemic transformation through unified resistance, emphasizing instead the multiplicity of movement discourses that are said to be incommensurable (Hardt and Negri 2004; Day 2005; Selbin 2010). Further, not only are counterhegemonic projects deemed to be unlikely, but they are also potentially undesirable.

The sources of postmodern skepticism on this count are many. In North America, the most sensational and lingering instance of cross-movement strife has been the extreme conflict between environmental activists and timber workers. Dramatic forms of confrontation, such as the numerous blockades of logging roads and the recent (and more surprising) corralling of a Greenpeace boat by loggers off the coast of British Columbia, have become common images of environmentalist practice. Longtime Green activists like Rudolph Bahro (1984), Murray Bookchin (1980, 1987), Dave Foreman (1991), Paul Watson (2002, 2005) and John Zerzan (2005, 2008a, 2008b) have portrayed resource workers and radical environmentalists as pursuing interests that are *fundamentally* exclusive. This presumed separateness is most commonly voiced through a "jobs *versus* environment" framework, which excludes any consideration of alternative conceptualizations. Laurie Adkin (1992a, 145) notes that many radical activists have become uncompromisingly hostile toward workers, as workers are considered to be "part of the problem" and any appeals for their support are viewed as a waste of time. Carroll and Ratner suggest that there is an "incongruity of social visions" between ecology and labor that "corporate-driven counter-movements" have successfully exploited. This incongruity arises from "the lack of ecological vision among trade unionists and the 'environmentalism without class' that tends to prevail in the visions of environmentalists" (Carroll and Ratner 1996, 429).

As Harter (2004), Jakopovich (2007), and Williams (2009a) suggest, a radical coalition between workers and environmentalists is a necessary development if one wants to stop the exploitation of workers and the land, but at the same time, such a coalition is not as natural as it may seem. In the view of many commentators, the mutually reinforced antagonisms existing between workers and environmentalists must be addressed before a meaningful coming together of Teamsters and Turtles can be achieved. Understanding the history of conflicts between workers and environmental activists can contribute to addressing further conflicts between class and environmental concerns. Only by examining the mistakes and missteps of environmental and labor groups, and the attempts to learn from and overcome these difficulties, can environmentalist and labor organizers attempt to forge new approaches to working together (Harter 2004; Jakopovich 2007; Shantz 2010).

The shift away from class analysis in ecology movements presents many problems, both theoretical and practical. Adam (1993, 331) has raised the question of whether such movements will "necessarily leave the deep structures of capitalism untouched and avoid taking on the prevailing distribution of wealth and power." More recently, many commentators (Jakopovich 2007; Williams 2010; Foster, Clark, and York 2011) have been drawn to ask the same question. The recent struggles of the ecology movement, including the disappointing outcome of the Teamsters and Turtles coalition, suggest that without a serious radicalization, which includes the contributions of workers, future attempts will continue to be constrained in their efforts to bring about fundamental change. By accepting the structure of existing society rather than directly confronting its underlying assumptions and class antagonisms the potential for co-optation is a pervasive and serious danger.

The case of Greenpeace is illustrative. There the acceptance of existing structural relations has reduced Greenpeace to an organizational weapon focused largely upon short-term success and with little interest in cosmological or ideological questions. Adkin (1992a, 149) has identified Greenpeace activists as "young, militant, imbued with a sense of urgency, and too impatient to stop environmental degradation to engage in the painstaking process of building alliances with organizations like the unions." Whether or not one agrees with the reasons provided by Adkin for the lack of alliances, the main point remains that connections have been limited. The failure to broaden the lines of engagement has greatly compromised Greenpeace's actions. Thus, rather than building direct action efforts on a broadened base of solidarity the elitist separation between "vanguard" and "masses" is maintained and the transformative potential of the direct actions is left largely unmet.

This situation has proven disastrous for ecology movements with ongoing impacts for nature as capitalist production proceeds almost without pause in the service of the specific interests of a relatively small core of elites. As Walker (2002, 8) notes:

> The U.S. economy is a ten trillion dollar goliath dominated by a corporate elite, a minority that distributes the nation's wealth on the basis of class ownership, not majority interest. That same corporate

elite determines the environmental risks that we all face. Environmentalists need not sell their cause short by settling for third-rate nostrums, enacted slowly, if at all. That's because workers have a common stake in the physical and social well-being of the world.

Of course, as I have suggested, this in no way means that such shared interests will be recognized and acted upon in relations of solidarity and mutual aid. Indeed, it has often been displaced in conflict. Indeed in a later chapter we will see, ironically, that rather than working to build working-class alliances, Greenpeace has set itself up as a corporate entity engaging, incredibly, in union busting against its own workers. Interestingly, as will be shown, green syndicalists took up the struggle of the Greenpeace workers, assisting them in securing their rights.

Movement away from analyses of class struggles has been a recurrent theme among the works of those within radical ecology who identify themselves as deep ecologists (see Devall and Sessions 1985). A main proponent of deep ecology, George Sessions (1988) has taken an extremely hostile position toward any attempts to situate ecological destruction within class relations in advanced capitalist societies. He argues quite unequivocally that the radical ecology movements can only assert autonomy from capitalist and socialist projects—crucial to any dark green movement—through insistence upon a distinctly anti-class posture. In Session's view, emphasis must be transferred to spiritual realms and to the development of human potential and maturity.

These perspectives are aspects of a broader utopian emphasis in ecology upon the transformation of values and the reconstitution of human needs, be they aesthetic, psychic, or material, enabled through an extension of rights discourses to include other species and ecological milieux. In this way they reflect and are expressive of the emphasis on "new values" or "postindustrial values" emphasized by new social movement theorists. Largely engaging in linguistic and expressive strategies of social transformation, utopian ecology "encompasses an important discussion about alienation and needs, including experiences of deprivation linked to the commodification of life, alienation from the body, and from nature" (Adkin 1992a, 144). For utopian ecology, anthropocentric human values as fixed within post-Enlightenment Western ideologies, that is, the privileging of human needs and denial of inherent rights of nature, are the cause of ecological destruction. Anthropocentrism involves the discursive separation of humans from nature and the objectification of nature for purposes of exploitation. Janet Biehl (1991, 20) argues that for utopian ecologists anthropocentrism has caused humans to lose track of a foundational "'oneness' of all nature" supposedly characterizing preindustrial social relations.

Given the essentialist inclinations in much of utopian ecology narratives, it is perhaps not surprising that discursive practices have tended to construct "humanity" as a bloc, undifferentiated by class and power, in which a universalistic human species itself is held responsible for biospheric destruction (see Devall 1988; Manes 1990; Watson 2005; Zerzan 2008a, 2008b). A consequential theoretical entanglement arising from a disinterest in the social articulation of attacks upon nonhuman nature is the blaming of those humans who themselves suffer at the hands of the same forces that are responsible for the destruction of global ecosystems. Dangerously ignored or discounted are divisions asserted through politically constructed differences of race, gender, and class. As Bookchin (quoted in Bookchin and Foreman 1991, 31) states, "when you say a black kid in Harlem is as much to blame for the ecological crisis as the President of Exxon, you are letting one off the hook and slandering the other." The "human" is always a political project. Examples of social division in the face of this "human" are too numerous to mention here.

The consequences of this discursive shift have been that long-range practical engagements of many utopian ecologists do not involve any active transformations of capitalist social relations (Adkin 1992b). This failure is most characteristic of those variants of utopianism articulated in a fundamentalist neo-Malthusian direction. For some deep ecologists (see Manes 1990; Watson 2005) the most desirable or necessary transformation is "drastically depopulating the Earth as if human numbers were all that mattered and the various kinds of

society that people can create are of little or no relevance to the ecological question" (Chase 1991). While claiming to be unconcerned
with political or social issues, such activists have developed what are
first and foremost political narratives, albeit of a reactionary nature.

Through such practices utopian ecology has been led away from
efforts to contextualize ecological crises within the persistent enclosure by uniquely exploitative forms of human social relations. By concealing the divisions and conflicts within these exploitative forms,
the critique of anthropocentrism can become an ideological cover for
those members of "humanity" who in asserting positions of privilege
have constructed not only nature but fellow humans—typically the
poor, blacks, and women—as mere "resources" to be exploited. Significantly, it is precisely among these inferiorized positions that the
impacts of ecological destruction are most severely experienced (Bullard and Wright 1986–87; Bullard and Wright 1987; Bullard 1990;
O'Connor 1998; Shantz 2010; Foster, Clark, and York 2011). Significantly too, it is also from these positions that some of the most interesting and poignant forms of resistance have emerged (Harter 2004).

The cautions raised by some radical environmentalists are important inasmuch as they do remind activists to be critical in their relationships. However, statements such as those offered by Foreman (and
also Watson) reveal an ignorance of such crucial intersections of power
as private ownership and control over production, which have much
to say about people's relations within larger ecological milieux. These
questions lead us to the very problems of political articulation raised
by Ernesto Laclau and Chantal Mouffe in their critical reworkings of
post-Marxism, notions that are examined in the next chapter.

Within the totalizing projects of utopian ecology, for which all
members of a "humanity," absent difference or articulation, are seen
as having an equal stake in ecological survival, the specificity of local
resistances is obscured. Instead through the assumption of ultimate
ends these activities are forced into a meta-discourse of nonanthropocentrism. Refusal to confront the uneven and conflictual constitution of human social relations and the integration of ecological
antagonisms with social antagonisms has displaced opportunities for a

broadened articulation of ecological activism (Bookchin and Foreman 1991; Jakopovich 2007; Foster, Clark, and York 2011). Thus ecological fundamentalists "have remained utopian in not emphasizing the importance of these strategic relations, and have instead almost forsaken the political process for the comfort of moral critique and futurology" (Frankel 1987, 242). The mistaken assumption of utopians is that "saving the earth" transcends ideology and is thereby capable of uniting people of all backgrounds in common cause. Nature, however, does not transcend ideology. It is always a political project; an outcome of hegemonic struggle.

Utopia, which the revolutionary syndicalist theorist Georges Sorel (1941) reviled as mere intellectualist projection, is restricted from an amplified resonance because of its silencing of negativity. In discussing the limits of utopianism the sociologist Paul Hirst suggests: "The utopians were not merely unworldly about the means needed to bring their perfect futures into being, they also envisaged them as a non-political and non-pluralist form of society without even the potential for antagonistic interests" (1986, 98). It is negativity or the presence of antagonisms, however, that everywhere confronts activists immersed in struggle.

Thus does a Sorelian conception of myth stand in harsh opposition to utopian dreamscapes of a future society in which the exclusion of antagonisms and the absence of power have been achieved independently and in wholeness (Sorel 1941; Laclau 1990). For radical ecology, as for any social movement, to repudiate the eclipsing of negativity within utopian social models requires creative activism through the perpetual articulation of alliances. Using the language of Dobson (1990), it might be said that while the utopians are "dark green" ecologically they remain "light green" socially.

Ecological Voluntarism

The overarching problem with much ecological analysis, radical or otherwise, and the great failure of vision that undermines the prescriptions for global renewal, rests with their emphasis on liberal voluntarism as the primary mechanism for social change. Simms (2005) actually holds out the hope, and indeed it is a hope shared by other, more radical, ecologists, as we shall see, that individuals in the West will simply see the light and renounce conspicuous consumption. As Simms concludes: "All we would need to do then, is follow Keynes' advice to free ourselves from the ephemeral satisfactions of conspicuous consumption and become those people who 'can keep alive and cultivate into a fuller perfection, the art of life itself and . . . not sell themselves for the means of life'" (2005, 188). Unfortunately the vast majority of people in the West have little choice but to sell themselves for the means of life. And the life situations of poverty and pain for those who are unsuccessful in making that sale are, especially under neoliberal regimes of workfare and gutted social programs, nothing that should be upheld as models for an ecological society. Yet Simms says nothing about collective and organized action to change the terms of life that base survival on waged labor or which encourage unhealthy and unsustainable consumption regimes.

Instead Simms offers the liberal standard of personal conversion. Thus Simms offers as the first solution to ecological destruction the rather offensive suggestion that people need mass psychologization. In his words: "We are still seriously in denial about global warming, both as individuals and as a culture. We are in denial about what changes it demands in our own lives. We need psychologists to help us stop rationalising our destructive behaviour, as much as we need wind farms for an alternative energy supply" (2005, x). Who is this "we" that Simms recommends for help, though? George Bush, Dick Cheney, and the president of General Motors, or the millions of people who are aware of, concerned about, and frightened by global climactic change? People who worry about it and talk about it every day but have no control over the structure and character of production or the distribution of resources? People who, because of the pressures and constraints of having to work, have little control over the structure, pace, and time of everyday life? Such considerations are also part of the ecological debt, but Simms says nothing about them. Exploitation and oppression as everyday lived experiences and factors in ecological destruction are largely absent from the analysis offered in his otherwise useful book.

At best he draws a sketch of a world of multiple conversions in small businesses, local currencies, and recycling. These are aspects of petit bourgeois fantasy, but there is little to suggest they have any prospect of addressing the extensive damage done to the planet. First, the private control of resources, financial and material, means that very few of those who might like to leave wage labor behind for a life of small or micro-business will be prevented from doing so. Even if they could, however, having to operate as a small business in a context of advanced capitalist competition, and the multinational monopolies arising from it, leaves the prospects for success (or for remaining small) somewhat questionable. Similarly the time it would take, not to mention the stiff opposition one might expect from those who control and profit from the monopolies, to build up a small business economy (while simultaneously waiting for the Wal-Marts and Pepsicos to wither away) may leave such an approach offering far too little, far too late.

Absent in too much radical ecological diagnoses or prognoses is the sense that the problem facing life on the planet relates to capitalism as a system or structure of social relations rather than simply misguided or irresponsible choices. Thus Simms can only express exasperation: "People in power in rich countries have taken their eyes off the ball. Instead of causing misery in poor countries by forcing them to pay illegitimate financial debts, they should have been worrying about their own ecological debts" (2005, ix). Indeed they should but there are well-known reasons why they do not. It's not because they've taken their eye off the ball either. Rather it is that their eyes have only ever seen an entirely different ball (one made of dollar bills). Similarly many ecology activists seem to expect that governments will voluntarily choose to undercut the economic and ecological conditions that have legitimized in law and defended through force, the very practices of the environmentally and socially destructive corporations. If they refuse, Simms can only bring himself to suggest people take them to court. Indeed. Such approaches are not particularly helpful if one is looking for a few suggestions about how actually to change the circumstances that have made global climactic change and other disasters possible in the first place.

Red + Green (+ Black)?

Socialists have long tried to develop an "environmentalism with class" in an attempt to find common ground between ecology and labor. Most (see Jezer 1977; Gorz 1980; O'Connor 1998; Foster 2000, 2002; Harvey 2007; Williams 2010; Foster, Clark, and York 2011) have argued that the specific problems surrounding a constructive engagement of workers with ecology might be addressed through an incorporation of Marxian analyses. Indeed, certain Marxist authors (Raskin and Bernow 1991; O'Connor 1998; Foster 2000, 2002; Harvey 2007; Foster, Clark, and York 2011) offer helpful criticisms of the limitations of environmentalism. In arguing for an imagined complementarity of Marxism and ecology, Raskin and Bernow (1991, 87) assail environmentalists for what they perceive to be an irresponsible and unsophisticated neglect of the "socioeconomic context of ecological disaster." In the view of another author (Rudig 1985–86), the "ungrounded" approach taken within much environmentalism has meant that initiatives are too often forced into either utopian or reformist responses. The most prominent Marxist commentators, Foster (2000, 2002), Harvey (2007), and Williams (2010), maintain that capitalist productive relations and commitments to profit at the expense of human or planetary need are most significant for an understanding of ecological destruction.

As Adkin (1992a, 145; 1992b) notes, eco-socialism is conceived most generally as "discursive practices that link ecological goals to a radical critique of capitalist society." Within eco-socialist discourse that has meant an understanding that the twin logics of capital accumulation and profit result in the pollution and contamination that workers experience directly at the workplace and in home communities (O'Connor 1998; Foster 2002; Harter 2004; Williams 2010; Foster, Clark, and York 2011). Eco-socialists have tried to make environmentalists aware that the compulsion of competition and growth encourage the use of technologies (such as the various machines used in the logging or pulp and paper industries) that result in unemployment at the same time as they intensify the destruction of diverse ecosystems. Globalization and the related threat of the capital strike likewise come under intense scrutiny within eco-socialist analyses (Bullard 1990; Harvey 2007; Foster, Clark, and York 2011). Eco-socialist arguments insist that "the labour-versus-environmentalist conflicts can be shown to stem from the trade-offs made necessary by a system geared towards the private appropriation of profit" (Adkin and Alpaugh 1988, 52).

Eco-socialism, in a very significant strategic shift away from non-socialist environmentalism, "identifies the capitalist biases in the state, judicial system, and cultural institutions, and it supports demands for greater access, accountability, and participation" (Adkin 1992a, 145). Eco-socialism has attempted a politically acute understanding of the state as an actor in a capitalist context. This shift has allowed eco-socialists to appreciate more fully than liberal environmentalism the various, and at times conflicting, involvements of state agencies in processes of ecological destruction.

The lingering problem for the eco-socialist project has been the lack of practical initiatives having any resonance in Green circles. Eco-socialists (see Foster 2002) had long assumed that a connection between ecology and labor would occur when the two sides saw a necessary relationship in eco-defense. The determining factor in the "new consciousness" was to be the involvement of socialist intellectuals (Adkin and Alpaugh 1988). There emerged, as a result, numerous attempts to insert a socialist discourse as "lightning rod" for an ecology/labor convergence, but with few real effects.

Perhaps most fatally, eco-socialist acceptance of structurally given identities and interests, as reinforced in a "jobs *and* environment" discourse, could not articulate the challenge to hegemonic conceptions of nature demanded by radical Greens. "Arguments are advanced about how environmental practices would create employment, but where is a radically different vision of an 'equilibrium' society whose dynamics are given not by the expansion of social labour and the consumption of goods?" (Adkin 1992a, 152). In accepting the domination of nature as the primary basis for "jobs" and through the continued equation of politics with the state, eco-socialism resists the more radical demands of ecology activists to forge "dark green" alliances that question the existing logic of production and consumption, and the defining of nature within it. Grundmann (1991) offers one of the clearest expressions of the anti-ecological possibilities of eco-socialism in calling for the domination of nature by humans (ironically as the starting point for overcoming ecological exploitation). Eco-socialism's apparent commitment to productivism and other traditional Marxist categories has contextualized "environmental relations" to mean *not* conditions of mutuality and complementarity with nature, but rather such forms of reproducible exploitation as tree farming. Even Pepper (1993, 221), in his otherwise excellent work, argues that Marxism, "wants to secure the material welfare of all humanity, through growth of productive forces via the 'domination' of nature."

From the perspective of much ecological thinking, traditional Marxism failed to make sense of the environment, typically relegating it to a supplement or accessory to the greater socialist cause (Clow 1986; Blackie 1990; Zerzan 2008a, 2008b), leaving undisturbed the presumption that nature serves as the stockpile of resources necessary for human freedom. For many Greens, eco-socialism, in failing to offer a counterhegemonic rendering of nature/society relations, is able to offer as an alternative little more than some form of the postwar Keynesian accommodation that rested upon the continued exploitation of nature (see Smith 2007). As a result, many Greens question whether the sort of social transformation of which eco-socialists speak is at all desirable. This lack of a dark-green vision accounts for the lack of appeal eco-socialism has for ecology's radicals.

Inasmuch as eco-socialism resists the colonization of workers and nature by the logics of profit and accumulation, it offers a radicalization of ecology beyond the parameters of liberal environmentalist discourse. By adhering to productivist, growth-dependent visions of human liberation and relations with nature, eco-socialism remains "light green" environmentally speaking. A lingering result of these tensions has been that relations between radical ecology and labor remain marked by separateness and festering tensions. "Into this battleground, our local Earth First! group has tried to bring some class consciousness of the variety prescribed by the Industrial Workers of the World" (Bari 1994, 14). Gaining some insight into the unique IWW/Earth First! alliance, forged despite enormous odds, is important given the crucial but difficult processes of alliance formation against the global capitalist order.

Toward Syndicalism

So we might now ask if a radical, counterhegemonic labor/ecology alliance can be formed given the failures of eco-socialism and the persistent distrust of Left ecology and organized labor within radical environmentalism? Do the lingering difficulties facing ecology and labor merely confirm postmodern doubts regarding counterhegemonic projects of the Left?

A tentative answer might begin by noting that most attempts to form a counterhegemonic point of attraction around ecology, "to class environmentalism," have pursued Marxian approaches. This approach has its own problems, as outlined above. Carroll and Ratner (1996) and Adam (1993), while encouraged by the presence of socialist visions within new movements, concede that these specific forms of new-movement socialism may actually be quite different from conventional Marxian understandings and often, in fact, owe more to anarchism, libertarian socialism, and syndicalism, both practically and philosophically.

Indeed Adkin (1992a, 148) suggests that more compelling challenges to capital in North America since the 1960s have emanated from anarchists and libertarian socialists. Others (Pepper 1993; Heider 1994; Harter 2004; Jakopovich 2007; Williams 2009a) propose anarcho-syndicalism as a more appropriate starting point for red/green alliances. Tucker (1991) and Jakopovich (2007) even suggest that much of the political distance separating movements such as ecology from workers might be attributed to a refusal to explore syndicalist strategies. Pepper (1993, 229) and Purchase (1994, 1997a, 1997b) argue that for a green socialism to be successful it would need to revive the syndicalist tradition, relying on militant labor-based organizations to confront the power of capital.

Pepper's optimism derives partly from his belief that the socialism of new movements shares certain commonalities with anarchosyndicalism. In this regard Tucker's work (1991) is instructive. He provides an intriguing argument for the similarities between French revolutionary syndicalism at the turn of the twentieth century and new social movements today. Tucker suggests that within French syndicalism one can discern such "new" themes as consensus decision making, direct participation, antihierarchy, dialogic process, decentralization, and autonomy (see also Hobsbawm 1979). These similarities are reflected also in the syndicalist emphasis upon direct action tactics, such as consumer boycotts and sabotage, as well as the contempt shown by syndicalists for the dominant radical traditions of their day (especially state socialism and social democracy).

Syndicalism refers to diverse movements and perspectives that take the collective self-organization and direct action of the working class both at the point of production, and within working class communities, as the basis not only for overcoming capitalism but for organizing a new, egalitarian society. While tracing its origins to the trade-union movements of the nineteenth century, the term syndicalism coming from the French word for unionism, *syndicalisme,* it has come to signify a radical or revolutionary approach to labor organizing that seeks to overthrow the wage relationship, capitalists, and class society rather than collectively bargain workers' place within the wage relationship.

Syndicalist unions, as opposed to bureaucratic unions, sought the organization of workers from the bottom up. Their strategies rejected large strike funds, negotiations, written contracts, and the supposed autonomy of trades. Actions took the form of "guerrilla tactics" including sabotage, slowdown, planned inefficiency, occupations, and passive resistance.

Perhaps the strongest and certainly the most enduring variant of syndicalism developed within anarchist movements in Spain and much of Latin America. Anarcho-syndicalism viewed the revolutionary self-organization of workers in radical opposition to capital, outside not only union bureaucracies but mainstream union frameworks themselves, limited as they were by collective bargaining over workers' contracts, as the means by which an anarchist society might be realized. Anarcho-syndicalism reached its highest level of popular involvement in Spain in the early decades of the twentieth century. The Confederation Nacional del Trabajo (CNT) played a major part in the Spanish Revolution and the resistance to the fascist regime of General Francisco Franco during the 1930s. The CNT was especially active in Barcelona during the revolution, running industries and providing social services in the region while organizing the armed resistance to fascist forces on the front lines.

Syndicalism also developed powerful movements in North America, most notably the Industrial Workers of the World (IWW or Wobblies), which was active in the United States, Canada, and Mexico, especially in the early 1900s and the One Big Union, which organized the Winnipeg General Strike in 1919. Destroyed almost completely by the Red Scare of 1919, the IWW has enjoyed something of a resurgence in the twenty-first century, especially among precarious workers in service industries often unorganized by the declining mainstream industrial unions. IWW perspectives with regard to capital emphasize workers' abilities and encourage the self-determination of workers and the importance of self-directed initiatives against capital. The IWW asserts that workers must organize themselves to fight employers directly. The symbolic unity of the working class and its break from capital is stressed in the single qualification for Wobbly membership. The only restriction to membership in the IWW is that no employer can be a member.

The IWW, as opposed to bureaucratic unions, sought the self-organization of workers beginning with the rank and file. As Montgomery (1974) notes, IWW strategies rejected large strike funds, negotiations, written contracts, and the supposed autonomy of trades. Furthermore, and of special significance for contemporary activists, the Wobblies placed great emphasis upon the nurturance of unity-in-diversity among workers. As Green (1974) notes, the IWW frequently organized in industrial towns marked by deep divisions, especially racial divisions, among the proletariat.

Montgomery suggests that direct action was "the main theme of a dozen years of fierce class conflict in America. During those years [1910–1922] a secondary theme of workers' control had recurred incessantly and become increasingly explicit" (517). Such actions, it should be noted, were not confined to IWW conflicts and Montgomery speaks of the emergence of a "new unionism" even within mainstream organizations. Syndicalist groupings were numerous and could be found even within the hated AFL.

Significantly, expressions of direct action were concentrated within modernized, large-scale industries. With assembly-line technologies and management styles, workers' resistance became covert, based in smaller, informal workplace groups. Again, responses often took the form of "guerrilla tactics" including sabotage, slowdown, planned inefficiency, and passive resistance, organized within the context of direct, face-to-face participation in informal work networks. Informal work groups, in the absence of legitimized control, became "a submerged, impenetrable obstacle to management's sovereignty" (Montgomery 1974, 518).

In addition to these organizing efforts, a primarily intellectual version of syndicalism was developed by the social theorist Georges Sorel in the 1910 and 1920s in France. Revolutionary syndicalism, as this variant was known, saw working-class direct action as the basis for a new society based on values of heroism and sacrifice, which stood counter to the apathy and social degeneracy of bourgeois society. Syndicalism, and worker direct action, stood also as a refutation of the rule of society by bureaucratic and technocratic professionals. For Sorel the general strike was most important not as a practical approach to labor organizing but rather as a "revolutionary myth" that served to rouse the fighting spirits of the working class and provided them with an image of the power of their unity in struggle. The vitality of the general strike was not so much material as ideological.

Syndicalism has enjoyed a resurgence recently in many parts of the world as workers seek an alternative to mainstream unions that seem unwilling to fight against multinational corporations. Many workers, including younger workers and workers in small workplaces that are often overlooked by mainstream unions, have turned to syndicalist organizing.

The Emergence of Green Syndicalism

Pepper (1993, 217–18) argues that a shift toward syndicalist-anarchist traditions might greatly aid environmentalism in a move away from its liberal tendencies. Though red/green coalitions are traditionally quite problematic, Pepper (221) believes they become more feasible when contemplated between greens and anarcho-syndicalists, given similarities in the organizing practices and political commitments to participatory democracy, autonomy, rank-and-file power, and direct action that greens and syndicalists share.

Recent developments show the convergence of labor and ecology perspectives and practices in a green syndicalist direction. During the early 1990s Roussopoulos (1991) noted the emergence of a green syndicalist perspective in France within the Confédération Nationale du Travail (CNT). Expressions of a green syndicalism have also been observed in Spain. There the Confederación General de Trabajadores (CGT) adopted social ecology as part of its struggle for "a future in which neither the person nor the planet is exploited" (Marshall 1993, 468). Likewise, syndical ecology has enjoyed some support in Australia, where it has enjoyed perhaps its longest tenure (see Pepper 1993; Purchase 1994, 1997a, 1997b).

In Australia, the "green bans" movement showed a number of features that were suggestive of a syndical ecology although the primary union organization behind the green bans was not a syndicalist organization (see Burgmann 2000; Burgmann and Burgmann 1998). Beginning in the early 1970s in New South Wales, the Builders Labourers Federation (BLF) worked to stop the destruction of green spaces, historic districts, and working-class communities by refusing to work on those projects. The BLF did all of this against its own economic interests, taking advantage of laborers' newfound economic clout in the midst of a massive development boom that was transforming Sydney and destroying low-income neighborhoods. Between 1971 and 1975 more than forty-nine bans halted projects worth more than A$5 billion (Burgmann 2000). Forest and island reserves were defended, and parks were saved from destruction. In what must have been a blow to the national bourgeoisie, the bans successfully ended plans for a car park adjacent to the Sydney Opera House that would have threatened the root systems of Moreton Bay fig trees. Perhaps most significantly, the BLF was able to make the connection between destruction of the environment and the destruction of working-class communities. The union opposed the eviction of tenants and refused to take part in gentrification projects. Significantly the union's actions inspired a groundswell of local opposition to redevelopment (Anderson and Jacobs 1999).

During 2000 the Electrical Trades Union resurrected the green ban tactic in an effort to halt construction of a thirty-four-meter light tower near the Melbourne Zoo. The union claimed that the light towers would harm the sleeping and breeding patterns of some animals. In September 2001 a number of community actions were held to support green bans against construction of a gas-fired power generator and its pipeline in Somerton, Victoria, because the pipeline would destroy the habitat of the endangered Growling Grass frog.

Other efforts have also emerged. Between March 31 and April 1, 2001, the CGT sponsored an international meeting of more than one dozen syndicalist and libertarian organizations including the CNT and the Swedish Workers Centralorganization (SAC). Among the various outcomes of the meeting were the formation of a Libertarian International Solidarity (LIS) network, commitments of financial and political support to develop a recycling cooperative, and the adoption of a libertarian manifesto, "What Type of Anarchism for the 21st Century?," in which ecology takes a very crucial place (Hargis 2001).

The IWW's Greenward Turn

In 1991 the Wobblies (IWW), following a union-wide vote, changed the preamble to the IWW constitution for the first time since 1908. The preamble now reads as follows:

> The working class and the employing class have nothing in common. There can be no peace so long as hunger and want are found among millions of the working people and the few, who make up the employing class, have all the good things of life.
>
> Between these two classes a struggle must go on until the workers of the world organize as a class, take possession of the means of production, abolish the wage system, *and live in harmony with the earth*. (emphasis added)

Those seven words present a significant shift in strategy regarding industrial unionism and considerations of what is to be meant by work. At the same time, their embedding within the constitution's original class struggle narrative draws a mythic connection with the history of the IWW and the practices of revolutionary syndicalism. The greening of the IWW was more explicitly expressed through a statement issued by the union's General Assembly at the time of the preamble change. It is worth quoting at length.

> In addition to the exploitation of labor, industrial society creates wealth by exploiting the earth and non-human species. Just as the capitalists value the working class only for their labor, so they value the earth and non-human species only for their economic usefulness to humans. This has created such an imbalance that the life support systems of the earth are on the verge of collapse. The working class bears the brunt of this degradation by being forced to produce, consume and live in the toxic environment created by this abuse. Human society must recognize that all beings have a right to exist for their own sake, and that humans must learn to live in balance with the rest of nature.

This philosophical shift has been simultaneous with the recent upswing in IWW activism over the last two decades. Although the IWW has never returned to the numbers of members it enjoyed in the 1910s and 1920s, the last decade has seen a revitalization of the radical union as it has organized a number of workplaces in North America. As it was historically, the IWW is a union that organizes the unorganized, including the unemployed. Significantly, the increases in direct actions around ecology have come from the largest workplace branches, not simply students or unemployed members. Ecological activism has encouraged a decentralization of formerly centrist union projects along with a revival of contacts with other industrial unions.

Curiously, little attention has been given to the most influential North American expression of green syndicalism. For this unique project, Judi Bari and other IWW and Earth First! activists attempted to build alliances with loggers in order to save old-growth forest in Northern California "and replace the corporate timber companies with environmentally responsible worker-owned cooperatives" (Chase 1991, 23). The unlikely context for a radical ecology–labor alliance was one of pitched struggle in which environmentalists of all stripes employed such diverse tactics as tree-sitting, blockades, lawsuits, and lobbying to stop destruction of the ancient forests by multinational timber companies, which were noted for such infamous tactics as felling trees into demonstrations. These environmental battles became some of the most heated in North America, eventually earning the title "timber wars." In response Bari sought to learn from the organizing practices of the IWW to see if a radical ecology movement might be built along anarcho-syndicalist lines. In so doing she tried to bring a radical working-class perspective to the agitational practices of Earth First! Her actions led to the formation of IWW/ Earth First! Local 1, a synthesis that brought loggers and environmentalists together as participants. Bari came to understand that "if we reduce our consumption of trees, . . . and if we stop the cutting of old growth, we will create the necessity for retraining workers and even a whole new kind of economy " (Paul McIsaac, quoted in Bookchin and Foreman 1991, 47). What is perhaps most interesting about the evolution of the IWW and the Redwood Summer of 1990 was the effort to unite radical ecology and timber workers through a series of political actions along with a unique attempt to develop an organizational infrastructure. IWW/Earth First! Local 1 provided an important, if underappreciated, "real world" project to effect a dialogue between radical ecology and labor through a greening of revolutionary syndicalism.

More recently, members of the IWW and Earth First! joined forces with rank-and-file members of the United Steelworkers of America (USWA) to support striking sheet metal workers at Kaiser Aluminum in Washington State (Harter 2004; Early 2009). Workers at Kaiser endured two years of strike and lockout, in 1998–2000, in struggle with a company owned by Charlie Hurwitz's Maxxam corporation. This was the very same company that owns Pacific Lumber, the logging operation clearing the redwood forests of California against which Local 1 fought. The IWW was instrumental in forming a worker-environmentalist coalition, the Alliance for Sustainable Jobs and the Environment, and organized a series of ongoing solidarity actions, including picket lines, flotilla pickets, and banner hangings at the Port of Tacoma where scab labor was deployed to unload a shipment of ore (Harter 2004). In the last action, the ship carrying ore was prevented from unloading its cargo and was forced to remain in port for twenty-four days rather than the typical seven (Earth First! 1999; Barnes and Kashdan 2002). As Harter (2004) suggests, this kind of action and the efforts of Earth First!ers and the IWW during the Kaiser strike and lockout shows the great potential for a truly united struggle that articulates and builds upon the interconnectedness of labor and the environment. As the EF! report on the IWW/EF!/Steelworker alliance put it: "When you have Charles Hurwitz exploiting both his workers and the land, it's a natural coalition."

Unlike the practice and perspectives of most of eco-socialism, green syndicalists have not directed the bulk of their energies toward alliances with official leadership and formal union structures. Rather, as we will see, green syndicalists have concentrated their efforts on two primary approaches to organizing beyond formal or official structures. On the one hand, green syndicalists have attempted to build alternative unions, organizing the unorganized, those who are not members of mainstream unions. On the other hand, green syndicalists have focused on building rank-and-file networks, committees and flying squads, or rapid-response direct-action teams, bringing together union members across union or local affiliations. Typically these efforts have involved organizing that brings together rank-and-file unionists, nonunionized workers, and community members within shared organizations, spaces, and actions.

In response to the collapse of Teamsters and Turtles many labor organizers and rank-and-file unionists believe that hopes for joint projects will be achieved on a smaller scale, primarily at local levels (see Walker 2002; Early 2009). Of course syndicalists are well aware that rank-and-file members do not control the mainstream unions, which has been a cause of much concern among syndicalists historically. At the same time, syndicalists have responded by attempting to build participatory networks of rank-and-file members, recognizing this as a prerequisite of workplace democracy as well as the primary means by which a radical working-class movement might develop from the bottom up. It is toward this face-to-face organizing among rank-and-file workers that green syndicalists have dedicated their efforts.

To be sure, the fact that union members opposed the Alaskan drilling by two to one gives cause for continued hope. It also shows the undemocratic, authoritarian, and problematic character of mainstream union structures and the structure of the AFL-CIO more broadly. It is these undemocratic and hierarchical structures that have been opposed by green syndicalists who attempt to draw on the democratic, participatory rank-and-file organizing practices of historic syndicalist unions such as the IWW and the Spanish CNT.

Appealing directly to workers and addressing their concerns and insecurities, and the connections between economic, social, and ecological crises, is crucial for environmentalists. In part it will assist in countering the role of union leadership who would seek to make deals with employers and/or government policy makers in order to preserve their own privileged positions within the existing labor hierarchy

(Walker 2002; Early 2009; Shantz 2010). According to labor organizer Charles Walker:

> Those union officials do more than argue that now is not the time for one or another environmental protection. They also attempt to mislead workers, by appealing to workers' need for work, and worker's understandable fear of joblessness. But if environmentalists take up the jobs issue head-on, and convince worker that now is the time to fight both for jobs and a safer environment, the environmentalists would stand a far better chance of realizing their ecological goals in time to matter. (2002, 8)

As Walker (2002, 8) notes: "Despite the failure if the AFL-CIO to join in a nation-wide alliance, the environmental movement's best hope is still the workers who are marching to a different drummer than the labour tops. Fighting for 'Jobs and Environmental Protections for All!' can cement a powerful alliance for change." At the same time, as has been shown repeatedly, the devil is in the details. How such an alliance might be formed remains an ongoing question. Green syndicalism provides one compelling, if overlooked, response.

By focusing upon radicalizing voices from the margins, particularly within the context of mainstream union organizing, I hope to contribute to the projects urged by Masterson-Allen and Brown (1990), Bullard (1990), Adam (1993) and Selbin (2010) to enrich our understandings of diverse contributions to ecological and labor discourses and practices—especially the relations of ecology to class discourses. The workers' ecology narratives of green syndicalism may offer some contribution to what Adam (1993) calls a "phenomenology of class"—descriptions that journey beyond caricatured economistic concerns of job security and income.

In the present context there remains a real need to bring into focus the differently placed and variously resourced actors, in movements, trade unions, and nongovernmental organizations (NGOs), that make up the interacting and sometimes competing networks of global justice movements. It is necessary to highlight the different attempts by different actors (peasants, industrial workers, students, caregivers) to forge mutual solidarities in pursuit of social, economic and environmental justice (Williams 2011). The focus on convergence spaces, what Routledge and Cumbers call "associations of differentially placed actors and resources which are put into circulation in a continual effort to make political actions durable through time and mobile across space," aids a necessary move away from more abstract claims about global justice networks (2010, 196). Geographically dispersed social coalitions show that place-based is not necessarily place-restricted and political action can be spatially extensive.

The present discussion addresses both the practical/strategic and theoretical aspects of ecological activism. By working to overcome the scarcity of available information concerning processes of radicalization and movement formation, it is hoped that this investigation may contribute to a situating of ecological antagonisms within broader counterhegemonic struggles.

The emergent greening of syndicalist theory and practice is significant in the questions it poses regarding the possibilities (and problems) for a radical convergence of social movements and the place of syndicalist practice in effecting a convergence between environmentalists and industrial or resource workers. Pepper (1993, 198) suggests that Greens should pay more attention to anarcho-syndicalist ideas, proposing that an infusion of anarcho-syndicalism might shake up the contemporary Green movement in North America just as syndicalism shook up the labor movement of the 1910s. Unfortunately, Pepper has had little to say about Local 1 or other manifestations of green syndicalism. In that he is not alone. Very little attention has been given to the implications of green syndicalism, and its emergence has gone largely unremarked in the socialist literature. This book offers an attempt to overcome this glaring oversight in the discussion of red/green alliances.

Green Syndicalism

1

Class Struggles

Marxism, New Social Movement Theories, and Ecology

What have been called the global justice or alternative globalization movements have been identified by numerous commentators as the most significant development in anticapitalist or antisystemic politics since the fall of the Berlin Wall and Soviet communism (see Routledge and Cumbers 2010). Especially since the events of Seattle in 1999 (but dating at least to the Zapatista uprising against neoliberal capitalism of 1994), the global justice movements have challenged the "End of History" triumphalism of neoliberal capitalism and posed prospects for an alternative global future based on justice and solidarity rather than profit and competition.

The aggressive character of capitalist expansion, that is, neoliberal "globalization," challenges contemporary social movements to build unity among the diversity of those threatened by the social and environmental dislocations wrought by global capital. R. B. J. Walker stresses the crucial need for social movements to develop what he calls a "politics of connection." Social movement analysis must avoid tendencies to speak of movements as singular without giving serious attention to the difficulties encountered by attempts to form alliances or broaden participation. "Whatever the rhetorical and tactical appeal of a woman's movement, or an environmental movement in the singular, it is an appeal that cannot disguise the differences and even intolerances among such movements" (1994, 699).

Examining spaces of convergence shows not only the interactions of solidarity that strengthen the movements (and the real ongoing

1

work involved in constructing and maintaining network relations) but also the real tensions and challenges that exist on a regular and often ongoing basis (Williams 2011). Notably, examples such as those presented in *Global Justice Networks* by Paul Routledge and Andrew Cumbers show the tensions and contradictions between the more mobile elites who can partake in global convergence spaces and the forced territoriality (by class, borders, racism, and gender among others) that constrain those who *are* the movement on the ground in local struggles but who cannot access the global aspect of the global justice movements of which they are fundamentally part.

Too often the only shared spaces or practices to receive extended analysis have been the ephemeral street spaces of the dramatic street protests outside meetings of global capital, as during the International Monetary Fund (IMF) or G8/G20 meetings. We must be sure to stress that convergence spaces, and the connections between participants, occur in disorganized and unstructured fashion, a reflection of the networked and horizontalist aspect of the global resistance to capitalism today (Routledge and Cumbers 2010).

The development of so-called global justice movements has given rise to wide-ranging discussions concerning the dynamics of social change and the strategies for transforming advanced capitalist societies. These various "newest social movements" theories assert that social movements such as the women's movements, the gay and lesbian movements, and the environmental movements represent truly novel sources of change (Halfmann 1988; Eckersley 1989; Rohrschneider 1990; Darnovsky 1995; Day 2005; Mouffe 2005; Laclau 2007; Selbin 2010). The essential tension underlying much of social movement theorizing, indeed the very thing against which these arguments are implicitly or explicitly formulated, is a strong sense of unease concerning class struggle and the position of industrial workers in collective movements for radical social change.

Certainly the class locations and consciousness of participants within recent social movements (especially students and radical youth) and the issues raised by those movements (e.g., environmentalism, lesbian and gay rights, feminism, global justice, and alternative globalization) have posed compelling challenges to class analyses. New categories and experiences of subordination have emerged as points for mobilization, and an awareness of these categories and the practices that sustain them has played an important part in overcoming the economism of much of Marxist theory. Class must be contextualized as it is lived, and the lived experiences of class include problems of race, gender, sexuality, and environment.

As John-Henry Harter (2004) argues, simply reasserting the primacy of class as a means of countering the claims of new social movements that labor is not suited to act as an agent of progressive transformation can only exacerbate the mutual distrust that exists between the different camps. However, in Harter's view, and this is a position shared by eco-socialists and green syndicalists alike, recognition by both labor and environmentalists that they have shared concerns and a common enemy could contribute to working relationships on a variety of campaigns.

As several authors (Adam 1993; Darnovsky 1995; Starn 1997; Tarrow 1994; Routledge and Cumbers 2010; Selbin 2010) stress social movements are resistant to unicausal explanations. According to Starn (1997, 235), the decision to mobilize "underscores the need to insist on social analyses that avoid the extremes of an ungrounded culturalism or a deterministic economism to examine the inseparable intertwining of cultural meaning and political economy in human experience." Even movements that are viewed, and indeed view themselves, as being expressive of "new values," such as environmentalism, have interesting intersections with class movements that are largely downplayed or overlooked in much of new movement discussion. For example, one might think of the significant and sustained efforts of union health and safety committees to control industrial impacts upon nature. To separate these efforts from "environmentalism" proper is purely arbitrary—especially so if one considers that environmental contaminants and their consequences are concentrated and most severely felt in working-class communities.

Amid the decay of Marxian analyses have arisen a series of theories by and about the "new social movements" that seek to address some of the fundamental issues of social theory, such as the nature of historical agency, the role of identity in politics, and the prospects for the radicalization and extension of democracy. Discourses around nature, gender, and labor suffer many of the problems of reductionism, essentialism, and unrealized syncretism, which are symptomatic of a certain disarray in "post-Marxian" social theory. While some versions of postmodernism would affirm this disarray in a Voltairean retreat to cultivate one's own particular theoretical backyard, I prefer to attend to questions regarding the difficult construction of counterhegemonies in advanced capitalist societies.

The relations between participants in the old hegemonic paradigm of the welfare state, particularly unions and labor parties and their varied relations to capitalist growth, have come under scrutiny by "new social movement" activists, within the context of neoliberal triumph and the decomposition of prior political formations. The ostensible capitulation of labor to capital via consumerism has posed seemingly impenetrable barriers to syntheses between elements of "old" and "new" movements. It is this complicity of organized labor in the expansion of capitalist relations that, perhaps more than anything else, has impelled the new movements' "retreat from class" (Wood 1986). Simultaneously, organized labor, with a "massified" and too often pacified constituency (where it has any constituency at all), often isolated from social movements, and forgetful of its own activist histories, has continued to decompose as a relevant force. Unable, even minimally, to disrupt legislative enactments such as the North American Free Trade Agreement (NAFTA) or, more recently, to halt the workplace closures and foreclosures on workers' homes that have marked the recent financial crisis, which represent direct assaults upon its own social positions, the labor movement seems an unlikely candidate to constitute a focus for any convergence of alternative rebellions (Shantz 2010).

The possibilities for social transformation raised within the new social movements have posed difficult questions about what is to be considered *radical* change and how such change relates to the projects of so-called "older" social movements, especially labor movements.

Some theorists (Harter 2004; Burkett 2006; Early 2009; Williams 2010; Foster, Clark, and York 2011) maintain that possibilities for cultivating a new radicalism will be dependent largely upon the capacities of new movements to articulate their demands in alliances with the traditional Left or labor. Only an alliance of new social movements with traditional Left forces is expected to provide opportunities for an effective challenge to the "old paradigm of politics" (Offe 1985).

Aronowitz argues that a new historic bloc might emerge out of what he calls "a micropolitics of autonomous oppositional movements," including those that arise from production relations. The new bloc might be constituted of those forces that "despite their particular oppositions, recognize the task of general emancipation" (1990, 167). Significantly, Aronowitz includes those "older" movements demanding self-management and the democratization of workplaces along with "new" movements such as ecology. Following Laclau and Mouffe (1985) and Harter (2004) it might be expected that broadened transformative struggles emerge out of specific, localist resistance through active construction and nurturance of moments of interdependence or the constitution of commonality out of contexts of practical discordance. These struggles raise new possibilities and open realms for creation and imagination as questions of identity and relation come to be (re)considered.

Such alliances have proved quite difficult to establish, however. The prominence of clashes between environmental movements and movements of labor cause one to wonder if there is much real hope for any radicalized alliances. It is an extremely complex question, one that incorporates a variety of related issues. For instance, one might ask further: "What kinds of alliances?" "What types of radicalization?"

Laclau and Mouffe (1985) provide a starting point for addressing these questions. They suggest that the economy can no longer claim a privileged position as a wellspring of political struggle. Social formations involve a plurality of possible antagonisms and cannot be reduced to a single logic. Furthermore, any social formation develops through ongoing political struggle. Class becomes decentered.

However, and this poses a key challenge for theorists of social movements who have been *too ready* to take this idea *too far*, decentering economic relations and denying them a position of determination does not imply that we should turn away from or abandon the specificities of class. Denying class a *privileged* role in politics or the transformation of social relations does not mean that social movements have no relation to questions of class. "Surely even a post-Marxist scheme will have to incorporate an understanding of the economy and class forces into its conceptual structure" (Boggs 1986, 16; See also Adam 1993; Carty 2008). However, there has been continued resistance to the inclusion of class conflicts and the efforts of workers within the political conceptualizations of new social movements both theoretically and practically. Indeed, the typical approaches to a decentering of class tend to leave unattended the hegemonic processes by which the significance of production relations is constituted (see Day 2005).

In recent years social movement and environmental theorists have devoted a great deal of energy to efforts that argue the demise of class struggle as a viable force for social change (see Eckersley 1989; Smith 2001; Day 2005; Jensen 2006; Zerzan 2005, 2008a, 2008b). These theorists argue that analyses of class struggle are unable to account for the plurality of expressions that hierarchy, domination, and oppression take in advanced capitalist or "postindustrial" global societies (see Bookchin 1980, 1986; Hardt and Negri 2001; Smith 2001; Day 2005; Zerzan 2008b). The result has been a broad turn away from questions of class and especially class struggle. Concerns have been raised that analyses of class inevitably assume one-dimensional identities of a fixed and determined character (see Hardt and Negri 2001; Mouffe 2005; Laclau 2007; Zerzan 2008b; Selbin 2010). Unfortunately, the response has too often been a denial of the significance of class struggle without a more critical analysis of the ways in which class struggle is conceptualized.

Both the orthodox construction of class struggle and the arguments raised against that conceptualization have been constrained by theoretically narrow visions of class struggle. Commentators have either taken class to mean an undifferentiated monolith (Bookchin

1986, 1987; Zerzan 2008a, 2008b) that acts, or more often fails to act, as the instrumental agent in history or else as a fiction generated to obscure hopelessly divided and antagonistic relations (Laclau and Mouffe 1985; Bourdieu 1987; Laclau 2007). What is generally missing from these otherwise disparate accounts is a dynamic understanding of people as workers and workers as activists.

Indeed one might argue that much of the difficulty arises from arguments over the sociologically constructed working class (e.g., the Marxist "totality" that posits a privileged role to workers) rather than the working class in its variety of daily negotiated manifestations. Certain theorists have examined the economistic construction of the working class as constituted by orthodox Marxism (see Laclau and Mouffe 1985 for an excellent analysis of the orthodox Marxist perspective of the working class and class struggles). The typical extension of such examinations, however, has been to reject the orthodox construction and, in rejecting it, to reject all ideas of class struggle and its revolutionary implications (Adkin 1992a, 1992b; Sandilands 1992; Hardt and Negri 2001; Day 2005; Zerzan 2008b).

As noted previously, this tension between class and social movement analysis has perhaps nowhere been more openly contested and hostile than in the case of the radical ecology movements (Jakopovich 2007; Williams 2009b; Shantz 2010; Williams 2010; Foster, Clark, and York 2011). As Kivisto (1986, 38) noted two decades ago: "Here in microcosm the fundamental issues that confront the new social movements coalesce." Indeed, this remains true despite some advances in alliance-building during the recent demonstrations against the World Trade Organization (WTO) and the International Monetary Fund (IMF) and World Bank.[1] The heated and often angry debates that have emerged in alternative globalization protests, as in

---

1. The city-by-city demonstrations against bodies of global corporate rule such as the WTO, World Bank, and IMF, are located away from the front lines of ecological destruction where industrial workers and environmentalists clash and are therefore not typical. Still, emerging rifts within those movements between direct actionists and trade unionists highlight the lingering difficulties in building alliances.

Toronto during the G20 meetings of 2010, show the tensions that remain and the importance of these questions in the current context. Some of these debates are detailed and analyzed in following chapters. That the most aggressive disagreements have occurred between social activist proponents of direct action and union spokespeople arguing against direct action in favor of legal channels is particularly telling. These are central issues to be addressed by organizers and activists in the present period, ones that challenge familiar notions of identity and organization. Therefore this chapter addresses the key issue of connecting workers and the ecology movement through a discussion of socialist, new social movement, and ecological theories and some of the obstacles that their framing of the issues has posed for a broadened articulation of antisystemic struggles.

Marxism

Marxists (Callinicos 1990; Smith 1994; Carty 2008; Williams 2010) have been especially critical of new social movements' theorists for remaining silent with regard to the crucial questions of convergence and universalization of social struggles. Marxists have attempted to answer these questions by asserting the existence of a historic agent whose self-realization will engender that imagined mastery of the social which renders possible the expulsion of negativity. The historic agent is, of course, the famous "working class," which is able to effect convergence and universality as the "natural" outcome of "losing its chains."

Marxists hold to a belief that the permanence of difference, the condition that threatens to interfere with and disrupt convergence, can be overcome through a total identity of the working class in socialist transformation (Aronowitz 1990, 168; Carty 2008). The Marxist solution, socialism as full positivity, offers a homogeneous and transparent society within which the negativity and opaqueness of the social disappear (Laclau 2007; Carty 2008). Socialism provides the objective reading of liberation that will bring about the end of history, ideology, and struggle.

But why should we be optimistic that the historical subject will do the job assigned it? The convergence of the revolutionary agent with its revolutionary tasks is, the Marxists tell us, all but assured (eventually) because the class "interests" of the proletariat are objectively counter to those of capital. Sharon Smith provides a typical offering of Marxist hope: "The working class has no interest in maintaining a system which thrives upon inequality and oppression" (1994, 40). According to classical Marxist theorizing, workers' real material interests are inscribed directly by their positioning within the real material conditions of existing social structure. Classical Marxism, according to Hall (1988, 44), "assumes an empiricist relation of the subject to knowledge, namely, that the real world indelibly imprints its meanings and interests directly into our consciousness. We have only to look to discover its truths." Within Marxist economism, classes constituted at the economic "level" determine hegemonic roles within the sphere of politics. This is given voice in arguments, such as those offered by Smith (1994) and Carty (2008), that working-class movements have greater hegemonic potential or transformative capacities given their "central" structural position in capitalist relations of production. Thus one's place in the political is referred back to origins in economy. "And class is nevertheless the key division within society" (Smith 1994, 45). Thus class is expected simultaneously to serve as the line of demarcation and point for convergence. (Nothing is said of a nature/human divide because such a dualism is accepted as pregiven and unchangeable—indeed, the "overcoming" of nature is nothing less than the human species realizing itself as human). In a passage that unambiguously expresses the lingering essentialism of many Marxists, Smith (1994, 47) pleads that "workers' *objective* role within the productive process places them in an *objectively antagonistic relationship* to capital" (emphasis in original). Never mind the inconvenient detail that more often than not relations between workers and capital have been marked by compromise and partnership. Clearly, it is problematical to assume, as Smith does, that antagonism is inherent to the relations of production. For instance, the discourses of "jobs" and "nation" reflect working-class strategies that are anything but antagonistic toward capital. Working classes within advanced capitalist contexts, far from being revolutionary, are, as Aronowitz (1990, 164) contends, "heir to a long tradition of compromise with capital." Indeed, the historic presence of non-antagonism, as exhibited by the working classes at various junctures, brings out what Stuart Hall (1988, 43) suggests is nothing less than "the whole dilemma of classical marxist theory in our time as a guide to political action." Simply put, this dilemma arises from the abject failure of classical Marxism to account for historic developments of consciousness and practice (Laclau 2007). Not only do such Marxist approaches entail a reductionism to class, for which all subjectivities have a necessarily class character; Marxist reductionism additionally supposes a necessary paradigmatic form, an appropriate consciousness, belonging to each social class (Mouffe 1988, 2005). The ongoing and in certain instances deepening conflicts between ecology and labor, and the persistence of anti-ecological perspectives among workers, even as ecology attempts the disruption of capitalist relations of production, offer testimony to the impossibility of such "objective" explanations.

According to Laclau (1991), classical Marxist theoretics are founded upon dual essentialist conceptions; one concerning society, the other as regards human agency. These variants of essentialism have been voiced, in the first instance, through a conception of society as a definable totality, upon which rest all of its partial elements; and, in the second case, through a conception of human agency that posits an ultimate homogeneity of the subject (Laclau 2007). Recently both assumptions have been brought to crisis. To understand the problems presently confronting theory requires an analysis of each crisis. It is precisely this task which is undertaken by Laclau (1988, 1990, 1991, 2005, 2007).

First, the crisis of social totality. Classical Marxism presents the social as a structural totality with its own identifiable and intelligible positivity, as society. This totality has assumed the character of an essential order for which social life merely expresses surface variations or tendencies. The founding totality is offered as an object of knowledge. Recognizing the underlying logic of the social order only requires peering beneath these surface manifestations (Laclau 1991). Thus Smith can argue about the objective centrality of class, as detailed above. "Against this essentialist vision we tend nowadays to accept the *infinitude of the social,* that is the fact that any structural system is limited, that it is always surrounded by an 'excess of meaning' which it is unable to master and that, consequently, 'society' as a unitary and intelligible object which grounds its own partial processes is an impossibility" (Laclau 1991, 25).

If we turn now to the essentialism regarding human agency we are confronted with similar problems which need be addressed. The Classical Marxist position assumes an ultimate subject whose identity can be fixed (see Laclau 2007; Carty 2008). The Marxist notion of false consciousness emerges to describe the condition wherein a subject fails to recognize its true identity. "And this implies, of course, that that identity must be *positive* and *non-contradictory.* Within Marxism, a conception of subjectivity of this kind is at the basis of the notion of 'objective class interests'" (Laclau 1991, 26). The overflow of meanings characterizing the social also holds when one speaks of subjectivity. Laclau (1991, 2007) inquires after what it means, then, to say that subjects fail to recognize themselves. His conclusion: "The theoretical ground that made sense of the concept of 'false consciousness' has evidently dissolved" (Laclau 1991, 26).

Recognizing this general failure in Marxist attempts to substitute a metaphysical postulate for pragmatic attempts to effect convergence actively, Mouffe (1988, 90) calls for a critique of the entire notion of class interests. Such a notion, it is argued, "entails fixing necessary political and ideological forms within determined positions within the production process." However, this conceptualization rests, according to Laclau and Mouffe (1985), on the incorrect assumption that social actors, on the basis of stable and essentially *pregiven* identities (and interests), simply enter into strategic relations with an already formed contextual exterior. It is exactly this type of assumption that is called into question by those inquiring after the new social movements. As Hall warns us, "[t]he logics of ideological inference turn out to be more multivariate, the automatic connections between material and ideal factors less determinate, than the classical theory would have us believe" (Hall 1988, 43). If interests, as Mouffe is led to contend, can never exist prior to the discourses constituting them, then they cannot be said to represent already existing social positions be they at an economic or at any other level. Furthermore, social groupings express multiple interests; these interests are often contradictory and oppositional, transforming over time. "A person's subjectivity is not constructed only on the basis of his or her position in the relations of production. Furthermore, each social position, each subject position, is itself the locus of multiple possible constructions, according to the different discourses that can construct that position" (Mouffe 1988, 90).

Solidarity, then, is always tenuous and only provisionally fixed "at the intersection of various discourses" (Mouffe 1988, 90). "How people come to *identify* themselves with some others in opposition to still other people is always a particular historical process which is not predetermined along a single political dimension, such as exclusion from production decisions, but rather follows complex patterns of inferiorization in the many spheres of life" (Adam 1993, 325).

As Laclau (1990, 202) notes, the articulation between the mode of production and the "political" is not derivable from any endogenous logic of the mode of production itself. Against any ideas of antagonism as being inherent to the relations of production, Laclau (1990, 221) argues that "antagonism is not established *within* capitalist relations of production, but *between* the latter and the identity of the social agents—workers included—outside of them" (emphasis in original). Given the contingency introduced by the recognition of exteriority in this relationship, Laclau concludes that "there are no grounds at all for the role of workers to be privileged a priori over that of other sectors in the anti-capitalist struggle." Furthermore, any specific grouping, including workers, can only occupy a partial position within anti-capitalist struggles. "This does not mean that workers' organizations cannot play an important hegemonic role in the direction of popular struggles in certain circumstances; but it does mean that this depends on concrete historical conditions and cannot be logically deduced from the mode of production" (Laclau 1990, 221).

According to Mouffe (1988) the emergence, at specific junctures, of a central position for a particular grouping only reflects the capacities of that grouping to constitute this convergence, rather than expressing any ontological privilege inherent to the group. Even this "center" is dependent upon the constant interplay of diverse forces that are extended from multiple positions of struggle.

Inasmuch as classes come into being they are constituted through discursive practices "with no necessary reference to any objectively given conditions" (Rustin 1988, 154). This constituting of classes occurs on the terrain of those hegemonic antagonisms over which they are engaged. Class struggles and even the processes of formation of classes are, furthermore, always ideological (Aronowitz 1990, 164). Again, this ideological character suggests that any social or political centrality of workers or trade unions is not strictly an outcome of necessary structural effects, as Smith (1994) might argue, but relates to specific contexts.

Elemental explanations of class have clearly been incapable of drawing any necessary connection between industrial workers and ecology. Indeed, as Harter (2004) points out, such attempts typically serve only to drive more of a wedge between movements. A class-centric typology of environmental activism, inherent within Marxian discourses, for which ecology is reduced to a representation of interests is clearly problematic. Ecology as floating signifier, ambiguous and contestable, cannot be constrained within unitary or reductionist class terms. This is crucial if any construction of class identities occurs on the very same terrain occupied by the circulation of those signifiers (Laclau 2007). Classes—more specifically, class solidarity—are the outcomes of social struggles, not the expression of economic structures.

It can no longer be said, then, that there is any logical or fundamental connection between radical objectives and the positioning of social agents with regard to the relations of production. Unity does not arise, then, as necessary political outcome from social relations of production or material interests (Laclau and Mouffe 1985; Mouffe

1988; Laclau 2007). Thus, there is no reason to privilege class as the point of origin for subjectivity. And at any rate, class is not the only grounds for social interests. "There are multiple forms of power in society that cannot be reduced to or deduced from one origin or source" (Mouffe 1988, 91).

If Not Class Then . . . ? To the Newest Social Movements

It is toward these multiple (other) forms of power that a recent wave of theorizing has turned in hopes of finding a solution to the problems of convergence and solidarity. Seeking to move beyond the limitations of classical Marxist constructions, some theorists of new social movements have argued for the substitution of other classes or of specific movements, such as new class (Eckersley 1989) or environmentalist (Touraine 1981) or anarchist (Day 2005) groupings, for a working class grown increasingly suspect. Ecology theorist Murray Bookchin, for example, inverts the Marxist position through a complete rejection of the proletariat and by inserting, in its place, a "classless class," that is, the cultural rebels of the new movements, as the truly privileged revolutionary subject. In this case we can see that the Marxist problematic has not been avoided. Structural location is still determining, even if for Bookchin it refers to one's *exclusion from* the relations of production (as unemployed or dropout, for example) rather than one's positionality *within* them (as industrial worker or service worker, for example). It is not simply that the Marxist perspective reduces to economy which calls it into question. Any approach that is founded upon a final narrative, be it one of race, gender, or even nature instead of class, becomes problematized.

Much of new, and "newest" (Day 2005), social movement theory is based upon a premise that capitalist societies have entered a new, possibly postindustrial, age in which class conflicts have given way to struggles over culture. This is said to be reflected in the class identities (or lack thereof) of participants in new movements (especially students and radical youth), and the issues raised by those movements (e.g., ecology, gay and lesbian rights, feminism), which have tempered class analyses in various ways. Various proponents of new movement theory over the years (Kivisto 1986; Melucci 1989; Tarrow 1994; Darnovsky 1995; Omi and Winant 1996; Black 1997; Hardt and Negri 2001; Smith 2001; Day 2005; Routledge and Cumbers 2010; Selbin 2010) have noted that the movements are, in large part, a response to the perceived hegemony of Marxist class analyses in previous struggles for progressive social change—analyses that are no longer adequate for an understanding of oppression under modern or postindustrial capitalism. In Kivisto's (1986, 32) view: "An important consequence of the emphasis on class divisions and class conflicts is that other modes of societal dissent and protest are devalued." In response, new social movements theorists give less attention to economic class divisions. Class conflict has seemingly passed over to new forms of conflict that have as their terrain the civic and cultural realms.

Of particular interest to the present work is the claim of new social movements theories that the working class has failed as an engine for radical change. Eckersley (1989, 205) notes that "much has been written in recent times about the decline . . . of the traditional 'blue-collar' working class as an innovatory political force." An argument is made that if the working-class struggle once held potential for a transformation of society, that time has since passed. So-called postindustrial society is deemed too complex for a simple two-class Marxian analysis in this view.

Ernesto Laclau and Chantal Mouffe (1985) have provided perhaps the most penetrating analysis and critique of the conception that views social division as arising from a duality of "opposing systems of equivalences"—in the case of Marxism, from the antagonisms of class. According to Laclau and Mouffe, the last time a dualist conception of social division could be reasonably posed was in the opposition between the "people" and the "ancien régime." After that particular moment the dualist understanding of antagonism "became increasingly fragile and ambiguous, and its construction came to be the crucial problem of politics" (1985, 151). It was, according Laclau and Mouffe, in answer to this problem that Marx developed the principle of class confrontation.

For Laclau and Mouffe this Marxian conceptualization was flawed from the start. In their words, "class opposition is incapable of dividing the totality of the social body into two antagonistic camps, of reproducing itself automatically as a line of demarcation in the political sphere" (1985, 151). They suggest that it was because of this fundamental flaw that Marxist theoretics have been in constant need of supplementary hypotheses that have sought to attach conditions to the historical realization of class struggle as the fundamental principle of political division. These supplementary hypotheses have included such imaginative constructions as "class consciousness," "false consciousness," or the "homogenization" of the social through immiseration.

The criticisms raised by Laclau and Mouffe have very serious implications when one turns from the realm of theory to the actual initiatives of the new social movements and to their visions of social change. Laclau and Mouffe suggest that any truly radical democracy must reject the dual opposition posed in Jacobin and Marxist political conceptions. Likewise, they call for the rejection of notions of privileged historical players and accept instead "the plurality and indeterminacy of the social" (1985, 152). They are particularly bothered by the idea that the working class represents the privileged agent in which the fundamental engine of social change is housed.

In *Hegemony and Socialist Strategy*, Laclau and Mouffe, through a fascinating and well-argued discussion of the problems confronting orthodox Marxism, critically address the idea of social totality. They suggest that it is the very lack of unity represented by the working class that provides the cause of the so-called crisis in Marxism. As a result corollary ideas such as the historical necessity of class struggle or "Revolution" as the founding moment in societal transformation are also called into question.

For new social movement commentators, the most obvious example of the lack of unity of the working class has been the recent rise of the new social movements themselves. These movements, which include the feminist, gay and lesbian, antiracist, and ecology movements have seriously challenged the ontological centrality of working-class struggle. That such movements have arisen in the highly industrialized capitalist nations of the West, where the Marxist vision would have been most likely confirmed, has supposedly added a final nail in the coffin of class struggle.

One significant result of such analyses has been that much time and energy are spent by new social movement theorists in an attempt to locate new forces for change (Eckersley 1989; Rohrschneider 1990; Bookchin 1986; Hardt and Negri 2001; Day 2005; Selbin 2010). These forces for change are seen as coming less and less from workers and more and more from a "new middle class," mobilized around "postindustrial" cultural values, who are viewed as having greater opportunities to challenge social relations or to improve their positions within them. It is the members of this new middle class who are said to provide the impetus for environmental, animal rights, and earth liberation movements. They are said to make up what Day (2005) calls "the newest social movements."

Neither should it be assumed (a rather too common error) that the struggles of the new social movements are necessarily radical or "progressive" (Laclau and Mouffe 1985; Mouffe 1988; Laclau 1990). Any radicality results from articulatory practices, given the partial character of all struggles. "Their articulation depends on discourses existing at a given moment and on the type of subject the resistances construct. They can, therefore, be as easily assimilated by the discourses of the anti–status quo Right as by those of the Left, or be simply absorbed into the dominant system, which thereby neutralizes them or even utilizes them for its own modernization" (Mouffe 1988, 98).

The "progressive" (also the "reactionary") is not determined along pre-given lines of demarcation (not even in relation to the means of production). "We cannot objectively identify what it is to be progressive and then set it in foundationalist cement. The point is rather to see how such identities as 'progressive' and 'reactionary' are historically derived and to develop forms of political solidarity and identification accordingly" (Daly 1994, 181). Answers are to be found in the processes of political articulation.

Ecology, for example, raises the question of the "progressive" or "reactionary" character of the working class and its supposed position of radical privilege. The working class (likewise ecology, as I shall detail) is neither essentially progressive nor essentially reactionary. Either outcome is a partial expression of ongoing engagements simultaneously internal and external to class. As Laclau and Mouffe (1985, 177) remind us, "the very orientation of the working class depends upon a political balance of forces and the radicalization of a plurality of democratic struggles which are decided in good part *outside* the class itself."

There is, then, no unique or privileged social grouping that derives a necessarily radical character from the location of its inception. The radical subject cannot simply be read off of some level or other of the social strata (Laclau and Mouffe 1985; Laclau 1990; Daly 1994; Day 2005). As Laclau (1990) asserts, it is the very category "privileged agent" that is being questioned, not which agent is finally to be privileged, as so many have believed (see Gorz 1982; Touraine 1981; Eckersley 1989; Bookchin 1987; Williams 2010). Following the critique made by Laclau (1990) it might be argued that these authors, in their search for a privileged actor, remain confined to a classical framework in which demands constituting a unified whole are realized through the efforts of a universal agent.

The Continued Significance of Class

It is obvious that workers occupy different subject positions influenced by factors such as race, sex, age, nationality, or income. No one needs a postmodernist, post-Marxist or poststructuralist discourse to tell them that (although one might be required to obscure the banality of such "revelations"). This does not, however, negate the fact that in a society based upon the private ownership and regulation of the requirements for existence, those who do not own must sell their labor power, thereby constraining their expressivity of subject positions. The fundamental act of theft by class has enormous implications for the articulation of peoples' lives under capitalism (Burkett 2006; Carty 2008). These implications cannot be ignored in the manner of those who seek to turn away, or in Wood's (1986) term retreat, from class. As Bowles and Gintis (1987, 206) note, any society that "allows a significant fraction of its members to live in conditions of financial insecurity and material distress expresses a degree of indifference or callousness toward its members which both exhibits and fortifies social division and invidious comparison rather than community." Even Laclau and Mouffe (1985) are careful to clarify that the extension of diverse forms of social conflict into a wide range of areas creates new possibilities for the construction of more democratic and egalitarian societies but does not mean the end of struggles over class. Likewise the fact that all of the new movements have representation in Latin America, Asia, Africa, and Eastern Europe warns against locating their genesis in a shift to postindustrialism or "postmodernism."

Overlooking these facts has deeply impacted new movements. Several commentators (Adam 1993; Aronowitz 1996; Epstein 1996; Brym 1998; Foster 2000; Carty 2008; Engler 2008; Williams 2010), however, have noted that the shift away from class struggle has fundamentally impaired the new social movements' capacities to enact any substantial and lasting changes to the existing sociopolitical structure. By turning away from issues of class, the new movements are open to criticism for having left major sources of domination and power largely untouched, both in theory and in actual practice.

> Not only is there no significant theorizing of this question among intellectuals linked to the new social movements (except among ecologists), but many intellectuals remain adamantly opposed to raising the question of global capitalism and the changing terrain of class relations on the premise that to speak the language of political economy is to sink into some version of marxist orthodoxy. (Aronowitz 1996, 94)

In Boggs' (1986, 13) early, but still accurate, assessment, their "failure to confront the issue of power has in the end only weakened, rather than empowered, those social forces capable of subverting the status quo." Thus, while the new social movements have been significant in broadening an awareness of complex and multifarious forms of hierarchy and domination, their reluctance to deal with class struggles has severely restricted their transformative capabilities. As Boggs (1986, 14) recognized, "the ongoing conflict between prefigurative (value-oriented) and instrumental (power-oriented) dimensions of popular movements has all too often been resolved in favour of the prefigurative." Perspectives that ignore or downplay political economy in favor of cultural issues or "postmodern values" and identities do a disservice by denying the ways in which the development of culture, values and identities are rooted in capitalist power relations.

Part of the problem must be attributed to the lack of understanding by social movement theorists and activists that removing economic forces from a position of analytical primacy does not mean that matters of class can be treated carelessly or abandoned. "Surely even a post-Marxist scheme will have to incorporate an understanding of the economy and class forces into its conceptual structure" (Boggs 1986, 16). Unfortunately such an understanding has been largely absent in the theoretics of the new social movements (Shantz 2009b). There has been a particular resistance to incorporating class forces and the efforts of workers. It may be argued that much of this resistance comes from a narrow and historically superficial understanding of class struggles. Furthermore, in the case of ecology, efforts to understand alliances have been impeded by a rigid construction of "official" environmentalism and a lack of attention to workers' contributions to "eco-defense." Even movements that are mostly clearly expressive of "new values," such as environmentalism, have important intersections with class movements. One might note in this regard the important ongoing efforts of union health and safety committees to limit harmful industrial impacts on nature. That these intersections have been conceptually separated from "environmentalism" proper in much new movement writing is purely arbitrary and, in fact, inaccurate.

Similarly, new movements also have real effects upon the exercise of property rights and state authority. To limit these movements to cultural expressions or manifestations of identity is to overlook their impact on interfering with state and capitalist violence or in shifting power relations socially (Adam 1993; Shantz and Adam 1999; Routledge and Cumbers 2010; Selbin 2010). What is needed is an approach that moves beyond both uncritical culturalism, as in much new/est social movement writing, and deterministic economism, to which Marxist analyses have often succumbed, to look at the interweaving of cultural meaning and political experience in social movements. In the following chapters, green syndicalism is examined as such an alternative approach, a red/green vision that moves beyond the dichotomous construction of new movements and socialism.

The construction of totalities is an affliction that befalls not only Marxist theorists. The idea of a privileged, unilaterally developed agent as the commanding force of social change should be obviously problematic. Such notions represent a gross misreading of a dialectical model of social change (a misreading that may have been made by Marx through an instrumentalist approach to Hegelian dialectics, according to Bookchin [1980]). Ironically, social movement critics of Marxism, including Murray Bookchin, repeat this error in their attempts to locate agents of change beyond the working class.

Ecology and Class Struggle

The concerns raised by social movement theorists have been expressed in even stronger terms from within the radical ecology movement (Bookchin 1980, 1993, 1997; Smith 2001; Watson 2005; Jensen 2006; Zerzan 2008a, 2008b). Often the radicalization of ecological antagonisms has involved a refusal to admit class and the structural context provided by capitalist property relations. This refusal is most characteristic within those articulations of radical ecology that shall here be referred to as fundamentalist, including many of the expressions that emerged within radical versions of ecology, including Earth First!, neoprimitivism, and *Green Anarchy*.

Where Marxism typically subsumed nature in its moral drama built out of the distinction between capital and labor, ecological thought has tended to collapse capital and labor together. Ecologists have often viewed capital and workers as "allies" in the exploitation of "nature." Workers turn up in ecological discourse as consumers intent on using up the natural environment (see Bahro 1984; Bookchin 1987; Foreman 1991; Watson 1994, 2005; Zerzan 2008a, 2008b). Thus workers, in a radical inversion of Marxian categories, become not the grave diggers of capitalism but rather a prop to capitalist social relations. The ostensible status of the working class as a co-conspirator in the continuation of industrial capitalist relations, most notably through the accommodations of Fordism, means, for some variants of radical ecology, that any economic or class interests of workers must inevitably reinforce the expansion of capitalist enclosure. Indeed, much has been written about environmentalists' distrust of and frequent denunciation of socialism and organized labor (see Pepper 1993; Carroll and Ratner 1996; Smith 2007; Zerzan 2008a, 2008b; Williams 2010).

Social ecologist and ex-Marxist Murray Bookchin (1987) argues that activism, to be radically Green, must be informed decisively by the moral considerations surrounding each and every manifestation of struggle. In his view, the political Left's historic preoccupations with the working class as an agent for radical social change have led to reduced ethical thoroughness on the part of social activists. It is for this reason, according to Bookchin, that antagonisms over ecology have been relegated to secondary or even insignificant status, often constituted as diversions from the "fundamental" pursuit of the "necessary" interests of securing jobs and "advancing" the workers' movement (see Sills 1975; Shapiro 1979). Thus Bookchin gives expression, within the specific context of radical ecology, to the concerns for "post-industrial values" that are central to much new/est social movement thinking.

Similarly, Earth First! cofounder Dave Foreman has criticized what he sees as a romanticizing of workers by leftist ecologists: "It does not follow from the huge guilt of the capitalists that all workers are blameless for the destruction of the natural world" (quoted in Book-chin and Foreman 1991, 51). Foreman posits, ironically, a latter-day lack of "class consciousness" on the part of workers as the main barrier to solidarity between ecology and labor. In response to eco-socialist visions Foreman claims that "too many workers buy into the world-view of their masters that the Earth is a smorgasbord of resources for the taking" (quoted in Bookchin and Foreman 1991, 51).

2

Radical Ecology and Class

From Fundamentalism to Green Syndicalism

Radical ecology has emerged as a potential point for linkage, or the nodal point, of a wide plurality of antisystemic struggles. Indeed, many have long expected that the "nature-society" question will provide the most likely focus for a coalescence of new social movements into a broadened counterhegemonic movement (see Olofsson 1988, 15). However, one problem persists. Ecology as a nodal point of solidarity has been wracked by conflict and torn by strife. While a radicalizing of movement discourses has been effected, there have been few alliances constructed around an ecological counterhegemony. One might readily conclude that the connective possibilities of ecology have failed to live up to advance billing. Examining ecology exposes a rather troubled mythopoetic, for which even a tentative fixing of radicalizing struggles has proved difficult.

Much of the impediment to radicalized green articulation derives from the location of ecological devastation within an anthropocentric discursive hierarchy, that is, human society, which accepts it as necessary, thereby inhibiting its constitution as antagonism. This "common sense" perspective operates around a society/nature duality, a hierarchical opposition in which the first term is provided a position of superiority (associated with a machine myth, i.e., progress, efficiency, stability, etc). This opposition serves to shape social practice as it enters institutions such as corporations, government, and unions and is extended in consumer culture. Radical ecology seeks to displace this oppositional hierarchy, opening spaces of difference and autonomy.

24

As Routledge and Cumbers (2010) note, even recent approaches to social movements are not sensitive enough to internal divisions. Yet one cannot even hope to understand the possibilities for radicalizing articulations between ecology and labor without first coming to grips with the complex internal interactions and manifestations emerging from within the constellations of environmentalist praxis. These constellations, I argue, reveal to us the tentative and difficult constitution of emergent struggles over ecological mythopoetics.

In attempting to address the radically antihegemonic transformative possibilities created within ecology, one must avoid the mistake of theorizing the environmental movement as a monolith, homogeneous in philosophy or practice. As is characteristic for other of the new social movements, the environmental movement is expressed through a complexity of struggles by which participants construct and reconstruct philosophical commitments and activist dispositions. These constitutive practices variously arise through differences that are often contradictory and antagonistic rather than complementary. "There is thus not one 'environmentalism' but many. There are competing discursive practices whose social bases are constantly forming and dissolving" (Adkin 1992a, 135). The character of ecological destruction engendered through industrial capitalist enclosures provides a context within which human relations to nature, previously constructed as relations of subordination in which the destruction of nature is normalized, can be rearticulated as relations of oppression to be contested and overcome.

However, one must make further distinctions among the types of ecological resistance that one finds within these relations of oppression (Laclau 1990). Perhaps most significantly, it cannot be assumed that each of these environmentalisms contributes to what Offe (1985) calls a "new paradigm" of politics. These discourses are not all subversive of the growth demands of industrial capitalist relations. For example, the spectacle of "green corporatism" reveals that there is nothing inherently radical about articulating "nature" to existing discursive formations (Simms 2005).

One of the difficulties facing efforts to constitute a radicalized articulation of ecology remains that nature has been more firmly affixed to hegemonic discourses such as consumerism or "resource-ism" than to liberatory discourses. "Ecology, as common sense, has been increasingly absorbed by dominant discursive formations and transformed into a narrow and limited environmentalism" (Sandilands 1992, 171). Understood in this manner, environmentalist discourse acts partly as an inhibitor to the liberatory potential of "nature"/ecol-ogy—it interrupts attempts to constitute nature as a site of antagonism. "The radical potential of ecology is undermined by the incorporation of concern for the environment into dominant discourses of growth, implying a project of continued exploitation" (Sandilands 1992, 165). This incorporation, however, tells us much about the indeterminate character of articulation. Environmentalism is possible because of the ambiguous character and radical unfixity of "nature." Quite simply, nature is open to a diversity of discursive constructions.

Laclau (1990, 235) notes that "the radicality of a conflict can depend entirely on the extent to which the differences are articulated in chains of equivalence." While some environmental actors (e.g., Sierra Club, Friends of the Earth) have been able to construct spaces of legitimate differences, others (Earth First!, Sea Shepherd Society) have worked to radicalize chains of equivalence through confronta-tional rhetoric and "no compromise" discourses (Lange 1990; Short 1991; Smith 2007). Inasmuch as ecology rejects the commodification and exploitation of nature upon which capitalist relations are built, it is articulated in subversion of the hegemonic paradigm and might be considered "dark green" (Dobson 1990). Where environmental-ism does not challenge the assumptions of productivism, growth, consumption, and the hierarchical relations of humans with nature it remains "light green" (Dobson 1990). Within the present research the "light versus dark" spectrum is further applied to the social analy-ses and visions of transformation expressed through ecology.

Politically, it makes all the difference if ecological discourse, for example, is conceived as the need for authoritarian state intervention to protect the environment, or as part of a radical critique of the irra-tionality of the political and economic systems in which we live, in

which case it establishes a relationship of equivalence with the emancipatory projects of other social movements. (Laclau 1990, 230)

According to a number of authors (Devall 1979; Bookchin 1987;
1990; Dobson 1990; Scarce 1990; Nash 1989; Johnson 1991; Adkin
1998; Watson 2002, 2005; Smith 2006, 2007; Jakopovich 2007;
Zerzan 2005, 2008b) environmentalist discourses diverge most pas-
sionately and virulently over understandings about the relationship of
humans with nonhuman nature. The character of ecological destruction provides a context within which human relations to nature, previously stabilized (and legitimized) as relations of subordination, can
be rearticulated as relations of oppression. However, one must go
further and distinguish among the types of ecological resistance that
one finds within these relations of oppression. For mainstream environmentalism—conservationism, green consumerism, and resource
management—humans are conceptually separated out of nature
and mythically placed in privileged positions of authority and control over ecological communities and their nonhuman constituents.
What emerges is the fiction of a marketplace of "raw materials" and
"resources" through which human-centered wants, constructed as
needs, might be satisfied. The mainstream narratives are replete with
such metaphors. Natural complexity, mutuality, and diversity are rendered virtually meaningless given discursive parameters that reduce
nature to discrete categories or units of exchange measuring extractive
capacities. Demand and convenience largely establish which members
of any eco-community are necessary within this humanly constructed
and imposed hierarchy.

For radical versions of environmentalism, emphasis is placed upon
human embeddedness within nature and upon the complementarity
of relations in nature. These distinctions say much about the indeterminate character of a "nature" that is open to a diversity of discursive
constructions. Environmentalism is possible because of the ambiguous character and radical unfixity of "nature."

The practices of mainstream environmentalism are largely confined within parameters marking hegemonic discourses. Mainstream

environmentalism "does not bring into question the underlying notion that man [*sic*] must dominate nature; it seeks to facilitate domination by developing techniques for diminishing the hazards caused by domination" (Bookchin 1980, 58). By disregarding the political articulations through which hegemonic assumptions have arisen and by adopting a utilitarian construction of nature, with ancillary narratives of domination, the mainstream is discursively led away from advocating any radical transformation of capitalist social relations. As Sandilands notes, "[d]ominant discourses of sustainable development, which represent the articulation of an environmental veneer with an agenda of continued capitalist expansion, have undermined attempts to link together processes of environmental and social change" (1992, 165). Typically proponents of the mainstream rely solely upon a rather narrow political process involving reformist appeals to legislative and judicial realms of the state. What most frequently results is a compromising pragmatism in which "winning almost always means losing something for the environment" (Scarce 1990, 7). Crucially overlooked are those relations of exploitation that sustain these hierarchical and utilitarian approaches to nature.

Eder (1990) argues that one of the most significant moments for the constitution of ecology movements as new political forces has been this reframing of human relations with nature as relations of exploitation. It is upon this terrain that radical ecological formations have become possible.

For proponents of radical ecology, including deep ecology, ecofeminism, and social ecology, the focus shifts toward human rootedness within nature and upon mutuality in relations among constituents of eco-communities. "By insisting upon the existence of a universe that is not subject to the ascription of mere otherness, seen logically as merely 'not living' or 'not human', ecology proposes to undertake not only a searching critique of the domination of nature, but of science and technology as well" (Aronowitz 1990, 114). What is discursively constituted is an image of ecological relations as diverse but interconnected strands in an intricate and irreducible web of life that includes humans within its nexus. Radical ecology "explicitly rejects any notion either of human primacy or the separation of humans from the rest of nature, and any possibility of humankind achieving mastery over nature through 'progress' in science and technology" (Clow 1986, 174).

Unfortunately the emphasis on relations between humans and nature, and the critical challenging of these relations as practices of domination and oppression, which has provided radical ecology with much of its potency, has obscured the struggles, domination, and oppression that makes up the category human itself. Radical ecology, in different versions, has tended to overlook issues of class. At the same time some attempts to bring a class analysis into ecology, particularly eco-socialism, have unsatisfactorily addressed human impacts on nature in the name of growth and development. This chapter addresses visions of class and nature, and tensions within those visions, as expressed within various approaches to environmental politics.

Scarcity and the Emergence of Fundamentalist Ecology

Unfortunately the attempt to return nature to the center of human understanding has given rise to tendencies within ecology that assert the need for human submission within nature and the privileging of the nonhuman over people and "society." Recently some radical ecologists have asked workers to give up all of their social gains of the postwar period in a "return to the Pleistocene" era that was lived, presumably, in naturally occurring caves. Elsewhere appeals to "let nature take its course" in matters of famine and AIDS, and wistful harkening after a "Green Adolph" (see Bahro, quoted in Biehl 1995) suggest more sinister currents within some strands of radical ecology.

I suggest that these manifestations relate to the emergence of a "fundamentalist" environmentalism and may be understood, in part, as reflecting a crucial confusion over natural scarcity and social scarcity. It is my contention that radical environmentalism, in the form of fundamentalist ecology, has all too easily become a Green chorus for neoliberal and neoconservative policies. It should not be taken as strictly coincidental that fundamentalist versions of ecology, exemplified in social philosophy by "deep ecology" and as a social movement by Earth First!, emerged in the mid-1980s, during the early stages of the neoconservative "revolution" and the return of scarcity.

Through the social transformations characterizing postwar Keynesianism, "a 'commodification of social life' has destroyed a series of previous social relations and replaced them with commodity relations. This is what we know as the consumer society" (Mouffe 1988, 92). Underlying the politics of this paradigm has been a pervasive and largely unchallenged commitment to growth. Offe (1985) suggests that it was only through illusions of growth as unlimited and beneficent that the readiness of labor to reduce broad demands for social change to limited questions of income distribution, and the corresponding willingness by capital to concede some legitimacy to organized labor, could become possible. Economic growth on the side of capital was matched with an increased capacity to consume on the side of labor. Specifically, the promise of unimpeded (because of the truce called between sides), boundless growth made the limited concessions to labor acceptable to capital, while the perceived desirability of "getting a piece of the pie" provided ideological cover for the co-opting and circumscribing of unions (Offe 1985). Significantly, the enlargement of consumerist relations into expanding social domains signaled a cultural displacement of militancy with profound consequences. Through the linkage of wages with productivity and a related diminution of the autonomy and resistance of workers, the way was cleared for the political constitution of workers as mere consumers and all that that would entail. As Ross (1996) has noted, this consequence has engendered the profound disappointment of intellectuals from Marcuse to Baudrillard.

Significantly (and usually overlooked), this alliance, with consumption as its underlying justification, enabled the displacement of class conflicts toward a mutual partnership in ecological conquest. Capitalist social relations, and specifically the introduction of commodity relations into ever-expanding realms, have engendered the fragmentation, domestication, atomization, and simplification of natural lifeworlds throughout the late twentieth century as diverse ecosystems have fallen prey to colonization by humans, with their constituents appropriated as factors of human production and consumption. Nature is reintroduced to us as "environment," a realm of capitalist profit and personal indulgence. Environment, nature's "brand name," becomes little more than a stockpile of "resources," reconstructed as a warehouse of riches existing solely for the gratification of ceaselessly multiplying human wants.

The insatiable consumer appetite, with its tireless development of wants disguised as needs, could only mean unthinkable assaults upon nature. "Unbridled economic expansion began to expose just how limited were the ecological prerequisites which had been taken for granted in the construction of postwar stability" (Adam 1993, 318). The encompassing appropriation of nature through human labor, permitted through hegemonization of the "logic" of capitalist accumulation and the corporatist conjoining of labor and capital in mass consumption regimes, has consequently raised rather poignant questions regarding possibilities for ecological survival of complex life on this planet. This is in no way an overly surprising turn of events within North America where news of abundance or richness in nature has been followed typically by rabid destruction of this nature and its "resources" (Ross 1996).

Eventually a new consciousness emerged concerning "limits to growth," which had its basis in a previously unexpected realm: nature. It became more and more evident that nature, the stockpile of resources, the vault of riches, the guarantor of utopias of the left and the right, was actually exhaustible. Various intellectual and political traditions, which had underestimated the contradictions between economic development and ecological integrity came, with greater or lesser difficulty, to recognize the presence of material limits. The efforts of the modern environmental movement introduced to us a newly conceived idea of scarcity with profound implications: natural scarcity (Ross 1996).

Equally significant for an understanding of environmental degradation, emerging concerns over natural scarcity have been accompanied by an extension of social scarcity. The past three decades have ushered in a now familiar series of social transformations character-izing finance-driven capitalist globalization.

Since the 1990s, the austerity programs of neoliberalism have brought about a new era of social scarcity marked by extensive cutbacks and the revoking of socioeconomic "rights." In place of the humani-tarian features of the postwar Fordist compromise there was (and con-tinues to be) an escalation of punitive initiatives regulating poor and marginalized populations. Welfare "reform," anti-immigrant legisla-tion and the dismantling of affirmative action policies offer but a few recent examples. A rhetoric of global competitiveness and the race to deregulate ushered in a new era of austerity in which entire sectors of the poor have been redescribed as immoral and irresponsible, living from the public purse but giving nothing in return. Contextualizing the poor as selfish "scroungers" allowed for a revitalization of neocon-servative discourses of family values, the work ethic, and race. In such a context, with elites facing limited, feeble, and fragmentary resistance to a concerted and systematic deployment of pro-scarcity policies the presence of organized scarcity became increasingly evident.

Notably, there has been much confusion of the two scarcities, natural and social. On one hand, this obfuscation may reflect an intentional effort to shore up austerity measures against marginalized populations. More innocently it also suggests a knowledge gap with regard to questions of resources, extraction, and processes of produc-tion and exchange.

> In these contexts and others, the admission of scarcity presents an opportunity to impose limits, cutbacks, concessions, and restric-tions, usually in the name of conservation and waste reduction. There is nothing more wasteful than market economics, and yet capitalism's mismanagement are more often than not turned into opportunities to punish its victims (Ross 1996, 21)

In an era in which the global significance of ecological damage is readily apparent, concerns over natural scarcity have made a return to the North (Ross 1996). However, these concerns must not be blurred in efforts to shore up austerity programs and the cynical regulation of selected populations.

Fundamentalist Ecology

Among the manifestations of a radicalized ecology are fundamentalist visions, including diverse expressions of "deep ecology" and eco-primitivism. According to Laurie Adkin (1992a, 144), ecological fundamentalism "refers to various forms of essentialism (claims about the sensual, spiritual, aesthetic, and developmental needs of humans as a species, and about the rights of other species) that are present (implicitly or explicitly) in different discourses." For fundamentalism, commodification of life (both human and nonhuman) is linked to alienation from the body, from nature, and from "authentic" human needs.

These positions are aspects of a broader fundamentalist emphasis upon the transformation of values and the reconstitution of human needs, be they aesthetic, psychic, or moral. Largely engaging in linguistic and expressive strategies of personal (rather than social) transformation, fundamentalist ecology "encompasses an important discussion about alienation and needs, including experiences of deprivation linked to the commodification of life, alienation from the body, and from nature" (Adkin 1992a, 144).

Movement away from questions of power underlying social scarcity has also been a persistent characteristic of fundamentalist ecology. Fundamentalist ecologists argue that radical activism, to be "deep green," must be informed most decisively by moral considerations.

Given the essentialist inclinations in the anti-anthropocentrist narratives of fundamentalist ecology, it is perhaps not surprising that their discursive practices have tended to construct "humanity" as a bloc, undifferentiated by power, in which a universalistic human species itself is held responsible for biospheric destruction (see Devall 1988; Manes 1990; Simms 2005; Watson 2002, 2005; Zerzan 2008a, 2008b). A consequence of such disinterest in the social articulation of attacks upon nonhuman nature has been the blaming of those humans who themselves suffer at the hands of the same forces responsible for the destruction of global ecosystems. Dangerously ignored or discounted are the distinct forms of power realized through politically manufactured differences of race, gender, and class. The "human" and the "natural" are, of course, always political projects, and examples of social division in the realization of these projects are all too familiar.

Fundamentalist Ecology and Neo-Malthusian Moralism

It does not require much creativity to imagine the sorts of paths that can lead from such beginnings. As we well know, for some deep ecologists (see Manes 1990; Watson 2002, 2005) depopulation is offered as a positive solution, without regard to the human suffering that would entail and without regard for the relationship of different social arrangements with ecological destruction. While deep ecologist Dave Foreman has suggested that nature should have been allowed to take its course in the Ethiopian famine, Paul Watson (1994, 128) has provided some insight into his calculus of population reduction: "To me, all of the human beings in California are not worth the extinction of one of the mighty and revered ancient forest dwellers we have chosen to call redwoods."

In a manner reminiscent of the conservation movement in the first decades of the twentieth century, fundamentalist ecology has also given rise to explicitly racist articulations (see Gusfield 1992). In one infamous passage, author Ed Abbey (1988, 43), one of the early proponents of deep ecology whose novel *The Monkey Wrench Gang* (1976) served as the inspiration for Earth First!, described Hispanic immigrants as "hungry, ignorant, unskilled, and culturally-morally-genetically impoverished people." Abbey (1986) argued for strict restrictions on immigration to protect the United States from being "Latinized."

Such positions reflect the antihuman turn in biocentrism, which lacks any analysis of human social relations and the integration of ecological degradation with social problems of domination, deprivation, or exclusion.[1] Blaming those who are preyed upon by the very processes that contribute to environmental degradation is one of the troubles arising from the confusion over questions of social scarcity.

Fundamentalist ecology has been too readily led away from contextualizing ecological crises within persistent social relations of scarcity. By concealing the divisions and conflicts within these exploitative relationships, the critique of anthropocentrism can become an ideological cover for those members of "humanity" who in asserting positions of privilege have constructed not only nature but fellow humans—typically the poor, blacks, and women—as mere "resources" to be exploited. Significantly, it is precisely among these inferiorized positions that the impacts of ecological destruction are most severely experienced (Bullard and Wright 1987; Bullard 1990; Bullard 1993; Foster, Clark, and York 2011). Significantly too, it is also from these positions that some of the most interesting and poignant forms of resistance to ecological damage have emerged (Bullard 1990; Miller 1993; Jakopovich 2007; Williams 2010).

Fundamentalists Against Workers: Anti-Labor Narratives in Fundamentalist Ecology

The recent return of scarcity in advanced capitalist societies has led some environmentalists to suggest that it is time for a "return to the state of liberal civil society before the emergence, in a time of relative abundance, of the welfare state, organized labor, and civil rights" (Ross 1996, 7). Paul Watson (2005) has been in the forefront of those issuing such calls. Referring to "antiquated rights of workers" he makes it clear that such rights must be suspended in the interest of nature.

The late union organizer and environmentalist Judi Bari (1994, 140) regularly argued against "the utter lack of class consciousness

---

1. Which is not to claim that biocentrism is inherently misanthropic, as the work of Judi Bari confirms.

[shown] by virtually all of the environmental groups." Speaking about Earth First!, Bari (205) has complained: "They don't give a damn about working people." Evidence for this claim abounds. Captain Paul Watson (1994, 129) has stated famously that "the logger is a nothing, an insignificance, a virus, a rot, a disease and an aberration against nature, and I for one will not weep a single tear at his demise." Elsewhere Watson (127) describes resource workers as "just pathetic foot-soldiers for the corporate generals of the logging industry." Indeed, many other fundamentalist activists became similarly hostile "and cynical toward workers . . . with environmentalists depicting workers as lumpen mercenaries" (Adkin 1992a, 145).

Any attempts to engage workers as agents for radical social change, as in Judi Bari's case, have been charged by fundamentalists with leading to reduced ethical thoroughness on the part of social ecology activists. Concerns preoccupying people in their roles as workers, such as securing jobs and "improving" the conditions of work, are given no status when viewed in relation to ecology. To the contrary, improvements in workers' material conditions are viewed as necessarily meaning an increase in their capacity to consume, and that is to be avoided. While fundamentalists are critical of consumer capitalism, "they typically also reject the possibility of articulating the interests of environmentalists to those of workers, because they view workers as subjects inextricably bound to the hegemonic model of development" (Adkin 1992a, 148). Anything tainted by association with the hegemonic model (such as unions or workers' rights) is shunned as impure or "inauthentic."

Refusing to confront the vastly uneven and conflictual arrangements of human social relations and the integration of ecological antagonisms with social antagonisms allows for an easy displacement of opportunities for a broadened articulation of ecological activism. Thus ecological fundamentalists "have remained utopian in not emphasizing the importance of these strategic relations, and have instead almost forsaken the political process for the comfort of moral critique and futurology" (Frankel 1987, 242). The mistaken assumption behind this utopian position is that "saving the earth" transcends ideology. Nature, however, does not transcend ideology. It is always a political project, an outcome of political struggle.

Some activists from labor-Left traditions, often through direct conflicts against misanthropic expressions within Earth First!, have become aware of the importance of developing a social understanding or analysis of environmental degradation (see Bari 1994; Purchase 1997a). "Not taking up ecological issues leaves these issues open for a green fascism and a situation where the cost of repairing the damage is taken out of the working class instead of the boss class" (Kauffman and Ditz 1992, 42). Given their views of workers and their stated aims not to change social structures, fundamentalist ecology remains especially susceptible to such formulations (see Biehl 1995).

Talking about Nature: Fundamentalism, Hard Primitivism, and Ecological Voluntarism

Much as in the contemporary natural foods movements studied by Gusfield (1992, 99), for fundamentalist ecology nature is only regained through "a world of individuals who carve out for themselves areas of detachment from the strong and overpowering institutions that surround them." The environmental voluntarism espoused by fundamentalist ecologists is directed at the market rather than at political engagement with the social relations underpinning market economies. In fundamentalist visions, "the hegemonic model is so all encompassing, so insidiously in control, that collective action is effectively impossible. The only strategy of resistance remaining is the accumulation of individual conversions" (Adkin 1992a, 149). Thus, fundamentalists are left to wait for the wave of moral conversion, a situation easily contributing to a "vanguardism of despair."

Not surprisingly, fundamentalist strategies become moralizing in tone. Individuals are called upon to change their consumption and other "lifestyle" practices and are chastised for failing to do so. The wasteful behaviors of individuals are held responsible for global ecological degradation. Thoughtless "worker-consumers" stand accused of bringing about biospheric devastation through their personal consumption practices. Individual selfishness is posed as a fatal flaw of humans as a species, especially for the "worker-consumers" who have had difficulties attaining the "higher consciousness" of the fundamentalists. Significantly, such appeals to "higher consciousness" have met with only limited success, confined ironically to "the gourmet, and alternative, consumer classes" (Ross 1996, 13). All the while, daily decisions over production and distribution are left unchallenged.

Among these revaluations are recent expressions of ecological primitivism. This is not surprising as a response to the dislocations and disruptions of industrial capitalism.

Contemporary primitivist concerns are in many respects quite similar to those expressed in nineteenth-century natural-foods movements, especially as they signify a reintroduction of narratives concerning the sacredness and authenticity of nature (a characteristic that is largely missing from other forms of contemporary environmentalism and the twentieth-century health foods movements discussed by Gusfield). "The body physical, as well as the body social and the body politic, is out of control, and only the will of the individual can regain control" (Gusfield 1992, 98). This "world out of control" might be summed up, in current ecology discourses, with only one word: consumption.

Natural scarcity, in the view of fundamentalists, means that one can no longer tolerate consumption in the form of what Gusfield (1992, 99) refers to as "unplanned periods of simple gratification." Each moment of consumption must be well considered, with attention given to possible consequences and outcomes. In an echoing of neoliberal discourse, individuals are lectured to show restraint, lower their expectations, and "tighten their belts." If they question these imperatives they are scolded for living beyond their (or the Nation's) means (see Ross 1996; Simms 2005).

None of the above discussion should be taken to suggest that there is no ecological crisis. Indeed, the Earth is under serious attack. What is most important is context. Attention must also be given to how we understand nature. In attempting to understand the articulations of "nature" within fundamentalist ecology it is helpful to bear in mind Gusfield's (1992, 99) discussion: "Nature becomes the symbol of opposition. It describes a morality and a source of knowledge that stems from an instinctual and unsocialized self that civilization, in its appeals and hierarchies, seems to have lost. Modern life is thus to blame for so much of the evil surrounding us." We might even recognize the emergence recently of a "hard primitivism" of the type identified by Gusfield (1992, 98) in his analysis of natural foods movements. This primitivism speaks of moral strength in the face of degenerate civilization. "*Civilization* is a word that spells danger, disenchantment, and distrust" (100). Fundamentalist ecology seeks a return to a past of unspoiled nature expressed presently as wilderness (in much the same way that fundamentalist conservatives speak of a return to "the family" unspoiled by such manifestations as single parents, working mothers, or mixed families).

It is particularly within arguments of radical ecology articulated outside of neo-Malthusian discourses, however, that one may distinguish the complex tensions of engagement between class and radical ecology. It is here that one sees the convergence of an imminent critique of both capitalist and socialist projects. Even those radical theorists (Bahro 1982, 1984; Bookchin 1987; Bookchin and Foreman 1991) who have otherwise appreciated the pressing need to move beyond capitalist domination toward ecological social relations remain suspicious of the roles workers might take in such transformations. This suspicion arises, in part, because "they view workers as subjects inextricably bound to the hegemonic model of development" (Adkin 1992a, 148). Again, the position of workers is inverted, so that rather than the grave diggers of capitalism, as in Marx, they become partners in the maintenance of capitalism. Workers organized collectively, therefore, cannot be trusted as any possible force for overturning those relations.

Rudolph Bahro, once a prominent theorist of the German Greens, unambiguously constructed condemnatory discourses regarding the position of workers within industrial capitalist relations. "In the case of capitalism the workers are part of the carousel of the capitalist formation" (1984, 184). Calls for workers to bring about the end of this formation, given their essential stake in the Western growth model, will necessarily result in failure. The supposed status of the working class as a co-conspirator in the continuation of industrial capitalist relations, most notably through the Keynesian capitulation, means that any economic or class interests of workers must inevitably reinforce the expansion of capitalist enclosure. Thus Bahro (183): "It would therefore be a most inappropriate strategy for survival to appeal to the interests of the working class."

Instead it becomes the task of all of humanity to end the industrial capitalist formation. Using highly charged language, Bahro (1984, 183) asserts that "it is the industrial system itself which is about to undo us—not the bourgeois class but the system as a whole in which the working class plays the role of housewife." Unfortunately, Bahro fails to appreciate the struggle contained within his own analogy. It does not take a radical feminist to realize that within industrial capitalist relations the category "housewife," rather than signifying positions of power, typically expresses identities formed through inferiorization. Given Bahro's statements and the implicit inattention to social cleavage, it is perhaps easier to account for some of the conservative positions taken by the Greens while in office in Germany, along with their subsequent decline as a relevant force for social change.

Social Ecology and Class Struggle

Anticlass perspectives are often vigorously expressed even among those radical ecologists who have been critical of biocentrism. Social ecologist Murray Bookchin has been especially critical of analyses and strategies that assign any centrality to a particular group such as the working class. Bookchin has gone beyond merely turning away from notions of class struggle to actively condemning them, even in their anarchist expressions. In *Toward an Ecological Society*, Bookchin (1980, 218) argues that it is "the very class nature of the proletariat . . . and its highly particularistic interests . . . [which] belie Marx's claims for its universality and its historic role as a revolutionary agent." Bookchin suggests that it is as class actors that workers are at their most reactionary. In his view, the fact of workers' exploitation by the bourgeoisie and their position within the factory system only reinforce workers' "actual one-sided condition under capitalism as a 'productive force,' not as a revolutionary force" (241).

Bookchin is rightly critical of the factory system and sees it as a major factor in the dehumanization of the working class. However, he goes a step further by suggesting that the factory system also assures the deradicalization of the working class. In *Post-Scarcity Anarchism* (1986), Bookchin argues that the factory system serves as the training ground for bourgeois society and for the instilling of bourgeois values. Through the imposition of a work ethic, the hierarchical organizations of management, and the demands for obedience, the factory system serves to indoctrinate workers as subservient upholders of capitalism. Bookchin (1986, 205) states that, in a sad parody of the Marxist vision, the "factory serves not only to 'discipline,' 'unite,' and 'organize' the workers, but also to do so in a thoroughly bourgeois fashion." This leads Bookchin (1987, 187) to argue elsewhere that socialist, anarchist, or syndicalist struggles focused around the factory give "social and psychological priority to the worker precisely where he or she is most co-joined to capitalism and most debased as a human being—at the job site."

For Bookchin, the only answer is to leave the job site and turn solely to struggles within the "community"—as though communities exist without workplaces. In Bookchin's view communities are somehow separate from the class positions of those who live in them. He argues that the workers who are so brutalized at the job site are able to shed those experiences and become different people within their communities. "Their human focus is the community in which they live, not the factory in which they work" (Bookchin 1987, 191). In Bookchin's analysis, as in liberal theory, "the most powerful form of collective organization in contemporary capitalism—the modern business corporation—is stripped of its communal status" (Bowles and Gintis 1987, 16).

This perspective leads Bookchin (1987, 1997) to insist that the efforts of socialists or anarcho-syndicalists who organize and agitate at the workplace are only strengthening the very aspects of workers' social beings that must be overcome if a radical transformation of society is to occur. Such work, he argues, only serves to distract from the potentially beneficial developments of consciousness that he expects to arise from activities within the community.

While not rejecting Bookchin's insights—of course community initiatives are important; certainly the disciplined regimentation of the workplace must be overcome—there remain difficulties that must be further discussed. First, if workers are to overcome their alienated class character, then they must at some point confront the growing contradiction between their developing community consciousness and the material confinement and dehumanization experienced at the job site. Rather than being simply left behind, or ignored, the job itself will be a crucial arena for struggle. The constitution of new identities as expressive human beings in transcendence of alienated class identities implies a successful struggle over the very structures of domination, regimentation, hierarchy, and discipline that exist concretely within the workplace. One cannot assume that the job site will simply wither away with the flowering of a new identity. More likely it will be impossible to develop fully the human expressivity of which Bookchin (1986) speaks, given the continued existence of this significant nexus of capitalist power, domination, and exploitation.

Appeals to humanity, conscience, and personality cannot be made in abstraction from the very material conditions that restrict and deform peoples' humanity, conscience, and personality. While struggles at the level of the workplace should not, indeed cannot, be elevated to the sole site of transformation, the corrective is not to abandon these struggles altogether. "The constitutive aspect of social interaction starts from the fact that individuals are recognized (in their own eyes and in the eyes of others) by their acts. The self as a social self is in continual need of definition, validation, and recognition through action" (Bowles and Gintis 1987, 150). Likewise, it is not enough simply to condemn or ignore peoples' identities as workers. Rather the fullest implications of this subject position must be understood through the activities and through the voices of workers themselves.

Rather than arguing for or against the workplace as opposed to the community, one must move forward to a fuller articulation of engagement carried out at both sites. That each realm of experience and action is an important site for transformation and struggle must be appreciated. That the workplace must be transcended and the community developed, or even restored, does not erase the fact that the process through which each can occur will not allow a retreat from one and a romantic preoccupation with the other. The development of community must be the dissolution of the factory system and all that it entails.

When attempting to articulate a fuller understanding of class struggles, it is worthwhile to remember that such struggles do not begin and end at the point of production. As Bookchin (1986, 249) himself has noted, without understanding the class implications, "it may emerge from the poverty of the unemployed and unemployables, many of whom have never done a day's work in industry." Likewise, class struggles entail extremely crucial ideological dimensions that extend far beyond any restricted notions of "class consciousness" or "superstructure." It is an ideological development that arises fundamentally from peoples' varied activities in a society ruled by the dictates of private property. Bookchin (1986, 249) comes up against this when he concedes that class struggle "may emerge from a new sense of possibility that slowly pervades society—the tension between 'what is' and 'what could be.'" This tension is precisely the contradiction that workers in struggle experience between their desires for self-determination and the limits of the workplace.

As important, such an understanding may infuse struggles over class with radically new visions of the vast terrain from which social change can emerge. A deeper understanding of class struggle concerns itself with the expression of ethical and cultural rebellions that occur along with economic rebellions. Out of this awareness the potential for an ecological understanding of class society and a class analysis of ecological society might emerge.

Certainly the historic anarcho-syndicalist and industrial union struggles have exhibited this conscious awareness that class struggle entails more than battles over economic issues carried out at the workplace (see Kornblugh 1964; Thompson and Murfin 1976; Salerno 1989; Rosemont 1997a, 1997b; Shantz 2010). Class struggles have been concerned with the broad manifestations of domination and control that are constituted along with the ruthlessly private ownership of the planet's ecosystems and their vast potentials for freedom.

One might argue that Bookchin's analysis represents a misreading of historical labor struggles or a rather too narrow understanding of socialism (see Deutsch and Van Houten 1974; Cleaver 2000; Hardt and Negri 2000; Day 2005; Williams 2010). That does not diminish, however, the resonance with which his views have impacted radical ecology and the new social movements in general.

Ecosocialism: Light Green Radicalism

In an early discussion of the modern environmental movement Jezer (1977) posited the importance of socialist engagement as an element in the political development of the movement and in forging strategic linkages to resist the ecological devastation wrought through the specific workings of capitalist economic relations. His primary concern was that without the active intervention of socialist ecologists the environmental movement would be susceptible to domination by the reform practices of liberal environmentalism. Jezer quite rightly argued that liberal environmental visions and practices are lacking any critical strategies for attacking matters of concern to workers, such as workplace exploitation or the coerced requirements of existence within capitalist exchange relations. Further, in accepting the permanence and legitimacy of capitalist relations, liberal discourse argues against any practical connections with workers within any formation of ecology as a possibly counterhegemonic force.

If one looks at the development of environmentalism since the time of Jezer's writings it appears that a dominance of liberal discourse has, in fact, been constituted. Liberal tendencies have shaped the parameters of much ecological practice. In recent years, however, through confrontations around ecology a radicalization of liberal discourses has emerged bearing resemblances to socialist critiques of class relations. Such radicalization has suggested (Rudig 1985–86; Adam, 1993) that there is developing what might here be termed an "organic socialism" among activists participating in various forms of ecological practice.

> What are more remarkable are the 'socialists' born not (or at least not only) of the labour movement, but produced out of the new social movements themselves. This other face of new social movement mobilisation includes a great many participants who understand their *praxis* within a comprehensive worldview which recognizes and supports subordinated people wherever they exist. (Adam 1993, 330)

This blurring of boundaries between radical liberalism and socialism, first theorized in the works of Thomas Paine (see Arblaster 1991), suggests that processes of articulation among different actors problematize essentialist and reductionist discourses and open possibilities for the rethinking of supposedly fixed identities. Specifically, within ecology it is through ongoing struggle "when capitalists attempt to mobilize workers into opposing environmentalists, that environmentalists come to see the importance of economic issues for the actors involved" (Adkin 1992a, 145). Because articulation is an ongoing process of struggle it cannot be assumed that such awareness by environmentalists is assured. However, it is within these emergent ecosocialist discourses that one can see the precarious and ambiguous nature of articulations between ecology and labor.

Marxist commentators, such as Raskin and Bernow (1991), O'Connor (1998), Foster (2000, 2002) and Williams (2010), provide insightful analyses of some of the failures of anticlass versions of radical ecology. In asserting the complementarity of Marxism and radical ecology, Raskin and Bernow (1991, 87) assail radical environmentalists for "their naive neglect of the socioeconomic context of ecological disaster. In Marxist arguments (see Rudig 1985–86; Foster 2002; Williams 2010) this "ungrounded" approach of radical ecology has meant that initiatives have often been forced into either utopian or reformist models of transformation. Much of this problem likely arises from the emphasis upon "industrialism" as the cause of ecological destruction rather than upon the capitalist uses of industry. Foster (2000, 2002) suggests that capitalist production relations and concerns for profit at the expense of human or environmental need are more significant for an understanding of environmental destruction than is industry itself.

From a Marxist perspective it is understood that the drive for capital accumulation results in the severe levels of pollution and contamination that workers experience directly at the workplace and at home (Faber and O' Connor 1993; Moore 1996, Foster 2000, 2002; Williams 2010; Foster, Clark and York, 2011). It is also recognized that the compulsion of competition drives the use of technologies, such as machines used in the logging and pulp and paper industries, which results in unemployment at the same time as it intensifies the destruction of nature.

Failure to comprehend such complex capitalist dynamics has played a part in the formation of those theories discussed earlier. Perhaps more significantly it has greatly hindered attempts to build a progressive alliance between radical ecology and labor. It is no longer, if it ever was, acceptable to criticize workers' actions without also providing a critical analysis of the wider networks of relations that condition the needs, concerns, and practices of workers. It is not only that workers must realize the destructive character of their jobs, but also that ecologists must understand workers' positions within capitalist society. Only then will the basic conditions be met for radical alternatives to the hegemonic capitalist model. With this mutual understanding and solidarity "the definition of conflict changes from 'environmentalists versus workers' to 'those who defend the conditions for a possible and desirable life versus those who defend practices and relations that make impossible such a life'" (Adkin 1992a, 136).

In arguing for a radical vision of democracy suited to the practices of the new social movements, one must acknowledge the possibilities for an articulation of movements between workers and ecology. It is only through open contact and mutual interaction that ecological and workers' struggles can become struggles for a radical ecology that expresses the transformation, culturally, morally, and economically, to a new, truly ecological society that may overcome the varied forms of hierarchy and domination that characterize contemporary capitalist society.

Failures of Socialist Visions

The radicalization of Green politics has convinced eco-socialists of the strategic importance of alliances to counter the hegemony of capital. "Because unions have been viewed as the representative bodies of citizens-as-workers, eco-socialists have been concerned to create forums for environmentalists and unions to meet and to work out common agendas" (Adkin 1992a, 146). Thus, priority has been given by eco-socialists to building coalitions between existing environmental groups and unions. In the United States these efforts have included the projects of Environmentalists for Full Employment and those of the Progressive Alliance (Adkin 1992a). In Canada the most notable efforts have involved the Labour and Environment Conference (Schrecker 1975), the Canadian Auto Workers (CAW) (Adkin and Alpaugh 1988), and the Windsor and District Labour Council (Adkin 1998). For the most part these efforts have met with only limited success or outright collapse.

Much of the distress of the eco-socialist project relates to the economistic priorities of traditional unionism. "In relation to environmental conflicts, they have tended to accept the logic of owners that profit is the only basis for economic growth and, hence, employment" (Adkin and Alpaugh 1988, 54). Corporatist unions still adopt a resource-management vision of human relations with nature while favoring current legislative approaches to environmental protection. "In accepting the domination of nature as the primary basis for 'jobs' and through the continued equation of politics with the state, unions have resisted the more radical demands of ecology activists to forge 'dark green' alliances which question the existing logic of production and consumption and the defining of nature within it" (Shantz and Adam 1999, 49). Leaving capitalist categories largely unscathed within union environmental discourses has allowed for their easy rearticulation along capitalist lines. Thus union environmentalism forms the workers' chorus of green capitalism in an all too familiar arrangement.

The stagnation of eco-socialism is not entirely attributable to the light green formation of traditional unionism. Eco-socialism's failure to radicalize forms of alliance is largely related to the limitations of *socialist* discourse as a possible convergence point in the formation of an alternative antihegemonic project. This failure is related to a persistent inability or unwillingness to transcend given bourgeois categories, that is, positivism and productivism, even as they collapse under continuous interrogation from radicals.

The privileging of "legitimate" means through union-centered activism and statist reforms, helpful in forming relations with workers, has stood diametrically opposed to the inclinations of activists raised on direct actions and decentered organizations. Conceptions of autonomy, participation, and cultural transformation that occupy the political ground of alternative movements have been only reluctantly engaged within eco-socialist strategies. "Arguments are advanced about how environmental practices would create employment, but where is a radically different vision of an 'equilibrium' society whose dynamics are given not by the expansion of social labour and the consumption of goods?" (Adkin 1992a, 152).

Eco-socialism's commitment to productivism and other traditional Marxist categories has contextualized "environmental relations" to mean not conditions of mutualism and complementarity with nature, but rather such forms of reproducible exploitation as tree farming. Guattari and Negri (1990, 13) voice the sentiments of many radicals in asserting that socialism, if it is to hold any relevance for alternative movements, "must be more than just the sharing of wealth (who wants all this shit?)—it must inaugurate a whole new way of working together."

The Marxist-socialist canon is assumed to be radical. From the perspectives afforded by vantage points within the ecology movements, as well as more recent alternative globalization and anarchist movements, however, it is not. For many of these movement activists, Marxism is characterized by progressivism, statism, authoritarianism, and centralism—conceptions that are, for the most part, shunned within the newest movements (Day 2005; Smith 2007; Routledge and Cumbers 2010; Shantz 2011). Instead the new politics allow for a renovation and renewal of long-eclipsed themes of radicalism such as anarchism, libertarian socialism, and syndicalism. More relevant to movement activists, though certainly not determinate, is the distinction between authoritarian and libertarian approaches to social transformation.

The shift away from productivism has allowed an emergence of positive themes such as solidarity, autonomy, and liberated desire. One might, therefore, ask: "Do the discourses of ecology suggest a renewal of political radicalism?"

Ecology emerges as a new radicalism that is launched against the machinism of the old Left. Traditional leftist discourses still express a lingering attachment to Enlightenment conceits of control through knowledge and reason and are properly understood as bourgeois inasmuch as they have supported progressivist ideas, albeit ones that are tempered with loving thoughts of redistribution (Smith 2001, 2007). One must question where such a radicalism might leave prior conceptions of work or even of workers themselves. Such an investigation implies that activists (re)read eco-discourses in a new light.

As Adkin suggests: "A more profound challenge was emanating from the radical ecologists, feminists, anarchists, and libertarian socialists" (1992a, 148). The movements of resistance that have emerged in the past several decades have aroused "a new conception of the emancipatory project of which socialism has been the leading proposal" (Aronowitz 1990, 123). Activist sensibilities bearing certain resemblances to marginalized libertarian or radical projects, for example, utopian socialism, anarchism, and anarcho-syndicalism (Tucker 1991; Roussopoulos 1991; Day 2005; Shantz 2010), as well as republicanism (Tucker 1991) and Romanticism (Scott 1990) have posed serious challenges to social theory. Confronting these questions and the problems they raise has required a critical rethinking of new movements' activism and those moments of continuity and discontinuity with the discursive strategies of earlier social movements.

Previously, radicalism had been characterized chiefly by progressivism, the idea that "the natural," with its mysterious and threatening forces, might be brought under human control as society moved through new, improved stages of human development, for the benefit of all humankind. Progressives of various stripes envisioned the taming of wild uncertainty in the post-scarcity march to the future. The making of history required that nature be made predictable. It was believed that the mastery of natural forces—especially through science and technology—would provide the basis for human freedom (Smith 2007). As Bookchin has argued, however, these utopian dreams have become ecological nightmares as the specter of global ecological catastrophe—deforestation, toxic contamination, ozone depletion, desertification, and species annihilation offer but a few examples—looms over us.

It must be emphasized that there is no natural, preordained affinity between radical ecology and leftism, as this work has already illustrated. One might even argue, going further, that traditional conservative themes (as opposed to neoliberalism or New Right fundamentalism) have been prominent in the politics of ecology, such as an emphasis upon restoration, conservation, preservation, and restraint. Indeed, early forms of environmentalism, such as conservationism, found expression through conservative or Romantic critiques of modernization (Worster 1979). Within such discourse the beauty and integrity of nature was to be defended against vulgar economic expansion.

Just as there is no privileged relation between ecological discourses and leftism, neither is there any necessary connection with conservatism. Ecological discourses, as some have said, are neither necessarily of the Left nor of the Right. Rather, they express shifting political commitments and orientations in a landscape of capitalist transformation. Green politics reveal many ambiguities and ambivalences. They reject progressivism and related optimism, yet they have managed simultaneously to articulate radical schemas suggestive of transformations well beyond those imagined within socialism. It is the volatile mix of contradictory forces that may account for the creativity and the radicalism of ecology.

While there may be—and clearly there has developed—some affinity between certain aspirations of ecology and those of the Left, the ecology movement is just as likely to pursue objectives that are directly opposed to traditional concerns of leftism, especially where those regard questions of productivism and security (see Offe, 1985). That reality becomes especially important when one attempts to understand the practices of radical ecology. Within the movements around ecology one finds a volatile interplay of antibourgeois discourses, both "progressive" and conservative. Indeed, radical ecology has emerged out of earlier critiques of capitalist and socialist categories. This history explains, in part, the distance that persists between ecology and the projects of both capitalism and socialism. It also means that anticapitalists have to develop clear perspectives that address the root causes of ecological destruction.

Green Syndicalism: An Alternative Red/Green Vision

As a corrective to the retreat from class in much ecological, new social movement, and "radical" thought, some activists have tried recently to learn the lessons shown by the history of the Industrial Workers of the World (IWW or "Wobblies"). As the next chapter discusses, the late Earth First! organizer Judi Bari used her knowledge of IWW organizing work to help build an alliance between timber workers and radical environmentalists in the redwood forests of Northern California. By showing that a radical working-class perspective may also contain a radical ecological perspective, IWW/Earth First! Local 1 contributed much to a radicalization of alliances within the ecology movement. Moreover, their efforts in Northern California provided a sharp and living critique of the common view among environmentalists (see Foreman 1991; Bookchin 1980, 1986, 1987; Watson 2005; Zerzan 2008a, 2008b) that class analyses and class struggle approaches have little to offer in the effort to bring about an ecological society.

This approach has led to the development of syndicalist practice informed by radical ecology—a "green syndicalism." Green syndicalists have articulated labor as part of the environmental community (see Shantz and Adam 1999; Bari 2001; Purchase 1994, 1997a, 1997b; Jakopovich 2007; Williams 2009a, 2009b). Within green syndicalism this assumption of connectedness between historical radical movements, including labor and ecology, has much significance. "We find ecological consciousness in both the history of the IWW and the philosophy and practice of earlier anarchists" (Kauffman and Ditz 1992, 41). This connectedness helps to explain why the IWW has become an important focal point for radical ecologists seeking to build alliances with workers.

These green syndicalist articulations are important in reminding (or informing) ecology activists and workers alike that there are radical working-class histories in addition to the histories of compromise that have preoccupied the thinking of social ecologist Murray Bookchin and fundamentalist ecologist Paul Watson alike. "Historically, it was the IWW who broke the stranglehold of the timber barons on the loggers and millworkers in the nineteen teens" (Bari 1994, 18). It is precisely this stranglehold that environmentalists are trying to break today. "Now the companies are back in total control, only this time they're taking down not only the workers but the Earth as well. This, to me, is what the IWW-Earth First! link is really about" (Bari 1994, 18). In her work, Bari forged conceptual bonds between the suffering of timber workers in the 1920s and ecological destruction today. The history of workers' struggles becomes part of the history of ecology in Bari's genealogy of the present.

Significantly, green syndicalists reject the productivist premises of "old-style" Marxists who often viewed issues such as ecology as external to questions of production, distracting from the task of organizing workers at the point of production. Within green syndicalist perspectives, ecological concerns cannot properly be divorced from questions of production or economics. Rather than representing "separate discursive universes," nature, producers, or workplace become understood as endlessly contested features in an always shifting terrain of struggle. Furthermore these contests, both over materiality and over meanings, contradict notions of unitary responses. Green syndicalists thus stress the mutuality and interaction of what had been discursively separated—nature, culture, workers (see Bari 2001).

> We are not trying to overthrow capitalism for the benefit of the proletariat. In fact, the society we envision is not spoken to in any leftist theory that I've ever heard of. Those theories deal only with how to redistribute the spoils of exploiting the Earth to benefit a different class of humans. We need to build a society that is not based on the exploitation of the Earth at all—a society whose goal is to achieve a stable state with nature for the benefit of all species. (Bari 1994, 57)

Through this expanded analysis of class struggles one may come to a more concrete understanding of the dynamic nature of conflict. No longer posited as one-sided or pre-given, it becomes clear that the struggles themselves lead to the emergence of entirely new issues and demands such as the quality of work and ecology.

The question becomes how these newly opening political spaces might contribute to deeper expressions of democracy and freedom. Laclau and Mouffe (1985) suggest that ecology and class might converge in new articulations that actually modify or transform the identity of participants such that the demands of each are rendered as equal. Thus a process of "hegemonic equivalence" changes the very constitution of the class and ecology forces engaged in social struggles. Following Boggs (1986, 231) one might expect an articulation of new social movement and class forces to occur as part of a transformation from a capitalist economy to an ecological community.

This suggestion is consistent with a key insight provided by radical ecology. "Unity-in-diversity is a basic attribute of healthy eco-communities. Why shouldn't it be a healthy characteristic for radical movements?" (Chase 1991, 10). Diversity is something to be cherished and cultivated as an important element of a new ecological society.

Green syndicalists insist that overcoming ecological devastation depends on shared responsibilities toward developing convivial ways of living wherein relations of affinity, both within our own species and with other species, are nurtured (see Bari 2001). They envision, for example, an association of workers committed to the dismantling of the factory system, its work discipline, hierarchies, and regimentation—all of the things Bookchin identifies and desires but denies as an aspect of class struggle (Kaufmann and Ditz 1992; Purchase 1994, 1997b; Jakopovich 2007; Williams 2009b; Shantz 2010). This vision involves both a literal destruction of factories and their conversion toward "soft" forms of small, local production. These shifting priorities express the novelty of green syndicalism—not the discourse of industrial management presented in the caricatures of its detractors.

Within green syndicalism one sees evidence of "deep green" perspectives that express new visions of relations between industrial workers and radical ecology. Green syndicalist perspectives are suggestive of some tentative synthesis. The emphasis still remains on possibility. Green syndicalist visions include elements that may be unrealistic or improbable.

Conclusion

According to Melucci (1992, 65) "the planetarization of the world system means that there is no longer an 'outside world': territories and cultures exist only as internal dimensions of the same system." Contemporary theorizing, then, stands at the "end of wilderness," where wilderness can be understood as any unspoiled realm outside of, or independent from, human penetration and interference. Nature is not an externalized objectivity marked by its designation as "environment" (or as "wilderness," which becomes a radical version of the same thing). Preservation presumes, though many fundamentalists seem to miss the point, social transformation and raises the question of how social relations might (and must) be reorganized. Such questions emerge within a context of radical unfixity in which nothing, including nature, can anymore be taken for granted.

While these are significant ecological matters, they have too often been conceived by fundamentalist ecology as external to ecological concerns with wilderness degradation and loss. Failing to confront adequately questions of social scarcity, or confused regarding whether the scarcity in question is social or natural in character, fundamentalists conclude that such matters are but diversions from the immediate task of emancipating nature from civilization. This is a mistake. Were they to look more closely they would find: "resource shortages and ecological degradation are *primarily a result* of the uneven social measures that manufacture scarcity all over the world for the economic and political gain of powerful interests" (Ross 1996, 7).

Unwillingness to attend to these matters has contributed to the social distance obtaining between radical ecology and other social movements, especially those organized around questions of race and class. It is impossible to understand the materiality of ecological crisis without attending to the structural inequalities that underlie social scarcity. The relationships between social scarcity and natural scarcity are crucial for ecological analysis.

The real consequences of such misunderstandings/views for radical ecology have been expressions of ambiguity or suspicion toward workers and toward the prospects for an articulation of environmental and workers' struggles that might confront the capitalist roots of current ecological threats. The typical response for many activists, despite the efforts of green Marxists and green syndicalists, has been a move away from class analyses altogether. Critical focus has shifted away from exploitation and toward discussions of hierarchy and domination more generally, and often vaguely, conceived.

In *Remaking Society* Bookchin (1989, 172) concludes that "the bases for conflicting interests in society must themselves be confronted and resolved in a revolutionary manner. The earth can no longer be owned; it must be shared." These statements represent truly crucial aspects of a radical vision for an ecological society. What is perplexing is that Bookchin does not draw the necessary implications out of his own radical conclusions. The questions of ownership and control of the earth are nothing if not questions of class.

As conflicts over nature deepen, economic crises intensify and the theft represented by property becomes delegitimized by the further destruction of varied eco-communities, there is the potential for greater mobilizations of people as workers in a diverse but united struggle for communitarian reconstruction. It is from a standpoint of unity-in-diversity (social and ecological) that a newer, richer understanding of class and class struggle must begin. Through open communication and alliance workers as environmentalists (and indeed environmentalists as workers) will add to this deeper understanding of class struggle.

3

The Feminization of Earth First!

IWW/EF! Local 1 and the Convergence of Class, Gender, and Radical Environmentalism

Commentators Larry Martel and John-Henry Harter identify the loss of union power in the woods of the West Coast of North America as the primary factor behind the recent crises in the forests. Martel argues that getting there requires nothing less than "a vast union machine in the woods" to ensure that workers "can no longer be blackmailed by the companies into trading off job and livelihood security for ancient-growth preservation" (1997, 34). Finding durable solutions to habitat destruction requires a reexpansion of unionization and a restoration of bargaining strength, according to Martel and Harter. As they see it, this is the best way to allow workers the power necessary to refuse divisive "jobs versus environment" strategies and hold companies accountable for both job loss and biodiversity destruction. Forest workers must be in a position to strike over jobs, wages, working conditions, *and* ecologically sensible practices. This cannot be done in the absence of organization. "More to the point, until strike capacity is increased, there will be tremendous pressure to harvest ancient growth, because there is no other more effective counterbalance to forest corporate profit imperatives than a union being able to stop work to enforce its demands" (Martel 1997, 34).

Martel suggests that environmental activists need to develop friendly relations with forest workers and goes so far as to argue that environmental canvassers could be trained as union organizers. His recommendations are strikingly similar to those actually attempted by Judi Bari and IWW/Earth First! Local 1. Unfortunately Martel makes no mention of this real organizing effort and the stunning obstacles it faced.

Among the more interesting of recent attempts to articulate solidarity across the ecology and workers' movements were those involving Earth First! activist Judi Bari and her efforts to build alliances with workers in order to save old-growth forest in Northern California. Bari sought to learn from the organizing and practices of the IWW to see if a radical ecology movement might be built along anarcho-syndicalist lines. In so doing she tried to bring a radical working-class perspective to the agitational practices of Earth First! as a way to overcome the conflicts between environmentalists and timber workers that kept them from fighting the corporate logging firms that were killing both forests and jobs. The organization she helped form, IWW/Earth First Local 1, eventually built a measure of solidarity between radical environmentalists and loggers that resulted in the protection of the Headwaters old-growth forest, which had been slated for clear-cutting (Shantz 1999b).

Wilderness Fundamentalism and the "Rednecks for Nature"

Emerging from the threatened landscape of the US Southwest in 1980, Earth First! (EF!) almost immediately established itself as the extreme edge of North American environmentalism. Arriving during a low ebb in the cycle of environmental activism, Earth First! provided an important voice for wilderness preservation against prevailing views that reduced nature to "our resources and private property" (Idaho Farm Bureau Federation, quoted in Short 1991, 181). Their position of "No compromise in defense of Mother Earth" quickly made them the bane of land developers, cattle ranchers, logging companies, the US National Park Service, the US Forest Service, and other environmentalists (Lange 1990; Short 1991).

The group's founders, most notably Dave Foreman, viewed confrontation and agitation as the only means to awaken an increasingly lethargic environmental movement that was clearly failing to protect wilderness ecosystems (Short 1991). Earth First! vigorously attacked mainstream environmentalists for being too close to the political establishment and too ready to make compromises that were not in the best interests of wilderness ecosystems.

In place of a "granola-crunching" pacifist image of environmentalists, which they were quick to deride, Earth First!'s founders identified themselves as "rednecks and cowboys for wilderness" (see Lange 1990; Short 1991). Throughout the 1980s and early 1990s Earth First!, with its extreme rhetoric and public commitment to direct action and "monkeywrenching,"[1] served as a striking symbol of a renewed radicalism in environmental politics. Armed with a broad sense of humor, they transformed the character of environmental protests by engaging in lively guerrilla theater, blockades, "tree sitting," and threats of sabotage[2] (Lange 1990; Short 1991). The group signaled a potentially important and necessary radicalization of environmentalism, both through its ecological sensibility and in the tactics deployed to realize that sensibility.

Inspiring EF! practice was an underlying philosophy of "deep ecology" or "wilderness fundamentalism" that provided an integral part of EF!'s political agenda (Short 1991). According to Laurie Adkin (1992a, 144) wilderness fundamentalism "refers to various forms of essentialism (claims about the sensual, spiritual, aesthetic, and developmental needs of humans as a species, and about the rights of other species) that are present (implicitly or explicitly) in different discourses." For eco-fundamentalism, commodification of life (both human and nonhuman) is linked to alienation from the body, from

---

1. Edward Abbey's novel *The Monkey Wrench Gang* served as political manifesto and spiritual guide for the group's early efforts (Short 1991). The 1975 novel presents vivid portrayals of various acts of sabotage in subversion of wilderness development projects.

2. Favored acts of sabotage in defense of ecology, or "ecotage," during the early years of Earth First! included pulling survey stakes and disabling heavy equipment.

nature, and from "authentic" human needs. Themes of ethics and identity predominate in fundamentalist discourses that are directed primarily toward the transformation of values within individuals (Adkin 1992a, 1992b).

However, it soon became clear that there was another, more ominous side to wilderness fundamentalism. List (1993, 6) suggests that EF!'s wilderness fundamentalism took on a "purist" fervor that held that "the core of social and political life should be reoriented towards wilderness preservation and restoration, instead of to other social issues." This biocentric orientation placed a commitment to wilderness ahead of other sociopolitical concerns such as struggles against racism, poverty, unemployment, and patriarchy. The fundamentalists implied that "real change in our behavior toward wild nature could occur without revolutionizing capitalist economic systems and social structures" (List 1993. 7). The essentialist narratives of fundamentalist ecology (see Devall 1988; Manes 1990) tended to construct "humanity" as a bloc, undifferentiated by power, in which a universalistic human species itself was held responsible for biospheric destruction, dangerously discounting politically constructed differences of race, gender, and class.

Indeed, there emerged a harsh neo-Malthusianism among fundamentalist ecology.[3] For some Earth First!ers (see Manes 1990)the first and best solution to environmental destruction is the mass reduction of human populations. While Dave Foreman was suggesting that nature should have been allowed to take its course in the Ethiopian famine, Paul Watson[4] (1994, 128) mused that "to a vastly reduced population wood could be made available without killing trees." No word from Watson regarding who among the population might be subject to reduction, although he did suggest that one redwood is worth more than all of the human residents of California. In a notorious Earth

3. A popular Earth First! bumper sticker proclaimed: "Malthus Was Right."
4. Paul Watson is the founder of the Sea Shepherd Conservation Society, a marine ecology group whose members identify themselves as the Earth First! navy.

First! article a writer using the pseudonym Miss Ann Thropy[5] "welcomed the AIDS epidemic as 'a necessary solution' to the 'population problem' (generously including 'war, famine, humiliating poverty' along with AIDS" (Bookchin quoted in Bookchin and Foreman 1991, 123). Perhaps not satisfied that the message had been understood, Miss Ann Thropy (1987, 32) continued: "To paraphrase Voltaire: if the AIDS epidemic did not exist, radical environmentalists would have to invent one." While insisting that they were unconcerned with political or social issues, the fundamentalists developed what were first and foremost political narratives, albeit of a reactionary nature.

Unfortunately, it's this version of Earth First! that came to represent the movement in the popular imagination. Yet the story is much more complex. For there emerged within Earth First! itself a countermovement of activists who attempted to bring sociopolitical analysis to their biocentric acts. By the late 1980s a grassroots opposition to the social and political shortsightedness of the "rednecks for nature" was beginning to take shape in the redwood regions of Northern California. The Northern California Earth First!ers (including Judi Bari, Daryl Cherney, Mike Rosselle,[6] and Pam Davis) rejected the misanthropy, machismo, patriotism, and antilabor biases of the old guard, condemning their comments on Ethiopia, immigration, and AIDS. Their actions, to reform Earth First! while fighting to preserve old growth ecosystems, would come to be among the most important examples of eco-defense in North America.

Local 1 and the Timber Wars

The environmental struggle over the redwoods of Northern California continues to be among the most heated in North America.[7] At the time

---

5. The article was written by Chris Manes, author of *Green Rage*.

6. Mike Roselle was the only Earth First! cofounder to identify himself as a political leftist.

7. In September 1998, Earth First! activist David "Gypsy" Chain was killed when a timber worker felled a tree onto his campsite.

of Judi Bari's work the fevered pitch of these conflicts had earned them the nickname "timber wars." Environmentalists were routinely subjected to violence with loggers driving through picket lines and felling trees into demonstrations. Hanging in the balance was the survival of one of the few remaining old growth ecosystems in the United States.

The context for the pitched battles raging in Northern California was one of rapid job loss and eroding communities.[8] Industry spokespersons denied responsibility for the decline in logging jobs, preferring to place the blame on environmentalists. Yet the timber companies (Louisiana-Pacific, Georgia Pacific, and Maxxam) removed trees at an incredible rate. Practicing "infinity logging,"[9] the logging firms were determined to take out every tree as quickly as possible.

As a long-time union activist and labor organizer, Judi Bari was well aware that the destinies of the forests and the forest workers were inextricably linked. In her view, blaming environmentalists or endangered species like the spotted owl for the loss of logging jobs was nothing but a cynical tactic on the part of logging industry spokespersons. She identified instead the rapid industrialization of logging during the past two decades as heavy machinery and mechanized practices such as clear-cutting came to replace labor-intensive and selective forms of logging. Additionally, processing jobs had disappeared because mill work was moved elsewhere as the companies pursued less expensive labor.[10] Smaller trees and fewer forests, of course, also required fewer hands. The only way to save both the forests and timber jobs was to change over to sustained yield logging practices, as many environmentalists were advocating (Bari 1994, 13).

8. According to Scarce (1990) the environmentalist Green Ribbon Coalition reported that 13,000 loggers were laid off in the Pacific Northwest between 1982 and 1988.

9. This charming notion comes from Louisiana-Pacific president Harry Merlo: "We log to infinity. It's out there, it's ours, and we want it all. Now" (quoted in Bari 1994, 12).

10. The automation of logging was specifically aimed at reducing labor costs.

Unfortunately, most timber workers were being successfully mobilized by logging companies against such practices. Management initiated a jingoistic "Yellow Ribbon Campaign," encouraging local families and businesses to display yellow ribbons to show their solidarity with the companies in the face of the environmentalist "menace." In some communities simply choosing not to fly a ribbon was dangerous (Bari 1994; Heider 1994; Purchase 1994).

The success with which management mobilized workers against environmentalists continued to be the immediate obstacle confronting environmentalists' attempts to change logging practices and end the slaughter of the redwoods. What was behind the success? Workers' fears over the imminent collapse of the forest ecosystems and concomitant loss of jobs, communities, and ways of life were easy enough to see, even if few environmentalists took these fears seriously. Judi Bari identified something else:

> That is the utter lack of class consciousness by virtually all of the environmental groups. I have even had an international Earth First! spokesman tell me that there is no difference between the loggers and the logging companies.
>
> I have heard various environmentalists say that working in the woods and mills is not an "honourable" profession, as if the workers have any more control over the corporations' policies (or are gaining any more from them) than we do. As long as people on our side hold these views, it will be easy pickins for the bosses to turn their employees against us. (Bari 1994, 14)

Bari knew that only the interests of the timber bosses would be served if environmentalists and workers continued to view each other as the enemy. She determined to do something to end this standoff, which had for too long impeded ecological defense. A possible solution gradually crystallized in Bari's mind—a radical timber workers' union organized along with Earth First!ers to save both jobs and ecosystems. The idea was soon realized as IWW/Earth First! Local 1, which brought together under one roof radical environmentalism and revolutionary syndicalism,[11] forming an improbable "green syndicalism." Bari immediately set out as a field organizer, against all odds signing up the Earth First! old guard's hated enemies—timber workers.[12]

Forest workers themselves, were they to organize against the destructive "cut-and-run" practices of the multinational forest giants, might be able to develop a sustainable harvesting operation. One of her earliest acts as a member of Earth First! was to conduct, together with long-time Wobbly musician and activist Dakota Sid Clifford, a seminar on the history of the IWW (Scarce 1990, 82). In the spirit and style of anarcho-syndicalism Bari recognized potentially instructive similarities with the praxis of radical ecology. Concluding a 1989 letter to the Wobblies' paper, *Industrial Worker*, Bari argued that "if the IWW would like to be more than a historical society, it seems that the time is right to organize again in timber" (Bari 1994, 18). The resulting synthesis was IWW/Earth First! Local 1.

Armed with an organizing style borrowed from the radical union's heyday Bari set out as an Earth First! field organizer, but with one remarkable difference. Local 1 immediately began signing up *timber workers* while publicly denouncing the timber corporations for their mistreatment of forests and forest workers alike. Bari recognized that workplaces offered promising bases of support. With that as her starting point, she found it surprisingly easy to make contact with

11. Revolutionary unionism, or syndicalism, sought the replacement of capitalism through working-class solidarity and control of production. The main proponents of revolutionary unionism in North America, the Industrial Workers of the World (IWW) had a rich history in the forests of the West Coast during the first decades of the twentieth century, organizing timber camps from California to British Columbia. Unlike mainstream unions, the Wobblies organized all workers regardless of race, ethnic background, gender, or language. They faced violent repression, including the arrests and killings of organizers. They were eventually broken in the 1920s.

12. So powerful was the image of Earth First! hostility to loggers that one of the few mainstream accounts of the planning for Redwood Summer came with the headline: "Eco-activist summer: Earth First! vs. the loggers in California" (Barol 1990, 60).

workers who did not accept the companies' views on the situation in the woods. Indeed over the course of two years, between 1988 and 1990, relations with timber workers gradually improved. A union local comprising timber workers and environmentalists was formed in Fort Bragg, California. Bari officially represented five mill workers, victims of a PCB spill at work, to the Occupational Safety and Health Administration (OSHA) (Purchase 1994). Newsletters countering management perspectives "spontaneously" appeared at two of the local mills. The industry publication "Timber Line" was greeted with "Timber Lyin'." Written from the point of view of workers and addressing such issues as health and safety problems and job loss resulting from clear-cutting, the paper called on workers to organize for the survival of their communities (Scarce 1990; Bari 1994). Workers also began to provide information that helped environmentalists organize effective tree-sits and blockades. After Louisiana-Pacific closed the nearby Potter Valley sawmill, which had employed 136 people, Darryl Cherney's song "Potter Valley Mill," which included two references to sabotage, became the most requested song on the local country music station. Mill workers even sold tapes of the song in Potter Valley.

Challenges developed quickly. In April 1990 one of the major timber companies, Louisiana-Pacific (L-P) announced 195 layoffs in Ukiah and Covelo and the closing of the Covelo Mill, at a time when the company registered record quarterly profits. L-P blamed environmentalists for interrupting the supply of lumber but shortly thereafter the company began shipping partially cut logs from California to its newly opened plant in Mexico. The machinery used at the Mexico plant had been transferred from the same mill in Potter Valley, California, that L-P had closed the previous year.

IWW/Earth First Local 1 responded with its first public demonstration of labor and ecology solidarity. Appearing at a Board of Superintendents meeting EF!, IWW, and L-P employees demanded that the county "use its power of eminent domain to seize all of L-P's corporate timberlands and operate them in the public interest" (Bari 1994, 136). One supervisor even met publicly with coalition members to discuss how the plan might be enacted.

An unanticipated turning point for the young labor-environment alliance emerged at an annual environmental law conference in Oregon in March 1990. Appearing on a panel with Judi Bari, timber worker Gene Lawhorn bluntly told the audience that Bari's timber worker–radical environmentalist alliance was doomed if Earth First! continued to advocate tree-spiking. This controversial tactic, in which environmentalists drove large spikes into trees to deter cutting, was perceived by loggers and mill workers as a very real threat to their lives because of the unpredictable breaking of saw blades. For Earth First!ers, however, spiking was almost an article of faith. With the audience anxiously awaiting her response, Bari spoke the words that would send shock waves through EF! circles: "I hereby renounce tree-spiking." Surprisingly, the Earth First!ers in attendance supported her. After discussing her decision, several Northwest groups agreed to denounce spiking formally (Scarce 1990). In mid-April a statement was issued citing the growing timber worker–radical ecology alliance as the reason for the break with EF! orthodoxy. Significantly, monkeywrenching itself was not renounced. The formal statement encouraged sabotage *by timber workers* as a means to disrupt the labor process and slow the cutting of trees. Workers were no longer viewed as necessary targets of sabotage, they were viewed as potential eco-saboteurs.

In his book *Ecodefense: A Field Guide to Monkeywrenching* (1989), Dave Foreman had argued that ecotage must be unorganized and the act of individuals alone. Local 1 countered that in order for eco-defense to be successful it must be based in the community. Individual acts of adventure cannot halt environmental destruction. Isolated from community support, individual adventurist acts further reinforce the divisions between environmentalists and local workers.

I have nothing against individual acts of daring. But the flaw in this strategy is the failure to engage in long-term community-based organizing. There is no way that a few isolated individuals, no matter how brave, can bring about the massive social change necessary to save the planet. So we began to organize with local people, planning our logging blockades around issues that had local community support. We also began to build alliances with progressive timber workers based on our common interests against big corporations. As our successes grew, more women and more people with families and roots in the community began calling themselves Earth First!ers in our area. (Bari 1994, 221)

Of course, timber workers were not the only workers in Mendocino County. Local Earth First!ers included students, carpenters, child-care workers, recycling center operators, and office workers (Bari 1994, 85). Many lived off of the land as fishers or homesteaders. One even owned a small sawmill. Bari emphasized organizing tactics that mobilized people in their local communities. She knew that many were already active in local watershed associations and did regular unpaid stream-restoration work. They were approached in terms of the interconnection between destruction of forests through clear-cuts and the damage done to local waterways.

Redwood Summer and the Feminization of Earth First!

Still, despite the best efforts of Local 1, the trees continued to fall. Hardt and Negri (2000) stress the importance of expanding local struggles against global capitalism, a necessity that became unavoidable within Local 1. Despite having strengthened relations with workers in a manner previously unimagined, the still troubling rate of logging and the continued hegemony of the transnational timber corporations caused the small group of activists to conclude that they could not protect the forests if their actions did not resonate beyond the isolated locale's tiny, rural population. Their solution was to organize a "Redwood Summer." Taking their inspiration from the tactics of the Civil Rights movement, Bari and her allies put forth an international appeal for "Freedom Riders for the Forest to come to Northern California and engage in non-violent mass actions to stop the slaughter of the redwoods" (Bari 1994, 222). The message of nonviolence, which marked a break with EF!'s prior stance and was cause for much controversy within radical circles, would be nurtured through workshops and creative strategy sessions to encourage novel approaches to activist community building. In the minds of the organizers, Redwood Summer would bring unprecedented international scrutiny to bear upon the timber corporations, in conjunction with a local show of resistance unlike any the companies had ever faced.

As organizing for Redwood Summer enjoyed cumulative success, expanding both the project's scale and its potential, incidents and levels of repression against the activists increased. Growing anxiety within the timber industry over the prospects of mass resistance was reflected in an escalation of violence against front-line activists who were punched, shot at, and run from the road by log trucks. Bari herself became the target for numerous death threats on behalf of corporate timber interests.

Clearly the radicalization of coalition practices across that carefully managed gulf separating timber workers and environmentalists was beginning to raise new possibilities for a realignment of forces in the woods. Such a shifting of sociopolitical terrain, if left unchecked, could have threatened an erosion of timber corporation hegemony.

Activists had long feared that timber supporters might actually make an attempt on the life of an organizer. "Bari, especially, was too dangerous, her wood worker–environmentalist union talk a chilling proposition for companies which operated effective monopolies over their workers' lives, secluded as they are from other sources of information and employment" (Scarce 1990, 85). Violence against anyone suspected of opposing the timber industry was readily deployed in the isolated timber-dependent communities (see Stentz 1993).

While Bari was driving through Oakland on the way to Santa Cruz to perform at a concert promoting Redwood Summer, a pipe-bomb placed under the driver's seat of her car exploded, nearly killing her. The blast tore through the car, badly injuring Bari, who suffered severe injuries including soft tissue damage and a shattered pelvis. Bari would never fully recover from her injuries and spent the rest of her life in debilitating pain. Her organizing partner, Darryl Cherney, riding in the passenger seat, was also injured. Within hours of the bombing, Oakland police along with the FBI arrested Bari and Cherney, claiming that the victims themselves had built and were transporting the bomb for use in a terrorist act.

Bari and Cherney told investigators the names of several individuals and a right-wing group that they suspected might have been responsible for the bombing based on previous threats. Instead of pursuing any of those leads, the FBI stepped up a propaganda campaign that attempted to portray Earth First! as a terrorist organization and Bari and Cherney as extremist bombers. The police even put forward a number of unsubstantiated claims that they had physical evidence linking Bari to the bombs. Police agencies provided major media outlets with ongoing supplies of incriminating "evidence" and rumor, which were utilized against the growing activist coalition to cultivate a fiction of environmentalist violence. This fictitious "equality of violence" allowed those responsible for violent acts, such as timber corporation supporters, the luxury of casting their activities as merely defensive responses to an eco-terrorist threat and hence justifiable. As Bari stated at the time: "So while the real Earth First! in northern California was renouncing tree-spiking, building coalitions with workers and peace activists, and responding to timber industry violence by calling for mass nonviolence, the public was being taught to associate us with bombs and terrorism" (Bari 1994, 300).

The FBI used their own baseless accusations as a pretext for a widespread investigation of more than 600 environmentalists across the United States. Documents obtained as part of a lawsuit launched by Bari and Cherney revealed that Oakland police were observing 300 activists groups and passing information to the FBI. In addition, the FBI maintained a database of 634 people who had so much as phone contact with Bari or Cherney. Many of these people were questioned by the FBI, which compiled numerous files on activists and their organizations. This broad campaign against activists was a clear attempt to disrupt organizing for Redwood Summer and discourage activists from traveling to Northern California. The searching of vehicles, raiding of homes, and harassing of activists uncovered nothing to incriminate anyone associated with radical ecology.

There were in fact early indications that the bombing was motivated by explicitly misogynist sentiments. Bari reports that one of the
death threats she received described the organizers of Redwood Summer as "whores, lesbians and members of N.O.W." (Bari 1994, 223).
As an outspoken defender of abortion rights Bari received numerous
death threats and hate letters from religious fundamentalists[13] (Purchase 1994, 135). Bari was convinced that the extreme forms of violence and hatred to which she was subjected related not simply to what
she was saying but that a woman was saying it.

Unfortunately, authorities chose not to follow these leads, preferring to focus on friends of the organizers. The FBI and Oakland
police almost immediately announced that the main suspects were
Bari and Cherney themselves. Incredibly, they accused the two pacifists of transporting the bomb for use in a terrorist act. The only evidence offered was that the bomb was in the back seat, where it would
have been seen by the activists. (Never mind that the epicenter of

13. Bari initially suspected that it was, in fact, a "pro-lifer," not necessarily
a timber supporter, who was responsible for the bombing. She became convinced
of this after receiving a detailed letter from the "Lord's Avenger" that contained a
detailed description of the bomb and offered a chilling explanation of why Bari was
wanted dead. "It was not just my 'paganism' and defense of the forest that outraged
him. The Lord's Avenger also recalled an abortion clinic defense that I had led years
ago. 'I saw Satan's flames shoot forth from her mouth her eyes and ears, proving forever that this was no godly woman, no Ruth full of obedience to procreate and multiply the children of Adam throughout the world as is God's will. "Let the woman
learn in silence with all subjection. But I suffer not a woman to teach, nor to usurp
authority over the man, but to be in silence" (Timothy 2:11)'" (Bari 1994, 224).
After the bombing Bari also received a steady flow of misogynist hate literature.
"The worst was from the Sahara Club, an anti-environmental group that wrote in
its newsletter: 'BOMB THAT CROTCH! Judi Bari, the Earth First bat slug who
blew herself halfway to hell and back while transporting a bomb in her Subaru, held
a press conference in San Francisco. Bari, who had her crotch blown off, will never
be able to reproduce again. We're just trying to figure out what would volunteer to
inseminate her if she had all her parts. The last we heard, Judi and her friends were
pouting and licking their wounds'" (Bari 1994, 224).

the blast actually showed that the bomb was under Bari's seat, out of view.) Under this pretext the FBI raided the homes of other activists and investigated supporters (Heider 1994).

In response, an international defense campaign was organized to clear the victims' names and continue mobilization in the redwoods. Activists, sensing corporate and state complicity in the ongoing and increasingly extreme manifestations of violence, united to halt FBI and police harassment of the victims, and environmentalists generally, and to initiate a serious investigation of the bombing. Greenpeace hired a private investigator to identify those responsible. The FBI's tactics were eventually called into question by the House Judiciary subcommittee on civil and constitutional rights. Cherney and Bari subsequently filed a lawsuit against the FBI and the Oakland police.

After eight weeks of slandering Bari and Cherney and attempting to discredit Redwood Summer, the authorities had to admit that they had no evidence, and all charges were dropped. The FBI and Oakland police never retracted their claims and never conducted a real investigation into the bombing. "Tried and convicted in the press, Bari and Cherney were set free" (Scarce 1990, 85).

The cynical efforts of the FBI, Oakland police, and local authorities greatly interfered with organizing for Redwood Summer, already hindered by the loss of the most experienced organizers. In addition, local law enforcement agencies actively worked to suppress the unionization effort (Purchase 1994). Activists faced continued incidents of harassment, intimidation, death threats, and violence.

Redwood Summer was not defeated, however. Despite the campaigns of disinformation and destabilization, organizers were not frightened away from their work in the forests. Unlike anything previously, the bombing and the incredible response of the FBI and Oakland police galvanized the environmentalist communities. New members from around the country were drawn into the movement, significantly from backgrounds quite different from those of the "mountain men"/"wilderness boys" and with new visions of ecological resistance (see Pickett 1993). The changes in EF! worldview and strategy initiated within Local 1 contributed to the growing prominence of women in Earth First! during Redwood Summer. After the bombing, more than twenty people came forward to take on key organizing roles in Bari's absence; three-quarters of them were women (Bari 1994; Purchase 1994). It was, in Bari's view, the feminization of Earth First![14] As she noted at the time: "Redwood Summer is an almost entirely women-led action. There are women holding the base camp together, there are women holding the actions together, even the attorney team is women" (Bari 1994, 43).

In June, in the first action of Redwood Summer, more than seven hundred people participated in a protest and rally at the L-P export dock in Samoa, California. Forty-four demonstrators were arrested while blocking log and chip trucks (Bari 1994). Other early actions included a Sacramento EF! protest at that city's export dock, a tree-sit in Murrulet Grove, and a "performance" by Urban Earth Women, for which they were arrested, at Maxxam's (Pacific Lumber Company or Palco, another logging firm) Marin headquarters. Several more demonstrations were held at the Maxxam offices in Marin. At one protest against Maxxam, activists from Latin America staged an action to emphasize the connectedness of ecological destruction in Northern California and in Central America. They were arrested for their efforts.

The climax of Redwood Summer was a July rally at Fort Bragg in which two thousand protesters marched through the town chanting:

14. Bari offers her insights into the feminization of Earth First! in an article by that title that appeared in *Ms Magazine* (and is reprinted in *Timber Wars*): "What is surprising is that I, a feminist, single mother and blue-collar worker, would end up in Earth First!, a 'no compromise' direct action group with the reputation of being macho, beer-drinking eco-dudes" (Bari 1994, 219). From the beginning Bari sought to overcome the typical gendered division of labor that existed in Earth First! "But Earth First! was founded by five men, and its principal spokespeople have all been male. As in all such groups, there have always been competent women doing the real work behind the scenes. But they have been virtually invisible behind the public persona of 'big man goes into big wilderness to save big trees.' I certainly objected to this" (Bari 1994, 220). Redwood Summer saw a transformation in the activities undertaken by women within Earth First!

"Earth First! Profits Last." In what could have been an explosive situation, the marchers were met by fifteen hundred angry supporters of the timber companies. Thinking quickly, activists Darryl Cherney and Pam Davis invited the counterdemonstrators to speak from the Redwood Summer stage. In a moment of symbolic significance for the young movement, "Duane Potter, a logger whom we had never met before, stood up and told the truth—that he used to log in the summer and fish in the winter, and now there are no logs and no fish" (Bari 1994, 74–75). The poignancy of Potter's plea, speaking to a sense of loss shared by many in the logging communities, aided a nonviolent resolution of the confrontation.

Redwood Summer's final action, held in August, also managed to avoid almost certain catastrophe through the patience of activists and their commitment to nonviolence. The ill-conceived plan called for a two-day concert named Redwoodstock, followed by a march through the town of Fortuna. All of this was supposed to occur in a notoriously hostile area and required a court order just to allow the assembly. The seven hundred protesters who marched through Fortuna were pelted with bottles and eggs by jeering counterdemonstrators. When the angry crowd attacked, pushing aside police officers, the protesters responded by sitting down and singing, which defused the situation

Overall, approximately 3,000 people took part in Redwood Summer, many from outside the United States.[15] By comparison, previous Earth First! actions had drawn no more than 150 participants. More than 250 activists were arrested. The actions preserved the two-thousand-year-old trees of Headwaters Forest, which had been slated for cutting. The commitment to nonviolence in relations with workers

15. Bari's only public appearance during Redwood Summer came during a women's rally at the FBI building in San Francisco. Two hundred women took part in that demonstration alone. After the bombing Bari, along with Darryl Cherney, sued the FBI and the Oakland police for violating their civil rights. Much of the support work was done by the Redwood Summer Justice Project. They can be contacted at P.O. Box 14720, Santa Rosa, CA, 95402 or by internet at www.judibari.org.

gained Local 1 a new level of respect in the local communities and allowed them to further develop the movement.

The "Redneck" Resistance to the Feminization of Earth First!

Still, old resentments within Earth First! remained. "Being the first women-led action, Redwood Summer has never gotten the respect it deserves from the old guard of Earth First!" (Bari 1994, 225). Some of Ecotopia's toughest battles were waged with the *Earth First! Journal,* the organization's newspaper. Bari's articles were edited beyond recognition, and Cherney's articles were not published at all. The *Journal* editors eventually canceled the Ecotopia EF![16] insert that was to have reported on the "Summer '91" action campaign (Bari 1994, 206).

The rivalry between Ecotopia and the old guard finally produced a showdown in March 1992 at a national conference of Earth First! activists. A few months before the conference, the *Journal* had published an article that advocated dressing up as a hunter and going into the woods to shoot hunters. While EF! had long encouraged hunt sabotage through such practices as noise making and alerting animals to keep hunters from making any kills, this article crossed a line for Ecotopia's activists. Some Local 1 supporters hunted to supplement their meals and were drawn to environmentalism because of growing concerns over habitat and species losses. In response, Ecotopia wrote a letter denouncing the article and withdrawing themselves from the contact list until the issue was addressed (Bari 1994, 196).

Their letter drew a wave of predictably negative responses in typically macho language. The contact from Santa Monica EF! snarled: "If you are not tough enough for Earth First! then I suggest you join the Sierra Club or the Audubon Society. If that is too radical, try the Green Party. Have a nice day!" (quoted in Bari 1994, 196). The Sugarloaf EF! contact chose to resurrect the misanthropic line, dismissing

16. The Northern California activists adopted the name Ecotopia for their EF! local.

Ecotopia's concerns as "humanist nonsense! Of course a few humans are endangered. So what! Plenty of damn humans here. The death of a few activists is not important in the evolution of Gaia. Are you warriors or whiners? I'd trade a hundred of you for one spiker" (quoted in Bari 1994, 196–97). The contact from Sugarloaf thus managed to bring together the old EF! standards of overpopulation, the brave warrior, and the worship of spiking.[17]

Bari's article against the group's lingering misanthropy, "Why I Am Not a Misanthrope," drew numerous responses. The *Journal* chose not to print thoughtful responses from Chris Manes and Murray Bookchin, instead printing Ken Shelton's angry misogynist attack, which referred to Bari's article as "an excrementious piece of eco-femme idiocy." The author's conclusion gave voice to the old guard's sexism, going so far as to blame women for the destruction of nature:

> Give us a break, Bari. Behind every aggressive white male stands a pampered female, wheedling, whining, and conniving, clamoring for more comforts and commodities. If you take any group of civilized people and set them down in the jungle with instructions to live like the Guatemalan Quiche, the women will set up such a din of bitching and caterwauling that the men will be forced to pave over the jungle and invent refrigerators and automobiles just to shut them up! (quoted in Bari 1994, 205–6)

Dave Foreman further tried to discredit the efforts of the Northern California activists. He characterized Local 1 as anarchists and class-struggle social justice leftists who had infiltrated Earth First! and led it away from its true purpose. Foreman spoke publicly against the organizers during Redwood Summer, thus providing timber executives with the opportunity to claim that the activists were such

---

17. Some members even debated whether or not it was consistent with deep ecology principles to advocate shooting humans. Bari could not help but wonder if this implied that the attempt on her life, if successful, would have been considered an ecological act by other Earth First!ers.

extreme radicals that even their "leader" disavowed their actions (Bari 1994, 89). Proclaiming his respect for private property, Foreman (1991) maintained that there was never any intention for Earth First! to engage in anticorporate activism. Rather, in his view, Earth First! was founded to deal with public land-use issues.[18]

Bari rightly recognized this respect for property as contradictory to biocentrism. The assertion that nature does not exist to serve humans, who are simply one part of nature, cannot be reconciled with the notion that the earth can be owned. Similarly, defense of biodiversity should not be deterred by the presence of a "private property" sign. Responding to Foreman's protests, Bari (1994, 105), playing on the Earth First! slogan, asked: "Should our slogan be No Compromise in Defense of Mother Earth on Public Land Only, And Only If We Don't Have to Confront the Corporate Power Structure?" Her answer, given through the work of Local 1, still resonates—a resolute "No."

Why the Wobblies?

From the perspective of organizers within IWW/Earth First! Local 1, it was important to root contemporary movements within historic, and ongoing, struggles. Attempts were made within Local 1 to articulate labor as part of an ecological cultural community through inclusion of radical labor movements. This helps to explain why the IWW became a focal point for ecological articulation with labor.

The activists of Local 1 found that contemporary workers in timber had little if any knowledge of historic IWW struggles, even in their own regions and industries, which is troubling given that we are speaking of the Western extractive industries where some of the most pitched Wobbly battles were waged. The manner in which social

---

18. Dissatisfied with the direction Earth First! was taking and the declining significance of the "Rednecks for Wilderness," Foreman left Earth First! in August 1990, ironically enough to take up a position with the reformist Sierra Club.

groups have their histories "stolen" from them is an important factor affecting the character of movement formation.

Local 1's efforts are important in reminding ecology activists and workers alike that there are radical working-class traditions that are not solely those of compromise. Significantly, this cultural excavation project of Local 1 made use of illustrations specific to the local cultural and political context in which they were engaged (as opposed to external "models"). The IWW confronted the power of timber companies and asserted the power of timber workers in the nineteen hundreds. The IWW provides a relevant example of how to organize against the companies that are currently exploiting workers while simultaneously destroying the natural world. Bari successfully forged connections between the historic (and ongoing) suffering of timber workers with ecological destruction as currently engendered. The history of workers' struggles becomes part of the culture of ecology in a cleverly constituted genealogy.

Bari tried to emphasize the similarities in the styles and tactics of labor and ecology against common depictions within radical ecology, such as the positions of Bahro and Bookchin. Toward developing this equivalent understanding green syndicalists have tried to engender an appreciation of radical labor histories, especially where workers have exerted themselves through inspiring acts that seem to have surprisingly much in common with present-day eco-activism. Attempts have been made within green syndicalism to articulate labor as part of the ecological "we" through inclusion of radical labor within an ecological genealogy. Labor, anarchy, and ecology all come together. This specific intersection of issues and concerns helps to explain why the IWW became a focal point for ecological articulation with labor.

"Clearcut the Bosses": The Deconstructive Politics of Local 1

For green syndicalists there can be no terms for compromise with bosses and capitalist relations. Such autonomy is necessary as an affirmation of integrity and solidarity. The politics of IWW/EF! Local

1 required a discursive connecting of timber workers and ecology within a context of shared exploitation.

> The first step is to stop blaming the loggers and millworkers for the destruction of the planet. The timber companies treat them the same way they treat the forest—as objects to exploit for maximum profit. We can't form an alliance by saying, 'Hey, worker, come help save the trees.' We have to recognize that their working conditions are not separate from or subordinate to the rape of the forest. They are part and parcel of the same thing. (Bari 1994, 14)

Sklair (1995) notes the significance of participation by capital's agents within local communities. The activists of Local 1 were confronted with a context in which the companies had long been engaged in efforts to organize loggers against environmentalists. These efforts, some of which are discussed above, contributed greatly to the incendiary conditions prevailing in the forests. At a hearing over the status of the spotted owl "[t]he timber companies closed the mills and logging operations for the day and bused 5,000 workers to the hearing, carrying anti-owl banners and cheering as speakers denounced environmentalists" (Bari 1994, 13). Timber companies established the jingoistic Yellow Ribbon Coalition to incite workers, their families, and local businesses to show solidarity with the companies against the environmentalist "menace." As Bari (1994, 13) reports, dissent (or even simply failing to participate) was dangerous since the threat of violence (as illustrated above) was ever-present.

Among the evidence of timber industry involvement in violence was a mandatory meeting at L-P's Somoa pulp mill during which management distributed fake press releases and openly encouraged workers to intimidate environmentalists. The purpose behind that meeting was only revealed after Pulp and Paper Workers Union Local 49 filed a grievance. L-P was not alone in agitating to turn workers against their potential environmentalist allies. Internal company documents reveal that Maxxam Corporation also distributed, to out-of-town newspapers, press releases that they knew to be false (Bari 1994).

Such actions raise crucial challenges that must be confronted by emerging alliances in the global age. As long as movement activists fail to disrupt these efforts, the prospects for convergence must remain limited.

Lacking the resources of big timber and having no "jobs" to dangle in front of workers, however, meant that activists had to engage primarily in symbolic acts. Much of this was attempted through confrontation with the local agents of capital and an open, explicit rejection of the prestige and deference typically exhibited toward them.

Bosses, thus, become constructed not as caring patricians who come bearing gifts of jobs, but as thieves who are robbing us of our presents and futures for their own greedy benefit: "The bosses are ecological thugs," and, "Evidence of the bosses' eco-terrorism is in all of our lives every day" (Kauffman and Ditz 1992, 42).

Here we see ecology engaged in acts of disruption through desecration. Within the syndicalist texts bosses are constructed not only as parasites—the traditional Wobbly mockery—but as eco-terrorists in an inversion of the common depiction of radical ecology. Thus, when viewing radical ecological discourses of recontextualization, "it soon becomes clear that the "good guys" are the ones *breaking* the law, since the law enables mining, logging, drilling, road building, developing and the accompanying concrete, steel, powerlines, parking lots, and wasteland, all of which replace wilderness and that which is *natural* and good" (Lange 1990, 485).

The irrational and unrealistic are redefined. After all, what could be more irrational than the destruction of one's home? Recontextualization, thus, serves as a rejection of hegemonic definitions and the prevailing relations of power, which only allow for a consideration of certain limited behaviors or outcomes.

IWW discourses with regard to capital also emphasize workers' abilities and encourage the self-determination of workers and the importance of self-directed initiatives against capital. "The IWW believes that wage-slaves must organize themselves to fight the bosses" (Meyers 1995, 73). The symbolic unity of activists and their break from capital is stressed in the single qualification for Wobbly membership. "The only restriction to membership in the IWW is that no boss can be a member" (73).

The constitution of a symbolic autonomy from the local agents of transnational capital has also entailed the use of extreme rhetoric: "We're a fighting, revolutionary union. If you want to kick boss butt with like-minded people, get in touch with us" (Meyers 1995, 73). Thus the amended Wobbly constitutional preamble, pulling no punches, "calls for class war, abolishing wage system and bosses, and seizing the machinery of production" (Kaufmann and Ditz 1992, 41).

Laclau and Mouffe (1985, 114) suggest that subversion is manifested as "symbolization, metaphorization, paradox, which deform and question the literal character of every necessity." Lange (1990) discusses the use of paradox, irony, parody, and contradiction as means to recontextualize or desecrate unfavorable contexts within the radical ecology texts of Earth First!.

Through the deployment of immoderate discursive practices IWW-EF! activists attempted to overcome the "otherness of workers and ecology," and the disruptive efforts of timber bosses to construct workers and activists as enemies. Green syndicalism suggests the smashing and rebuilding of the social frontiers of ecology such that resource workers are included as part of the make-up of the ecological "us." Thus these texts must be understood as disruptive counterarticulations, largely through desecration, within a context in which activists have little material strength. Armed with little more than their senses of humor, the prankster guerrillas set upon their enemy with a fusillade of mockery. They thereby reject the entire context within which they can be either marginalized or assimilated; they occupy their own ground. Green syndicalism foregrounds those spaces where the presence of an anti-ecological other impedes movements of convergence around ecological resistance.

Forms of confrontational rhetoric may be situated as the desecration or recontextualization (*detournement*) of hegemonized contexts or identities. Desecration involves the production of controversial texts against codified strictures governing acceptability. This strategy involves forms of rhetorical extremism. Recontextualization "occurs when a text appears in but alters the expectations in which it is under-stood and evaluated. Reconstruction transforms the entire context; a rhetor rises to the occasion by changing it" (Lange 1990, 477). These acts of redescription are often, as we have seen, antagonistic or "violent." Green syndicalism is clearly engaged in the recontex-tualization of capital ("the bosses") through discursive tactics that invoke humiliation and condemnation. This engagement is seen in the attempts to redescribe capitalists not as the guardians of community welfare but as uncaring, voracious "land rapists." Indeed, much of green syndicalist engagement involves the humiliation of capitalists (and assorted anthropocentrists) through the ridiculing of their prin-ciples, language, dress, and ideas. From the current research one may identify various manifestations of these deconstructive acts within green syndicalist praxis.

Scission for ecology is, of course, metaphorical (we are talking about pacifists, remember). Within the organizing mythic of ecology, scission must be understood as an ironic and largely satirical attempt at *creating* an "us/them" bifurcation under conditions of materiality disfavoring such a separation. Such a metaphor must be constantly constructed and reconstructed, as the activists of Local 1 have dis-covered. Furthermore, it is always tenuous and susceptible to collapse; activists must be vigorous and vigilant about maintaining it.

Green syndicalism, in exposing the equivalent connecting of mul-tiplex antagonisms, foregrounds those spaces where the presence of an anti-ecological other impedes movements of convergence around an ecological nodal point. Green syndicalist themes as expressed in anti-work, control, anti-boss, and sabotage narratives are here under-stood as asserting a symbolically constituted autonomy from the megamachine.

Emphasis upon working-class autonomy from capital has been a crucial characteristic of historic syndicalist theoretics.

> Syndicalist discourse stressed the importance of autonomy, the fear
> of dependence and corruption, the association of luxury with ego-
> ism, and the debilitating consequences of the growth of the division

of labor. Working-class independence, the syndicalist leitmotif, was not simply a way to increase the economic and political power of labor; it simultaneously, and primarily, created the conditions for moral development, collective solidarity and the overcoming of dependence. (Tucker 1991, 90)

Even if, as some autonomist Marxists (Negri 1984, 1989) suggest, the possibility for a working-class break with capital now exists, such a separation can only be the result of active articulation. This active constitution might even be called *class* struggle inasmuch as it is engaged over questions of ownership and control of production and "resources."

Broadening the Movement

Judi Bari maintained that Earth First! was primarily a direct action group and viewed its theories and policies as the result of practice, valuable for informing and revising strategies and tactics. The crucial matter was the development of radical ecofeminist praxis. One necessity facing Earth First! was to broaden the group's focus. The early-1980s identity of the movement as concerned only with wilderness Bari (1990) viewed as self-defeating. As she argued, it is impossible to address seriously the destruction of wilderness without addressing the social relations responsible for the destruction. The time had come for the Earth First! movement to stop viewing itself as separate from social justice struggles. In Bari's view, the ecology movement is but one strand in a multiply woven fabric of resistance.

In her view the power that manifests itself as resource extraction in the countryside manifests itself as racism and exploitation in the city. An effective radical ecology movement (one that could begin to be considered revolutionary) must organize among poor and working people. Only through workers' control of production and distribution can the machinery of ecological destruction be shut down.

Ecological crises become possible only within the context of social relations that engender a weakening of people's capacities to fight an organized defense of the planet's ecological communities. Bari (1994) understood that the restriction of participation in decision-making processes within ordered hierarchies, prerequisite to accumulation, has been a crucial impediment to ecological organizing. This convinced her that radical ecology must include demands for workers' control and a decentralization of industries in ways that are harmonious with nature. It also meant rejecting ecological moralizing and developing some sensitivity to workers' anxieties and concerns. "And it seems to me that people's complicity should be measured more by the amount of control they have over the conditions of their lives than by how dirty they get at work. One compromise made by a white-collar Sierra Club professional can destroy more trees than a logger can cut in a lifetime" (Bari 1994, 105).

Bari asked how it could be that there were neighborhood movements targeting the disposal of toxic wastes but no workers' movement to stop the production of toxics. She argued that only when workers are in a position to refuse to engage in destructive practices or produce destructive goods could any realistic hope for lasting ecological change emerge. The only way to bring the system to a standstill is through mass-scale noncooperation, what an earlier generation of syndicalists knew as the "General Strike." Bari's vision for Earth First! combined a radicalization of the group's initial ideas of biocentrism and an extension of the decentralized, nonhierarchical, federative organization, the nascent syndicalist structure of EF!, into communities and workplaces.

While agreeing with the old guard that efforts should be given to preserving or reestablishing wilderness areas, Bari saw that piecemeal set-asides were not sufficient. The only way to preserve wilderness was to transform social relations. Earth First! had to be transformed from a conservation movement to a social movement. Earth First! needed to encourage and support alternative lifestyles. To speak of wilderness decontextualized the destruction of nature.

Where Dave Foreman sought to keep the movement small to maintain its "purity," Bari (1990) recognized that the profound social transformations necessary to preserve nature would require large-scale participation. She was convinced that the participation of large numbers of women in the radical ecology movement led to increased openness to Earth First! in logging communities (Purchase 1994). Isolated and individualistic forest actions that separated environmentalists from sympathetic loggers had been a huge tactical mistake on the part of Earth First!.

Rather than "watering down" the movement, as Foreman charged, Redwood Summer brought new people into the movement and gave them experiences in direct action. It also provided a vital example of community-based coalition building under extremely disagreeable circumstances. Local 1 provided a new approach that encouraged many environmentalists to rethink strategies for building a sustainable green future.

Syndicalism, Ecology, and Feminism

According to Judi Bari, a truly biocentric perspective must further challenge the system of industrial capitalism, which is founded upon the "ownership" of the earth. In her view, industrial capitalism cannot be reformed since it is founded upon the destruction of nature. The profit drive of capitalism insists that more be taken out than is put back (be it labor or land). Bari extends the Marxist discussion of surplus value to include the elements of nature. She argues that a portion of the profit derived from any capitalist product results from the unilateral (under)valuing, by capital, of resources extracted from nature.

Because of her analysis of the rootedness of ecological destruction in capitalist relations, Bari turned her attentions to the everyday activities of working people, as noted above. Workers would be a potentially crucial ally of environmentalists, she realized, but such an alliance could only come about if environmentalists were willing to educate themselves about workplace concerns. Bari held no naïve notions of workers as privileged historical agent. She simply stressed her belief that for ecology to confront capitalist relations effectively and in a nonauthoritarian manner requires the active participation of workers. Likewise, if workers were to assist environmentalists it was reasonable to accept some mutual aid in return from ecology activists.

To critics, this emphasis on the concerns of workers and the need to overcome capitalist social relations signified a turn toward workerist analysis, which, in their view, undermined her ecology. Criticisms of workers and "leftist ecology" have come not only from deep ecologists, as discussed above, but from social ecologists such as Murray Bookchin and Janet Biehl, who otherwise oppose deep ecology. Social ecology guru Bookchin has been especially hostile to any idea of the workplace as an important site of social and political activity or of workers as significant radical actors. Bookchin repeats recent talk about the disappearance of the working class (1997, 57), although he is confused about whether the working class is "numerically diminishing" or just "being integrated." Bookchin sees the "counterculture" (roughly the new social movements like ecology) as a new privileged social actor and in place of workers turns to a populist "the people" and the ascendancy of community. Underlying Bookchin's critique of labor organizing, however, is a low opinion of workers, whom he views contemptuously as "mere objects" without any active presence within communities[19] (see Bookchin 1980).

Lack of class analysis likewise leads Janet Biehl (1991, 134) to turn to a vague "community life" when seeking the way out of ecological destruction. Unfortunately, communities are themselves intersected with myriad cross-cutting and conflictual class interests that, as Bari showed, cannot be dismissed or wished away. Notions of community are often the very weapon wielded by timber companies against environmentalist "outsiders."

---

19. Bookchin (1997, 51) goes so far as to claim that the "authentic locus" of anarchism is "the municipality." This is a rather self-serving claim given that Bookchin has staked much of his reputation on building a "libertarian municipalist" tendency within anarchism. It also runs counter to almost all of anarchist history.

Biehl recognizes the ecological necessity of eliminating capitalism but her work writes workers out of this process. This exclusion is directly expressed in her strategy for confronting capital: "Fighting large economic entities that operate even on the international level requires large numbers of municipalities to work together" (1991, 152), not specific social actors—workers—with specific contributions to make, but statist political apparatuses—municipalities. To confront "macrosocial forces like capitalism . . . [Biehl proposes] . . . political communities" (152). All of this is rather strange coming from someone who professes to be an anarchist.

Biehl (1991, 151) even states that the "one arena that can seriously challenge" current hierarchies is "participatory democratic politics" but makes no reference to the specificity of the workplace in this regard. Yet within capitalist relations, the workplace is one of the crucial realms requiring the extension of just such a politics. And that extension is not likely to occur without the active participation of people in their specific roles as workers. Bari, concerned with encouraging this participation, did not have the luxury of overlooking the everyday concerns of workers.

As a longtime feminist and unionist, Judi Bari was well aware of tendencies within the labor movement, and the Left generally, to treat concerns of gender or environment as subordinate to the larger movement or, worse, as distractions. Bari was no vulgar materialist given to economistic analyses, however, and she rejected Dave Foreman's characterization of Local 1 as simply "leftists" or a "class struggle group." She too remained sharply critical of Marxist socialism and what she saw as its acceptance of the domination of nature. As she repeatedly stressed, Local 1 was not seeking to overthrow capitalism solely for the benefit of the working classes. They sought a new society in which neither workers nor nature were exploited or abused. That society was one that would achieve a balance with nature for the sustenance of all species.

For inspiration Bari turned to nonauthoritarian traditions of socialism, which she viewed as "beyond leftism." Specifically, her materialism took the form of syndicalism—revolutionary libertarian unionism.[20] Bari developed her green syndicalist approach as an attempt to think through the forms of organization by which workers could address ecological concerns in practice and in ways that broke down the multiple hierarchies of mainstream trade unionism. She recognized in syndicalist structures and practices certain instructive similarities with the contemporary movements for ecology and radical feminism.

Historically, anarcho-syndicalists and revolutionary unionists fought for the abolition of divisions between workers based upon, for example, gender, race, nationality, skill, employment status, and workplace. Revolutionary unions, such as the IWW, in fighting for "One Big Union" of all working people (whether or not they were actually working), argued for the equality of workers and the recognition of their unity as workers while realizing that workers' different experiences of exploitation made such organization difficult.

Like radical feminists, anarcho-syndicalists have argued for the consistency of means and ends. Thus syndicalists organize in nonhierarchical, decentralized, and federated structures that are vastly different from the bureaucratic structures of mainstream trades unions, which have been largely resistant to participation by women. The alternative organizations of anarcho-syndicalism are built upon participation, mutual aid, and cooperation. Anarcho-syndicalism combines the syndicalist fight against capitalist structures and practices of exploitation with the anarchist attack on power and awareness that all forms of oppression must be overcome in any struggle for liberty. The IWW fought for the recognition of women as "fellow workers" deserving economic and physical independence (i.e., self-determination) and access to social roles based upon interests and preferences.[21]

---

20. For a detailed discussion of green syndicalist theory see Shantz (1999a).

21. As Purchase (1997b, 32) awkwardly overstates: "Moreover the IWW . . . was the first union to call for equal pay and conditions for women and actively sought to set up unions for prostitutes—and in doing so achieved far more for the feminist cause than any amount of theorising about the evolution of patriarchy could ever hope to have done."

Regarding the affinity between anarcho-syndicalist organization and "second wave" feminist practice Peggy Kornegger (1996, 161) has commented: "The structure of women's groups bore a striking resemblance to that of anarchist affinity groups within anarchosyndicalist unions in Spain, France, and many other countries." Kornegger laments that feminists did not more fully explore the syndicalist traditions for activist insights.

Besides, as Purchase (1997b, 28) argues, industrial unions "are composed of people—feminists, peace activists and ecologists included and are simply a means by which people can come to organise their trade or industry in a spirit of equality, peace and co-operation." As Barry Adam (1993) argues, the exclusion of workers from new social movement discussions is both arbitrary and inaccurate.

> Exactly what sense we are to make of such sweeping dismissals of centuries of sustained resistance to the encroachments of capital and state by ordinary working people is quite unclear. . . . Besides, in the absence of state-supported industrial [or green] capitalism trades unions and workers' co-operatives—be they bakers, grocers, coach builders, postal workers or tram drivers would seem to be a quite natural, indeed logical and rational way of enabling ordinary working people to co-ordinate the economic and industrial life of *their* city, for the benefit of themselves rather than for the state or a handful of capitalist barons and it is simply dishonest of Bookchin to claim that anarchism has emphasised the historical destiny of the industrial proletariat at the expense of community and free city life. (Purchase 1997b, 28)

The concerns raised by Foreman, Bookchin, and Biehl are well taken. Indeed, much Old Left thinking, of various stripes, did fail to appreciate the causes or consequences of ecological damage. However, as Graham Purchase (1997b, 25) has pointed out, the reasons for this are largely historical and practical rather than necessarily theoretical. The ecological insights of social ecologists like Bookchin (e.g., ecological regionalism and green technologies) are not incompatible with syndicalist concerns with organizing workers.

Ecofeminism and Deep Ecology: A Possible Synthesis?

Judi Bari was ultimately convinced to become a member of Earth First! because of her appreciation for the philosophy of deep ecology. "This philosophy, known as biocentrism or deep ecology, states that the Earth is not just here for human consumption. All species have a right to exist for their own sake, and humans must learn to live in balance with the needs of nature, instead of trying to mold nature to fit the wants of humans" (Bari 1994, 220).

However, she also understood deep ecology to have revolutionary implications, which she tried to develop in practice. Her intention was to articulate a vision of deep ecology that was profoundly social in its analysis, recognizing the interrelations of global capitalism, human oppression, and the destruction of nature. She refused to accept conceptions of deep ecology which privileged nature over humans as though human were somehow not part of the natural world. Biocentrism, if it were to make a useful contribution to environmental politics, would need to be demystified.

> I certainly believe that the Earth comes first. . . . But I don't think you can separate the way our society treats the Earth from the way we treat each other. And that includes feminism, and that includes support for labor and oppressed peoples. At a time when we need to make connections and build coalitions in order to stand up to an unprecedented right-wing anti-environmental assault, Earth First! is becoming more isolated and more single-issue. (Bari 1994, 215)

Unlike critics such as Janet Biehl (1989, 1991), Bari saw no inherent contradiction between deep ecology and ecofeminism.[22] Biehl,

---

22. The term *ecofeminisme,* coined by French author Françoise d'Eaubonne in 1974, has come to stand for a widely divergent and complex body of ideas ranging from "Goddess worship" (see Gray 1993) to socialist feminism (see Merchant 1993). Bari's version of "ecofeminism" most nearly resembles socialist ecofeminism, although she clearly draws her inspiration from long-eclipsed traditions of socialism

like Bari, has criticized deep ecologists' lack of sensitivity to divisions and boundaries within human societies. Unlike Bari, however, she sees no way of developing awareness of such divisions from a deep ecological perspective. In Bari's view, both deep ecology and ecofeminism promote holistic visions of nature as consisting of interconnected and interdependent parts. Both seek informed interactions with natural processes instead of control through disruption and domination. Where Biehl chose to reject deep ecology Bari preferred to seek a critical synthesis.

Bari and Biehl have, in distinct ways, approached both ecofeminism and deep ecology from materialist vantage points that sought to overcome the alienation between men and women and humans and nature not through appeals to some sort of spiritual covenant, but through specific political practices and social transformations. Our understandings of nature, as well as human nature, are only the outcome of social and political engagements that must be addressed in any radical ecological analysis.

For Bari, the crucial contribution made by ecofeminism lay in drawing the connection between the treatment of women within patriarchal society and the treatment of nature.[23] Ecofeminist materialism views ecological problems as rooted in the emergence of capitalist patriarchy and corresponding ideas that nature must be exploited as part of human progress beyond conditions of scarcity (see Merchant 1993; Biehl 1989). The destruction of subsistence-based economies oriented toward producing use values via consolidation of "a capitalist economy dominated by men and a domestic sphere in which women's labour in the home was unpaid and subordinate to men's labour in the marketplace" resulted in "the alienation of women and men from each other and both from nature" (Merchant 1993, 51).

such as anarchist communism (see Kropotkin 1955, 1994) and revolutionary syndicalism (see Kornblugh 1964 and Dubofsky 1969) rather than Marxism.

23. For fascinating accounts of the oppressive conjoining of women and nature historically see Barker-Benfield (1973) and Gusfield (1992).

Indeed, Bari's (1991) response to the misanthropes began from the perspective of her feminism, arguing that the crimes identified by the misanthropes were largely the crimes of men, often against the needs and interests of women.[24] By characterizing as "human" deeds that were predominantly carried out by men, Bari rejected the misanthropes' claims to biocentrism, instead identifying their analysis as a form of androcentrism.[25] In this way the misanthropes conveniently and arrogantly avoid "any real analysis of who is responsible for the death of the planet" (Bari 1994, 84). Among those responsible she includes the misanthropes themselves, who preserve the status quo by failing to recognize the distinctions between oppressor and oppressed.

Bari (1991) could not accept the misanthropes' conclusion that the source of ecological problems was "humankind." To do so would mean refusing to acknowledge those cultures that have lived in relative harmony with nature for much of their history or exempting them from the category of "human" altogether (Bari 1994, 82). Likewise, accepting such a conclusion ignores the differential culpability for environmental harm among inhabitants of ecologically destructive cultures. Misanthropic arguments dishonestly collapse distinctions of class, race, gender, and age into the catch-all "human," ignoring the ways in which social inequalities and power relate to ecological crises. The atrocities on Manes's list, for which he finds "humanity" guilty, have not been perpetrated by all humans and do not speak to the vast forms of resistance by which humans have fought such atrocities. The only conclusion, for Bari (1994, 82) was that "it is not humans-as-a-species, but the way certain humans live, that is destroying the Earth." Specifically, the modes of living characteristic of industrial capitalism

24. Chris Manes argued that the burden of proof rests with nonmisanthropes because the history of humanity is one of wars, massacres, and ecocide. This is of course incorrect. Manes's description could rightly be said to apply only to the last few thousand years of human history, and only with regard to certain societies.

25. This includes the deep ecologists' preoccupation with "overpopulation." Both Biehl and Bari have recognized that such notions have served as cover for a broader attack on the bodies of women and women's reproductive choices.

are responsible for ecological destruction. Misanthropy, in Bari's view, serves to maintain these modes of living by refusing to recognize the distinctions between exploiter and exploited.

For Bari, biocentrism, rather than suggesting a privileging of nature over humans, simply expresses the view that all species exist for their own sake regardless of their utility for humans. Humans are situated as one of the many species that are a part of nature, not its crowning jewel. Nature, she argues, behaves in a biocentric manner regardless of whether humans understand it anthropocentrically. The revolutionary implications of biocentrism rest in the deconstruction of values and practices that privilege humans even while undermining the conditions of their continued existence on the planet.

Bari, while rejecting deep ecologists' misanthropy, did not follow social ecologists like Biehl and Murray Bookchin in accepting humanism, anthropocentrism, or notions that humans were a "higher" form of nature.[26] Rather, Bari sought a way out of the anthropocentrism/ecocentrism duality, preferring a decentered ecology that focused upon interrelationships, connectedness, and conflict. Likewise Bari refused the essentialisms underpinning radical ecofeminist dualities of male/female, mind/body, science/myth and culture/nature. Instead she attempted a route out of these hierarchies through practical alliances that transform the identities of participants in ways that resist essentialist definitions.

With respect to their analyses of social and political relations there is much agreement between the perspectives of Biehl and Bari. Differences relate to the overall thrust of their undertakings. Where Bari attempted a materialist understanding of the emergence and perpetuation of antinature (anthropocentric) views within social hierarchies and authorities in order to grasp their ideological significance for ecological organizing, Biehl's work has been preoccupied with developing a materialist refutation of all critiques of anthropocentrism, arguing

26. Bookchin refers to humans as the "second nature" that stands above "first nature" (nonhuman nature) as its consciousness. See Bookchin (1990, 1997).

that such ideological domination cannot be overcome "until we rid ourselves" (1991, 5) of relations of domination. Thus Biehl has backed into a rather vulgar materialist position as part of her defense of social ecology.

In the end, the crucial difference between their analyses relates, once again, to the questions of class and work. Biehl's attempts to rethink ecofeminism have not addressed the specificities of women as workers, preferring vague references to differences between rich and poor. More specifically her work says little about the particular experiences of women working in male-dominated movements (e.g., EF!) or communities (e.g., timber).

Inevitably and unfortunately, this underdeveloped class analysis leads Biehl to succumb to the same universalizing trap she finds so worrisome in deep ecologists. Thus she can state after parting with ecofeminism: "I am committed to the concept that ecology is a movement that should speak for a *general* interest of human beings *as a whole*" (1991, 5; emphasis in original). Such claims do little to unravel the circumstances that inhibit such potential, like the accumulation and expansion of capital, or that influence the multiple forms by which such "general interests" might be articulated, such as "green capitalism" or "eco-trade." Romantic notions of general interests offer no more grounding for ecological transformation than do the other mystical notions that Biehl condemns in some ecofeminism.

Active Alliances

The "phenomenology of alliance formation" offered within the present discussion allows for some understanding of those struggles that inhibit or encourage the forging of unity and limit the formation of alternatives, something that has been regretfully lacking in much of the work on global social movements. Through analysis of the politics of connection a number of issues emerge for sociological consideration.

The alliance around Local 1 was organized in opposition to the agents of transnational capital and their global order of local ecological and community destruction. Specifically, activist responses were targeted directly at the local sources of destruction. They engaged in the disruption of local agencies with which they came into direct contact in their daily lives (rather than the more global or distant institutions whose interests these agencies are serving). The hegemony of transnational corporations was disrupted through local campaigns, both economic and political, of interference and counterinformation.

However, the present exploration reveals the significance of broadened expressions of local struggles and the difficulties faced by such undertakings. While the local is crucial for the formation of resistance, Local 1 activists soon realized that external linkages must be cultivated if movements against global intrusions are to move from the margins. Recognizing the limits of mainstream political channels from which they were, in any event, largely excluded, they turned to symbolic politics, sensational activism, and extreme forms of rhetoric. Castells, Yazawa, and Kiselyova (1996, 22) suggest that marginal movements or movements for radical alternatives are typically rendered invisible by corporate mass media until they "explode in the form of media events that call public attention, and reveal the existence of profound challenges to everyday normalcy."

Following Castells, Yazawa, and Kiselyova we might understand Redwood Summer as *l'action exemplaire* directed to increasing outside awareness of the destruction of Northern California wilderness and community. Such spectacular forms of activism bring "the attention of the world to the movement's claims, and is ultimately intended to wake up the masses, manipulated by propaganda and subdued by repression" (1996, 50). Here the media savvy of Local 1 (especially after the bombing) was a crucial weapon in the battles over images and messages.

Acts of ecological sabotage, as communicative acts, serve to maintain public awareness of environmental issues and to encourage discussions and debates. They provide a direct reminder to the agents of capital that their destructive actions are not supported by all community members and that unacceptable acts will not be without consequences. The renunciation of tree-spiking and the commitment to nonviolence offer especially significant symbolism. Specifically they represented a movement away from short-term actions, which workers found threatening, toward longer-term community-based strategies. Above all they sent a clear public message that no longer would workers be considered the enemy.

The present discussion also allows us to better understand the relationship of the state to processes of globalization. The actions of police and Federal authorities (leaving aside speculation about FBI involvement in the bombing) serve to remind us that direct domination is still an aspect of governance in the global age. Those who attempt to operate outside of the limited and circumscribed spheres of "legitimate" action or "normal" politics will be subject to repression.

Distinct subject-positions, "worker" and "environmentalist," harden within various labor and ecology discourses as poles for the fixing of antagonisms as separate and exclusive. The activities of Local 1 demonstrated that ecology and labor "identities" are not mutually exclusive. Rather, there is some basis for a translation of positions. Green syndicalism suggests that the transformation of social relations will allow for the construction of new identities. Those who study social movements need to remember that identity does not exist prior to acts of transformation. Rather, transformation is an aspect in the construction of the actors engaged in bringing it about (see Laclau 2007).

The affirmation of identity is expressed through the imaginative, novel, and playful cultivation of cultural experiences in often unexpected directions, both deconstructive and constructive. Local environmentalists and workers unite in fighting to preserve wilderness and traditional ways of living, which are being sacrificed to serve the demands of global capital and consumer culture. Activists make appeals to the integrity of local environments and communities and the necessity of self-determination and control over decisions that affect residents and nature.

Finally, when viewing the activities of Local 1, it is necessary to recognize that the social relations characterizing global capitalism engender a weakening of people's capacities to fight a coordinated defense of the planet's ecological (including human) communities. Bari

(1994) insisted that the restriction of participation in decision-making processes within ordered hierarchies, as obtains under capitalism, has been a crucial impediment to ecological organizing. Similarly, the persistent absence of workers' participation in decision making, of which Sklair (1995) speaks, allows coercion of workers into the performance of tasks that they might otherwise disdain, or that have consequences of which they are left unaware. It is significant too that the lack of control regarding the conditions of their own sustenance, and related uncertainties about the future, result in workers competing with one another over jobs or even over the slight possibility of jobs. As one timber worker put it: "But without organization, well what good's it going to do me to quit when Joe Blow down the road is going to go ahead and take my job" (quoted in Bari 1994, 256). Workers are left more susceptible to threats of capital strike or environmental blackmail (Bullard 1990). The issue is one of formal power and decision making, of which blue collar workers have little within capitalist economic and political arrangements. The compromises made by professional environmentalists can wreak more harm on the environment than do the job tasks of specific blue collar workers. Criticizing workers abstractly, in the manner of some prominent radical ecologists of the 1980s and 1990s, is not only wrongheaded, it is self-defeating for movements seeking to defend the earth.

Postscript

One year after the bombing, Judi Bari and Darryl Cherney filed their civil suit, claiming false arrest and unlawful search in violation of the Fourth Amendment to the US Constitution. They also claimed that the FBI and Oakland police campaigns constituted politically motivated attempts to stop their organizing work, in violation of the First Amendment. Defense motions and appeals designed to discourage the plaintiffs kept the case from coming to trial for over eleven years, five years after Judi Bari's death. This was clearly a case that the FBI and Oakland police did not want to get anywhere near a courtroom.

The Verdicts

On June 11, 2002, after six days of trial and seventeen days of deliberations, a US federal jury delivered a verdict in favor of Bari and Cherney against four FBI agents and three Oakland police officers. In a stunning decision, the jury awarded Cherney and Bari's estate compensation of US$4.4 million: $2.9 million was awarded to Bari's estate and $1.5 million to Cherney.

The jury found that six of seven FBI and Oakland police defendants had framed Bari and Cherney in an attempt to break Earth First! and destroy Redwood Summer. This conclusion is reflected in the fact that 80 percent ($3,525,000) of the $4.4 million total was awarded for violation of the activists' First Amendment rights protecting political speech and assembly. The verdict clearly shows that the jury found that the FBI and police were motivated by an attempt to disrupt Bari's and Cherney's environmental and labor organizing work. The rest of the award covered violations of Fourth Amendment rights regarding false arrests and unlawful searches.

FBI agent Frank Doyle was found to have violated Bari's and Cherney's First Amendment rights and was found guilty of two violations of Bari's Fourth Amendment rights and one violation of Cherney's Fourth Amendment rights. Doyle was the agent in charge of the bomb scene and had instructed an FBI bomb school at a logging company clear-cut only one month before the bombing. He was also relief supervisor of the joint FBI-OPD terrorism squad that compiled files on Bay Area political groups.

John Reikes, head of the FBI's terrorist squad, who briefed Oakland police on Earth First! the day of the bombing, was found to have violated Bari's and Cherney's First Amendment rights. FBI agent Philip Sena, who was involved in a secret investigation of EF!, was also found guilty of two First Amendment violations, as was OPD officer Mike Sims, who also violated Bari's Fourth Amendment rights. OPD officer Michael Sitterud constructed evidence in the bombing and was found in violation of Cherney's First Amendment rights. Officer

Robert Chenault, who provided a fraudulent search warrant affidavit, was found guilty of violating Bari's and Cherney's Fourth Amendment rights. This was only the third jury trial in a civil rights suit against the FBI, and the damage award was the highest ever.

From COINTELPRO to "Homeland Security": Political Repression Then and Now

The trial's historic outcome takes on increased significance in light of recent and ongoing attempts by the US government, particularly under former president George W. Bush, to curtail civil liberties in new "homeland security" legislation that simultaneously provides government with increased powers of surveillance. Part of Bush's plans removed restriction on the FBI and gave them greater powers of surveillance, arrest, search, and seizure.

Many critics have warned that this legislation leaves increasing numbers of progressive groups vulnerable to labeling as terrorists in order for the state to expand its programs of repression and control. Indeed, that has already been the case in the hundreds of racial profiling arrests in the United States based on nothing more than the arrestee's ethnic background. In addition, the use of antiterror laws against protesters at the Republican National Convention in 2008 suggest the broad scope of application of such laws in an effort to stifle dissent. As well, critics point to the designation of radical environmental groups, such as the Earth Liberation Front, as domestic terrorists. Even more critics point to the five-year sentences dealt to environmentalists associated with the Stop Huntington's Animal Cruelty campaign, for nothing more than posting websites critical of animal abuse within food industries, as a frightening example of the abuses associated with current "homeland security" legislation.

The verdict against the FBI and Oakland police suggests to many that the public will not accept these extensions of state power. At the very least it sends a warning about the dangers of granting increased powers to an agency with a habit of trampling on citizens' civil rights. As Cherney stated after the finding: "The American public needs to understand that the FBI can't be trusted. Ten jurors got a good, hard look at the FBI and they didn't like what they saw." The verdicts against the FBI suggest to many that the public is not nearly as willing as the government to sacrifice hard-won civil liberties to the altar of "security."

Lead attorney Dennis Cunningham expressed his hope that the verdict will give pause to politicians intent on tearing up civil rights protections in the wake of September 11. With reference to former attorney general John Ashcroft, Cunningham noted: "Ashcroft is doing precisely the wrong thing to abandon the (Levi) guidelines and let the FBI go after dissent with a free hand. It's clear that their intention is not about fighting terrorism, it's about suppressing dissent. That's what the FBI has always been about. Hopefully, it will make Congress think twice about giving them a free hand" (quoted in Shantz 2003, 169). The Levi guidelines arose out of Senate investigations in the mid-1970s that found that the FBI routinely violated citizens' constitutional rights in the regular course of their investigations. Concerns over the possible removal of the Levi guidelines in any "homeland security" legislation were echoed by many observers of the Bari and Cherney trial, including Nkechi Taifa, director of the Equal Justice Program at Howard University. As she stated at the end of the trial: "This jury verdict is yet another indication of what is in store should Ashcroft's plans to loosen the longstanding Levi guidelines become a reality. The 1990 Bari bomb fiasco occurred despite the existence of these clear guidelines prohibiting such outrageous activity by the FBI. What will be the limits of government abuse if there are no guidelines in place?" (quoted in Shantz 2003, 169).

Indeed, for anyone contemplating the abuse of powers under "homeland security" policies, the FBI's own recent history is quite telling. From the beginning the bombing and the actions of the FBI suggested to many the workings of the agency's supposedly defunct counterintelligence operation, COINTELPRO. This infamous program has been linked to the practices of "neutralization," including the targeted killings of leading activists. COINTELPRO practices included regular violations of First Amendment rights, disregard for

established laws, and interference with judicial process. Under COIN-
TELPRO, the FBI made use of informants, disinformation campaigns,
false arrests, raids of activists' homes and offices, and malicious pros-
ecutions without evidence. All of these practices were present in the
FBI treatment of Bari and Cherney, despite the canceling of COIN-
TELPRO around thirty years ago. As Paul Wolf, author of the report
COINTELPRO: The Untold American Story, stated with regard to the
Bari and Cherney case:

> Despite its carefully contrived image as the nation's premier crime-
> fighting agency, the FBI has always functioned primarily as Ameri-
> ca's political police. This role has included not only the collection of
> intelligence on the activities of political dissidents and groups, but
> also counter-intelligence operations to thwart those activities. . . .
> There is no better example than the Judi Bari case to show that the
> FBI kept on well into the 1990s using covert action tactics against
> political movements and activists which they perceived as threats to
> the established order. . . . In spite of knowing full well from their
> own expert's testimony that Bari and Cherney were innocent vic-
> tims, the FBI and Oakland police continued to lie to the media . . .
> saying they had plenty of evidence they were the bombers. (quoted
> in Shantz 2003, 170)

The verdict was reached despite the fact that lawyers for Bari and
Cherney were prohibited by the judge from discussing this lengthy
and well-documented history of interfering with political groups,
most notably the Black Panthers and the Socialist Workers Party. Prepared statements by historian Howard Zinn and attorney Flint Taylor,
both experts on COINTELPRO, were not allowed as evidence. The
fact that this evidence was kept from jurors may explain the lack of a
guilty verdict on the conspiracy charges.

The trial clearly shows that the FBI, rather than limiting their
work to "going after terrorists," might use its powers to attack political activists and opponents of government and corporate interests.
The trial also shows that the FBI is ready and willing to portray political opponents as terrorists, as they did with Bari and Cherney, if that

is required. As Zinn and Taylor suggest in their statements, this has always been the FBI's practice if not its explicit mandate.

Beyond the Criminalization of Dissent

There has been much talk, especially since September 11, 2001, about the criminalization of dissent. Indeed there has been, in North America, an escalation of repressive measures against political opposition movements of various sorts. These repressive measures have ranged from legislation expanding state powers of surveillance and detention to increased police powers against participants in political demonstrations. The Bari and Cherney trial serves as an important reminder that this criminalization of dissent is an outgrowth of long-standing, rather than simply recent, state practices. This trial brought some of these practices out into the open for all to see. It revealed the real character of the FBI and police as defenders of corporate, in this case timber, interests.

As Judi Bari made clear at the time of filing the suit: "This case is not just about me or Darryl or Earth First!. This case is about the rights of all political activists to engage in dissent without having to fear the government's secret police" (quoted in Shantz 2003, 171). As Bari also recognized, that fear will not dissipate with the outcome of any state-managed court case, but will only disappear with the development of social relations that respect and protect the people and the planet. It is this fight for social and ecological justice, a fight for real justice, that is the true legacy of Judi Bari's life and work.

4

Green Syndicalism

An Alternative Radical Ecology

The greening of syndicalist discourses and practices is significant not only in offering practical examples of rank-and-file organizing and alliance building between union members and environmental activists. It also raises a number of interesting possibilities and questions regarding anarcho-syndicalism and ecology, indeed questions about the possibilities for a radical convergence of social movement organizing. While most attempts to form labor and environmentalist alliances have pursued Marxian approaches, more compelling solutions might be expected from anarchists and libertarian socialists. Numerous others (see Pepper 1993; Heider 1994; Purchase 1994, 1997a; Jakopovic 2007; Williams 2009a, 2009b) suggest that Greens should pay more attention to anarcho-syndicalist ideas, though few of those authors have examined green syndicalism in any detail. Pepper argues (1993, 198) that an infusion of anarcho-syndicalism might shake up the contemporary Green movement in North America just as syndicalism shook up the labor movement of the 1910s. Indeed Martel (1997), Harter (2004), and Early (2009) argue that confronting "jobs versus environment" blackmail requires nothing less than militant labor-based organizations, arming workers with the necessary weapons to confront the power of capital and to strike over ecological concerns.

Green syndicalists have tried to emphasize the similarities in the styles and tactics of labor and ecology against common depictions within radical ecology, as in the positions of Foreman, Watson, and Bookchin. Toward developing this mutual, or equivalent,

102

understanding green syndicalists have tried to engender an appreciation of radical labor histories, especially where workers have exerted themselves through inspiring acts that seem to have surprisingly much in common with present-day eco-activism. Attempts have been made within green syndicalism to articulate labor as part of the ecological "we" through inclusion of radical labor within an ecological genealogy. Within green syndicalist discourses, this assumption of connectedness between historic radical movements, especially those of labor and anarchy, and ecology has much significance. As I have suggested, green syndicalist articulations are important in informing or reminding ecology activists and workers alike that there are radical working-class histories in addition to the histories of compromise; workers are not always willing pawns.

The previous chapter examined specifics of green syndicalist organizing and connections between syndicalism, ecology, and feminism in practice. Still, little has been said about green syndicalism and its specific red/green vision. This chapter attempts to correct that oversight by offering a discussion of the varied perspectives, the different theoretical and practical strands, that make up a syndicalist ecology.

Murray Bookchin's Antisyndicalism

Upon first reading, it might appear curious to seek an ecological or anti-industrialist theoretic within anarcho-syndicalism. Syndicalism is supposedly just another version of narrow economism, still constrained by workerist assumptions. Certainly, that is the criticism consistently raised by social ecology guru Murray Bookchin (1980, 1987, 1993, 1997). Bookchin's work has served as a major focal point for much discussion, at least in libertarian-left and anarchist environmental circles. Even, Marxist ecologists, in journals such as *Capitalism Nature Socialism*, have given much time to discussions of Bookchin's writings.

His recent (1995) rediscovery of social anarchism aside, social ecologist Bookchin has displayed a long-standing hostility to the possibilities for positive working-class contributions to social movement struggles. Bookchin's critique rightly engages a direct confrontation with productivist visions of ecological or socialist struggles that, still captivated by illusions of progress, accept industrialism and capitalist technique while rejecting the capitalist uses to which they are applied (see Rudig 1985–86; Blackie 1990; Pepper 1993). These productivist discourses do not extend qualitatively different forms, but merely argue for proletarian control of existing forms. Bookchin's critique of the workplace, by asserting the inseparability of industry from its development and articulation through technology, offers a tentative beginning for a post-Marxist discussion of productive relations and the obstacles or possibilities they might pose for ecology.

Severe limits to Bookchin's social theorizing are encountered, however, within the conclusions he draws in his attempt to derive a theory of workers' (non)activism from his critique of production relations. Bookchin (1987, 187) makes a grand, and perilous, leap from a critical antiproductivism to an argument, couched within a larger broadside against workers, that struggles engaged around the factory give "social and psychological priority to the worker precisely where he or she is most co-joined to capitalism and most debased as a human being—at the job site." In his view, workers become radical despite the fact that they work rather than through their work experiences.[1] He concludes that the efforts of socialists or anarcho-syndicalists who might organize and agitate within the realm of the workplace are typically only strengthening those very same aspects of workers' identities that must be overcome in the radical transformation of social relations. And moreover *this is correct*, insofar as workplace discourses are limited to purely corporatist demands of a quantitative nature (Gramsci 1971; Telò 1982). However, within Bookchin's schema the Marxist error is repeated, only this time in reverse. For Bookchin, workers' relations to capital, rather than being objectively antagonistic as in the Marxist rendering, are depicted as being necessarily conciliatory. In

---

1. For interesting accounts of the radicalization of workers in response to unsatisfying or degrading workplace experiences, see Zimpel (1974) and Sprouse (1992).

each case workers' positions are drawn as one-sided, derivable from a supposedly external and objective realm, in abstraction from the diversity of their often contradictory expressions, and outside of any transformative articulation. Bookchin, as with the Marxists, substitutes an abstraction "the proletariat" for the complex web of subject positions—including that of ecologist, feminist, and worker—constitutive of specific subjectivities.

Bookchin is correct in asserting that categories "worker" and "jobs" as presently constituted are incompatible with ecological survival. Likewise, industrial production has already been rendered ecologically obsolete. But how can the authoritarian "realm of economic necessity" (Bookchin 1980) ever be overcome except through direct political action at the very site of unfreedom? There is no disagreement with Bookchin as regards the importance of overcoming the factory system; a difference emerges over the position of workers' self-directed activism in any democratic articulation toward such an overcoming. It cannot be expected, except where an authoritarian articulation is constituted, that industrialism will be replaced by nonhierarchical, ecological relations without workers' confronting the factory system in which they are enmeshed.

It is difficult to follow the logic of Bookchin's leap from a critique of industrialism as "social relations" to his explicit rejection of any and all working-class organization. Bookchin insists upon a grass-roots politics, including any of the new social movements, but he is unclear how a movement might be grassroots and communitarian and at the same time excluding an articulation with people in their subject-positions as workers. What he actually recommends sounds more like the radical elitism so often attributed to ecology (see Adkin 1992a, 1992b).

Bookchin's rigid dualism of community/workplace further interferes with his critique of syndicalism. The idea, which Bookchin attributes to syndicalism, that social life could be organized from the factory floor is but a simplistic caricature. "This caveat is, of course, pertinent to all institutions comprising civil society. It would be impossible to nurture and sustain democratic impulses if schools, families, churches, and the like, promoted an antithetical ethos" (Guarasci and Peck 1987, 71). While he rightly criticizes those, such as Earth First! cofounder Dave Foreman, who permit a wilderness/culture duality, he falls into a similar trap himself in his vulgar separation of workplace and community.[2]

Finally, Bookchin's biases are especially curious in light of his own ecological conclusion regarding the resolution of ecological problems, that conflicting social interests be resolved in a revolutionary manner such that private property regimes are dismantled and the earth returned to its status as commons. He provides a crucial beginning for a radical convergence of ecological social relations articulated beyond a "jobs versus environment" construction. In turn the further step must be taken, even if Bookchin himself fails to do so, to confront issues of ownership and control of the earth as, first and foremost, matters of class.

Theoretical Syndicalism and Radical Working-Class Histories

For his part, R. J. Holton (1980) explicitly rejects the characterization of syndicalism as economistic. He suggests that such perspectives result from the gross misreading of historic syndicalist struggles. In the works of Melvyn Dubofsky (1969), Jeremy Brecher (1972), David Montgomery (1974), and Kenneth Tucker (1991) one finds substantial evidence against the positions taken by radical ecologists such as Bookchin, Dave Foreman (1991), and Paul Watson (1994). Guarasci and Peck (1987) stress the significance of this class-struggle historiography as a corrective to theorizing that objectifies labor. Tucker (1991) argues that much of the theoretical distance separating new

---

2. Bookchin's criticism of workers' organizations becomes even more curious given his attachment to technological solutions to ecological degradation. He remains unclear, for example, on the matter of who might design, construct, repair, or recycle his much desired eco-technologies (see Purchase 1994). For a discussion of the technocratic and anthropocentric dimensions of Bookchin's writings see Marshall (1993).

movements from workers might be attributed to a refusal to explore syndicalist strategies.

Historic anarcho-syndicalist campaigns have provided significant evidence that class struggles entail more than battles over corporatist concerns carried out at the level of the factory (see Kornblugh 1964; Brecher 1972; Thompson and Murfin 1976; DeCaux 1978; and Tucker 1991). In an earlier article, Hobsbawm (1979) identifies syndicalist movements as displaying attitudes of hostility toward the bureaucratic control of work, concerns over local specificity, and techniques of spontaneous militancy and direct action. Similar expressions of radicalism have also characterized the practices of ecology. Class struggles have, in different instances and over varied terrain, been articulated to engage the broader manifestations of domination and control constituted alongside the enclosure and ruthlessly private ownership of vast ecosystems and the potentialities for freedom contained therein (see Adkin 1992a, 140–41).

From a theoretical standpoint Tucker's (1991) work is instructive. His work provides a detailed discussion of possible affinity between French revolutionary syndicalism and contemporary radical democracy. Tucker suggests that within French syndicalism one can discern such "new" movement themes as consensus formation, organizational egalitarianism, participatory democracy, dialogic process rather than command process, decentralization, and autonomy.

French syndicalist theories of capitalist power place emphasis upon an alternative revolutionary worldview emerging out of working-class experiences and offering a challenge to bourgeois morality (Holton 1980). Fernand Pelloutier, an important syndicalist theorist whose works influenced Sorel, argues that ideas rather than economic processes are the motive force in bringing about revolutionary transformation. Pelloutier vigorously attempted to come to terms with "the problem of ideological and cultural domination as a basis for capitalist power" (Holton 1980, 19). Reconstituting social relations, in Pelloutier's view, becomes possible when workers begin developing revolutionary identities, through self-preparation and self-education, as the means for combating capitalist culture (Spitzer 1963). Thus, syndicalists have characteristically looked to labor unrest as an agency of social regeneration whereby workers desecrate the ideological surround of class domination, for example, deference to authority, acceptance of capitalist superiority, and dependence upon elites. According to Jennings (1991, 82), syndicalism, distinct from authoritarian versions of Marxism or Leninism, "conceived the transmission of power not in terms of the replacement of one intellectual elite by another but as a process of displacement spreading power out into the workers' own organizations." This displacement of power would originate in industry, as an egalitarian problematic, when workers came to question the status of their bosses. "This was not intended as a form of left 'economism' but rather as a means of developing the confidence and aggression of a working class threatened with the spectre of a 'sober, efficient and docile' work discipline" (Holton 1980, 14). Toward that end syndicalist movements have emphasized "life" and "action" against the severity of capitalist labor processes and corresponding cultural manifestations.

It might be argued that, far from being economistic, syndicalist movements are best understood as countercultural in character, more similar to contemporary new social movements than to movements of the traditional Left. Syndicalist themes such as autonomy, anti-hierarchy, and diffusion of power have echoes in sentiments of the new movements. This similarity is reflected not only in the syndicalist emphasis upon novel tactics such as direct action, consumer boycotts, or slowdowns. It also finds expression in the extreme contempt shown by syndicalists for the dominant radical traditions of its day, exemplified by Marxism and state socialism, and in syndicalist efforts to divorce activists from those traditions (Jennings 1991). Judi Bari (1994, 2001) emphasized the similarities in the styles and tactics of labor and ecology against common depictions within radical ecology, as exemplified in the positions held by Bookchin. In this the place of the IWW is especially suggestive.

The IWW, as opposed to bureaucratic unions, sought the organization of workers from the bottom up. As Montgomery (1974) notes, IWW strategies rejected large strike funds, negotiations, written contracts, and the supposed autonomy of trades. Actions took the form of "guerrilla tactics" including sabotage, slowdown, planned inefficiency, and passive resistance. Furthermore, and of special significance for contemporary activists, the Wobblies placed great emphasis upon the nurturing of unity-in-diversity among workers. As Green (1974) notes, the IWW frequently organized in industrial towns marked by deep divisions, especially racial divisions, among the proletariat.

Interestingly, Montgomery (1974) notes that concerns over "success" or "failure" of strikes were not of the utmost importance to strikers. Strikes spoke more to "the audacity of the strikers' pretensions and to their willingness to act in defiance of warnings from experienced union leaders that chance of victory were slim" (Montgomery 1974, 512). This approach to protest could well refer to recent ecological actions. Such rebellious expressions reflect the mythic aspects of resistance, beyond mere pragmatic considerations or strict pursuance of "interests."

Contemporary workers have little, if any, knowledge of historic IWW struggles, even in their own regions and industries. In my view, green syndicalist articulations are important in informing or reminding ecology activists and workers alike that there are radical working-class histories in addition to the histories of compromise; workers are not always willing pawns.

Workers' Control: Ecology Enters the Machine

Why have workers' and environmentalists been so readily mobilized against one another? Partly the success enjoyed by companies in stirring workers' anger against environmentalists is attributable to quite tangible fears, for example, job loss or the demise of traditional ways of living. However, in addition to such material concerns, Judi Bari identified such sociocultural factors as the social and cultural distances which have existed between activists and workers and an ignorance of workplace issues and "realities" on the part of ecology. Bari (1994, 140) referred to this situation as the disturbing lack of class consciousness, or even rudimentary awareness of class issues, among almost all environmental groups.

Theorists of both deep and social ecology tend to overlook or disregard radical working-class histories. All workers' movements are simply categorized as "productivist" and discarded (Smith 2001). The possibility that ecology movement activists might learn from workers' struggles is discounted out of hand. Such totalizing approaches to labor, in which the multiple efforts of workers are always and forever productivist in nature, forbid any discussion of the indeterminacy of social-movement practices. Productivism and nonproductivism, however, reflect processes of struggle rather than pregiven outcomes.

Both social ecology and wilderness fundamentalism (deep ecology) are alike in their tendency to fix immutable capacities to workers and to technology (as eternally subject to the exercise of capitalist control). Any possibility for the active development of workers' antagonism to capital is excluded from these accounts in which only capitalists create and workers are objectified as mere appendages. Antagonism and struggle are treated as anomalous manifestations rather than as the perpetual features of labor/capital relations, or capitalist social relations generally. Fearing anything associated with the megamachine, radical ecology has avoided attempts to situate work relations within struggles over ecology. Failing to appreciate their significance in concerns for ecology, questions of control and decision making are rendered invisible in analyses that serve only to obfuscate the intensely political character of work relations.

A vastly different position emerges from green syndicalist praxis. Green syndicalism emphasizes the permanently emerging character of relations between labor and capital, recognizing the prevalence of antagonism and contestation. (Indeed, the accent is placed on class struggle.) This perspective allows for recognition of the imaginative capacities of labor as an autonomous intervention in the productive process. With this insistence on creativity and autonomy, against any permanent fixing of constant and unilateral control by capital, emphasis is shifted toward possibility and opportunity, however uncertain they may remain.

As the ones most often situated at the nexus of ecological damage, workers in industrial workplaces may be expected to have some insights into immediate and future threats to local and surrounding ecosystems (see Harter 2004; Burkett 2006; Foster, Clark, and York 2011). Such awareness derived from the location of workers at the point of production/destruction may allow workers to provide important, although not central, contributions to ecological resistance.

However, this possibly strategic placement does not mean that any such contributions are inevitable. Those people who suffer most from ecological predations, both at workplaces and in home communities, are also those with the least control over production as presently constituted through ownership entitlements and as sanctioned by the capitalist state (Faber and O'Connor 1993; Peet and Watts 1996; O'Connor 1998; Foster 2002; Burkett 2006; Harvey 2007; Williams 2010; Foster, Clark, and York 2011). These relations of power become significant mechanisms in the oppression not only of workers but of nonhuman nature as well. Without being attentive to this web of power one cannot adequately answer Eckersley's (1989) pertinent questions concerning why those who are affected most directly and materially by assaults upon local ecosystems are often least active in resistance, both in defending nature and in defending themselves. Thus the questions of workplace democracy and workers' control have become crucial to green syndicalist theoretics.

"The IWW stands for worker self-management, direct action and rank and file control" (Miller 1993, 56). For green syndicalism, workers' control becomes an attempt by workers to formulate their own responses to the question "what of work?" Within the IWW, decisions over tactics are left to groups of workers or even to individual workers themselves. Worker self-determination "on the job" becomes a mechanism by which to contest the power/knowledge nexus of the workplace.

Labor insurgency typically articulates shifting relations within transformations of production and the emergence of new hegemonic practices. Times of economic reorganization offer wide-ranging opportunities for creating novel or unprecedented forms of confrontation on the part of workers. The offensives of capital can provide a stimulus to varied articulations of renewed militancy. Such might be the case within the present context of capital strike, deunionization, and joblessness characterizing cybernetized globalism. Of course the emphasis must always remain on possibility, as there is always room for more than one response to emerge.

Green syndicalists recognize that ecological crises have only become possible within social relations whose articulation has engendered a weakening of people's capacities to fight a coordinated defense of the planet's ecological communities. Bari (1994, 2001) argued that the restriction of participation in decision-making processes within ordered hierarchies, prerequisite to accumulation, has been a crucial impediment to ecological organizing.

The persistent lack of workers' control allows coercion of workers into the performance of tasks that they might otherwise disdain, or that have consequences of which they are left unaware. Additionally the absence of self-determination results in workers competing with one another over jobs or even the possibility of jobs. Workers are left in a situation in which they are highly vulnerable to threats of capital strike or environmental blackmail by corporations and governments alike (Foster 2002; Burkett 2006; Harvey 2007; Foster, Clark, and York 2011). This vulnerability is perhaps the greatest deterrent to labor/ecology alliances. Without job security and workplace power workers cannot provide an effective counterbalance to the power of capital.

Having developed a keen awareness of the prevalence of management attempts to constitute a monopoly over knowledge, and actively contesting those efforts toward monopolization, green syndicalism largely avoids the utopianism that might be attributed to previous theories of workplace democracy or workers' control. Following the general critique of syndicalist approaches leveled by critics, it might be said, however, that green syndicalists remain utopian if they assume that developments toward participation will engender substantial transformation simply through perpetual diffusion into everexpanding claims to power. One must be cautious in believing that any increased involvement in decision making might "take on a life of its own." Such claims, however tantalizing, are overly optimistic.

When we speak of "control" it is perhaps helpful to keep in mind that there are at least two senses in which the concept might be applied. There is a moderate sense, that is, defending prior conditions of job performance against innovation, and a radical sense, that is, challenging capital for control of an industry. It is in this latter sense that green syndicalists imagine workers' control. "Such awareness has to question unflinching deference to experts, as part of a more general attack on centralized power and managerial prerogatives" (Guarasci and Peck 1987, 70). Again, for green syndicalism, workplace control provides examples that raise the possibility that things can be done differently. They can reveal that shifting of interests by which workers come to challenge prevailing parameters of labor-capital antagonisms.

It is no longer acceptable simply to criticize the actions of workers without a critical understanding of how hegemonic relations of power impel or delimit people as workers. Green syndicalism asserts that it is not only when industrial workers realize the destructive character of their jobs but also when radical ecologists understand workers' positions within the complex interstices of power comprising capitalist social relations that radical alternatives to global capitalism can be developed. With these alternatives "the definition of conflict changes from 'environmentalists versus workers' to 'those who defend the conditions for a possible and desirable life versus those who defend practices and relations that make impossible such a life'" (Adkin 1992a, 136).

Radical ecology, outside of green syndicalism, has failed to appreciate these negative consequences of diminished workers' control for participation in more explicitly political realms. Only through a development of political confidence can such activism be engaged. Furthermore, the degree of workplace democracy can depend largely upon the influence of supposedly exterior concerns such as impacts upon nature. In recognizing the relationship between workplace articulation and political participation green syndicalism poses a challenge to received notions within ecology.

Participation as conceived by green syndicalism cannot come from management. Direct participation is understood as contributing to worker self-determination, constituted by workers against the veiled offerings of management that form part of eco-capitalism. Eco-capitalist visions leave the megamachine and its power hierarchies intact and thus offer no alternative. Production remains undemocratic, and profitability is the final word on whether or not resources should be used. Thus, eco-capitalism introduces to us the wonders of biodegradable take-out containers and starch-based golf tees.

Green syndicalism emerges, then, as an experiment in more creative conceptions of workplace participation and production. For Purchase (1994, 1997a, 1997b), productive control organized around face-to-face, voluntary interaction and encouraging self-determination might be employed toward the freeing up of vast quantities of labor from useless though profitable production, to be used in the playful development of life-affirming activities. Thus a common theme of working-class radicalism becomes an important element of an ecological theoretic. Leftists have long argued that eventually human needs must become the primary consideration of production, replacing profitability and accumulation. Such critiques of production must now go even further, raising questions about the "needs" of ecosystems and nonhumans.

A Brief Note on Health and Safety

Health and safety issues appear to offer the most encouraging possibilities for an intersection of ecology and labor. Ecological engagement, especially around health and safety concerns, may provide a means to overcome what Guarasci and Peck (1987, 61) following Braverman (1974) identify as the pivotal predicament for workplace democracy: "the elitist impulse inhering in large-scale enterprises and rendering working people incapable of any but unsophisticated, unspectacular degrees of political engagement." Health and safety issues, perhaps more than any others, encourage the development and sharing of workplace knowledge along with direct application of that knowledge to matters of immediate concern, both for workers and their communities. "We are victims where we work and where we live: first on the factory floor, but also 'downriver' in working-class communities" (Kauffman and Ditz 1992, 42).

Perhaps most significantly, health and safety issues situate workplace democratization and control within a context of larger social mechanisms. Attempts at democratization cannot be separated from the social relations in which they are embedded, and possibilities for success are greatly related to contextual characteristics. Assuming that workers do not prefer to poison themselves and their families, the ecological health of workers' communities provides for an immediate barometer of democracy in the productive sphere, where effects become personalized in the community or even in the body, and a possible convergence point in the reconstitution of workplace culture (e.g., partial suggestions about how we might live). Guarasci and Peck (1987) relate the diffusion of democratization to workplace culture—what they call "shopfloor political culture"—which is contingent on informal work groups. Agitating for health and safety can contribute to the development of a knowledge-based workplace culture. Against processes of deskilling, indeed as a specific reskilling outside of mere job performance, health and safety efforts suggest a possible transcending of the "expert elitism" identified by Guarasci and Peck (1987) as a serious inhibition to efforts of democratization.

Struggles over health and safety reveal a contradiction in which the establishment of interests in a public sphere, such as citizens' rights to a clean environment, runs up against a private space, the workplace, in which these interests are interrupted. Ecology, in corroding the distinction between private and public, offers a radically new constitution of the workplace as political space. The system of legitimized hierarchies, subordinate relations for workers and nature, maintained in the workplace is politicized as the public/private demarcation is displaced through a proliferation of interests, often articulated as health and safety initiatives, which dissolve the needs hierarchy (the acceptability of pollution, for example) of the workplace. As workers learn about what goes into their bodies, their homes, and their neighborhoods, ecology may play some part in the process that Guarasci and Peck (1987) refer to as "activating more broadly liberative sentiments."

Ecology and Violence Reconsidered:
Ecotage and Eco-defense

Signs of ongoing rebellion among workers can be found typically in such activities as sabotage, wildcat strikes, slowdowns, and absences. Wobbly (IWW) activists explicitly agitate for "deliberate inefficiency" as a means to encourage the desecration of work hierarchies. Sabotage is also an implicit critique by workers' of the practices of their employers. "As long as people feel cheated, bored, harassed, endangered, or betrayed at work, sabotage will be used as a direct method of achieving job satisfaction—the kind that never has to get the bosses' approval" (Sprouse 1992, 7).

As yet, however, little attention has been given to acts of sabotage engaged by workers with eco-defense as the primary or sole consideration. For green syndicalists the desired tactics against corporate-sponsored destruction of the environment include such direct, nonbureaucratic forms of action as shop-floor sabotage, boycotts, green bans, and the formation of class-wide solidarity outside of the workplace, within workers' home communities.

Again, ecological sabotage cannot be understood in the literal sense as it pertains to individual acts against specific processes or machinery. Ecotage is enacted more broadly against the entirety of social relations that make up the megamachine. Ecotage expresses utter contempt for the industrial manifestations of planet-destroying anthropocentric ways of living. Each act of ecotage, whether destroying logging roads or dismantling machinery, should be recognized as an element of an attempt to immobilize the megamachine or at least to disrupt its legitimising mythology. Acts of ecotage, as communicative acts, also serve to maintain public awareness of environmental issues and to encourage discussion and debate.

The role of ecotage in broader strategies of eco-defense was a key issue in the organizing work of Judi Bari and IWW/Earth First!

Local 1. A critical moment for that alliance emerged unexpectedly during an annual environmental law conference in Oregon in March 1990. While participating in the conference's "Labor and the Environment Panel" Bari was challenged by co-panelist Gene Lawhorn, a millworker, who argued that for any radical ecology/workers' alliance to survive as a sustainable, broadened movement it would be necessary for Earth First! to renounce tree-spiking. Loggers and millworkers had long expressed concerns that spiked trees could be quite dangerous, perhaps even deadly. Since tree-spiking represented most directly an attack upon workers, there was little reason to expect that they would engage in alliance-building activities with any group that advocated such a tactic. At that time, however, belief in the necessity of tree-spiking was almost an article of faith for many in Earth First! For many radical environmentalists, as long as there was logging there could be no compromise over such a seemingly effective practice.

In mid-April 1990, after much discussion among activists throughout the North Coast region, tree-spiking in Northern California and Southern Oregon was publicly renounced by the various Earth First! groups in those areas. A statement prepared by seven Northern California Earth First!ers, including EF! cofounder Mike Roselle, cited the emerging timber worker/radical ecology alliance as the primary motivation for the decision about spiking. Rather than denouncing broader manifestations of monkeywrenching, however, the activists shrewdly encouraged alternative forms. Significantly, within those forms was explicit recognition of ecology's new allies. An awakening to the specificity of workers as potential activists, given their unique talents and location at the point of production, was revealed in the environmentalists' subtle shift in emphasis toward the sabotage of machinery and facilities *by mill workers* as means for grinding the industry to a halt. This reconsideration of tactics would prove a defining moment in the convergence of radical ecology with labor, one that exposed deep divisions over the aspirations and strategies of radical activism.

Paul Watson, the self-proclaimed "originator of tree-spiking," was particularly offended by the decision of Local 1 not to spike. Watson

(1994, 125) continues to believe that spiking trees "is one of the most effective tactics yet developed to protect old-growth forests." Because of the decision to retire spiking, Watson (1994, 127) considered Bari and Local 1 as the "weak link" in Earth First!, denouncing them as "anthropocentric socialist types, whose hearts bleed for the antiquated rights of the workers." Within the controversy over tree-spiking the divisions of ecology in constituting non-anthropocentric *praxis* are laid bare.

Despite Watson's claims, tree-spiking is almost entirely ineffectual as a tactic. Most important, the renunciation of spiking represented a move away from attacks upon workers to emphasis upon community-based strategies. The renouncement of tree-spiking sent a clear message that no longer should workers be considered "the enemy." Thus the decision signified a decisive moment in the alliance of labor and Earth First! radicalism. Awareness was at last developing that workers are not to blame for destruction wrought by corporate logging practices over which they have little control. The IWW and EF! activists who publicly issued the statement of renouncement affirmed that tree-spiking only served to threaten the safety of loggers and mill workers, and that the actual impact upon corporate logging was negligible. "'Their livelihood is being destroyed along with the forest,' said our written proclamation. 'The real conflict is not between us and the timber workers, it is between the timber corporations and the entire community'" (Bari 1994, 293).

In order for eco-defense to enjoy long-term success as a strategy it must become community based. Individual acts of heroism, while often necessary, are not by themselves enough to halt ecological destruction on a sustainable basis over time. Furthermore such actions, when they occur as isolates from community support, can and do serve to alienate possible allies. This recognition should not be taken as an argument against even extreme acts of eco-defense, but rather is meant to suggests that such acts require grassroots involvement if they are to have any lasting legacy in fighting assaults upon nature. "Such actions are problematic if it is assumed that they can be substituted for more above-ground work. But if they can be situated within a broader politics, as one tactic among many, then they can give the above-ground movements more room to manoeuvre, making them both more visible and more credible" (Campbell 1994, 181).

For green syndicalism, workplace organization founded within a context of broadening concern over relations with nature offers one of the most significant realms for developing community-based forms of eco-defense. Bari noted, quite significantly, that it was often timber workers themselves who provided the crucial information, otherwise unobtainable, that allowed activists to engage successfully in blockades, tree-sits, and sabotage without being found out by the police or the companies. Likewise, personal discussions have made me aware of practices of industrial workers regularly engaging in a variety of "radical" activities, both overtly and covertly, in defense of nature. These actions are quite often, as in cases that involve sabotage of destructive machinery, in direct conflict with the "requirements" of the job or the supposed economic self-interests of workers. Such activism suggests still-heroic forces posing powerful challenges to the hegemonized workplace relations and identities attacked by anti–working class radical ecologists such as Murray Bookchin, Dave Foreman, and Paul Watson.

The controversy over ecotage raises the "Luddite question" in green syndicalism. Lyons (1979, 398) argues for the reasonableness of Luddite suspicions of technical progress by offering one Luddite maxim: "'Minimize blind, dramatic change: so act as to prevent more blind change than you cause—either by minimizing the blindness of inevitable change, or by minimizing change that must inevitably be blind'." The principal stimulus for Lyon's concerns is the realization that human knowledge of how to do something ("know-how") always races ahead of the broader knowledge required for determining whether to do the thing ("know-whether"). Know-how, as narrow skills for achieving short-term goals, such as the development of technology, must outstrip the slower, uncertain processes—evaluating any possible outcomes or consequences of every action—involved in the more complex and difficult know-whether knowledge. This tendency relates to the character of each form of knowledge and cannot be attributed simply to capitalist applications, as some Marxists would have it.

Acts of "propaganda by the deed," while not likely to be understood broadly within a depoliticized social context "can make a difference to those people who are already concerned about the situation, and who have become frustrated with other methods of dealing with the issue" (Campbell 1994, 181). Eco-defense is, for activists, understood as distinct from corporate violence. Acts of ecotage are creative and constructive, not directed toward individual profit or the extension of control. Reminiscent of Romantic themes, ecotage is partly a defense of community and the shared heritage of nature. It is simultaneously a reminder to bosses that destructive industrial practices occur in a community context with extensive consequences and that not all community members support such practices.

Green Syndicalism and the Question of Work

The green syndicalist responses might be understood, most interestingly, as characterizing a broader revolt against work. "The one goal that unites all IWW members is to *abolish the wage system*" (Meyers 1995, 73). Ecological crises make clear that the capitalist construction of "jobs" and "workers" are incompatible with the preservation of nature. It is, perhaps, then, not entirely paradoxical that green syndicalism should hint at an overcoming of workerness as one possible outcome. As organizer Charles Walker argues: "A plan to take up a fight for jobs and the resulting social security would benefit from workers' rich tradition of fighting for jobs, by fighting to reduce the work day" (2002, 8). Labor struggles over the workday recognize that one of the central absurdities of capitalism is the situation in which many workers are overworked with ten-, twelve-, and fourteen-hour workdays, while millions of other workers are left with no work at all. Concerns over jobs and joblessness could be addressed without expanding work, or without making additional demands on nature, if the workday was shortened and more people given access to work over shorter periods. Of course such a shift, and workers' struggles over the workday, have always confronted and been opposed by capital's demands for surplus value extraction and profit, which seek to get more work out of workers and extract more from nature.

Green syndicalism conceives of the transformation of "work" as an ecological imperative. What is proposed is a radical alteration of work, both in structure and meaning. Solutions to the problems of work cannot be found merely in the control of existing forms. Rather, current practices of production along with the hierarchy of labor must be overcome.

The meaning of work is once again on the agenda and gaining increasing relevance for contemporary struggles. Within movements such as ecology, work is being examined from novel and challenging perspectives and with a growing sense of urgency. Beyond prior theoretical understandings, either as *the* basis for identity (as in classical Marxism) or, conversely, as being of no relevance to social transformation, the category "job" is (re)opened as a crucial site of struggle. "What about work?" is returning as a key question for transformative politics in the new millennium.

There are perhaps two principal, but very different, impulses for an emergent critique of work: first, the antiproductivist visions of social relations coming from social movements—most significantly ecology—that have encouraged a rethinking of the character of work; and second, the cybernetized restructuring of global capital with its "jobless recovery" and institutionalized levels of unemployment (Aronowitz and DiFazio 1995; Aronowitz and Cutler 1998). The first impulse tends toward radical and critical approaches to the decline or end of jobs, while the second is commonly reflected in expressions of anxiety, desperation, and political reaction.

Numerous authors (Polanyi 1944; Black 1995; Bridges 1995) have discussed the historic emergence of "jobs"—meaning "work for wages"—as something distinguished from the performance of work—meaning specific tasks engaged to meet direct needs. This transformation was closely related to enclosure of common lands and the separation of home life and work life as people left villages to work in the factories of the cities (Polanyi 1944; Thompson 1963). Through industrialism work became transformed into jobs (Bridges 1995). The new job-work gradually contributed to the destruction of traditional social relations and served to undermine prior ways of living. "The job is a social artifact, although it is so deeply embedded in our consciousness that most of us have forgotten its artificiality or the fact that most societies since the beginning of time have done fine without jobs" (Bridges 1995, 44).

According to futurists such as Bridges, we have recently entered a new period signaled by further transformations in what is to be meant by jobs. "Now, once again, we have come to a turning point at which the assumptions about living and working that people had grown comfortable with are being challenged" (Bridges 1995, 45). Fellow Nostradamian Jeremy Rifkin (1995, 60) argues that "the global economy is in the midst of a transformation as significant as the Industrial Revolution." He suggests that we have entered a "new economic era" marked by a declining need for "mass human labor." As computers, robots, and telecommunications networks and other cybernetic technologies replace human workers in an increasing range of activities we have entered "the early stages of a shift from 'mass labour' to highly skilled 'elite' labour accompanied by increasing automation in the production of goods and the delivery of services" (Rifkin 1995, 60).

Bridges (1995) suggests that changes in technology and the global market have transformed work relations in such a manner as to suggest the disappearance of the very category "job." Cybernetization of capital has provided a context in which it is not unreasonable for workers to expect that their jobs will be eliminated (Aronowitz and Cutler 1998). Bridges (1995) suggests that each increase in productivity seems to make jobs redundant.

Corresponding to that change may be a shift in peoples' perceptions of work. More and more, people are "searching for alternatives to jobs and job descriptions" (Bridges 1995, 46). Rifkin (1995, 58) suggests that the "jobs" question is "likely to be the most explosive issue of the [present] decade."

More interesting than the futurists are those calling for the outright abolition of work in its job form. Recognizing that the category "job" signifies a dependency relationship disguised as independence (the "freedom" to consume) work abolitionists call for workers of the world to relax in a gleeful rejection of the leftist mantra of full employment (see Black 1995). The abolitionist appeal is not a project for further integration of the working classes through preservation of jobs at all costs and over-reliance upon parliamentary mediation toward that end. Rather it expresses traditionally anarchic or libertarian sensibilities that journey beyond the reductionist contortion that has seen work come to be equated with jobs. This unconventional approach is made manifest primarily through emphases on creativity, self-determination, and conviviality of relations. The category "jobs" is understood as marking a restriction of peoples' capacities to care for themselves and those within their communal/ecological groupings and is therefore rejected as a point for a radical activist convergence.

Work abolitionism suggests a movement simultaneously "of class" and "against class," that is, against the commodification of creativity and performance. Jobs or employment within the "anti-class" milieux refer to the idea that one must sell oneself to any function in order to receive sustenance—the imperative of wage labor. The category "jobs" speaks to the compulsory character of involvement in production, enforced via relations of economic and political control and power. Questions of what one is doing are removed given this construction, of course. Work is no longer done for its own sake but for secondary effects, such as wages, which are not characteristic of or inherent to the work itself. It might be said that jobs form a condensation point for complex relations of power around the trading of time for money, or what Zimpel (1974) quite poignantly refers to as "a transaction of existential absurdity."

Jobs, as characterized by an extension of organizational control over people as workers, signify a system of domination practiced through forms of discipline that include surveillance and time management. The regimentation and discipline of the job serves to habituate workers to hierarchy and obedience while also discouraging insubordination and autonomy. Jobs as regimented roles replace direct, creative participation and initiative through arrangements of subservience.

Bob Black (1985) argues that employment is capital's primary and most direct coercive formation, one that is experienced daily.

Antiwork themes are not new, of course. They find antecedents in Fourier, Lafargue, and even (especially?) in Marx's critique of alienated labor. For radical abolitionists (see Negri 1984), the liquidation of wage labor is not a given; it is a question of political struggle.

Here a convergence between antiwork theorizing and the analyses developed within autonomist Marxism are particularly interesting. Drawing from Marx's analysis of automation within a wage system, autonomist Marxists have argued that the cybernetization of capital will not usher in a leisure society (who would want it anyway?) but would instead encourage an enlargement of the realm of work as labor displaced from primary and secondary industry becomes reabsorbed by "the tertiary, quaternary, or quinary sectors as farther and farther flung domains of human activity are assimilated within the social factory" (Witheford 1994, 106). Cybernetized capital, through the commodification of expanded and novel realms of human activity, can maintain wage labor, "incessantly recreating its proletariat, unless it is forcibly interrupted by the organised efforts of workers to reclaim their life-time" (Witheford 1994, 108). Perhaps more than other activists, abolitionists have increasingly come to understand jobs, under the guise of work, as perhaps the most basic moment of unfreedom, which must be overcome in any quest toward liberty. Too often, previously, the common response has been one of turning away from workers and from questions about the organization of working relations. Green syndicalism suggests that radical politics can no longer ignore those questions which are posed by the presence of jobs, however. Indeed it might be said that a return to the problematic of jobs becomes the starting point for a reformulation of radicalism, at least along green lines.

So, what forms has the organization of "workers-against-work taken"? Earlier Wobbly demands for a four-hour day may be understood as an expression of opposition to the extension of capitalist control over labor and the reduction of workers to one-dimensional class beings. They suggest a movement for autonomy wherein labor achieves some distance from capital and the extension of control over creativity. The shortened workday might be best understood as the opening of creative time, outside of capitalist discipline and command, and the expansion of time available for such "frivolous" undertakings as bringing about the end of industrial capitalism. In limiting the duration and intensity of the workday labor asserts its own project counter to that of capital.

The mythic use of the general strike by Wobblies might also be understood in this manner. Anarcho-syndicalists have long argued that for cooperative, community-based ways of living to endure workers will have to stop producing for Capital and State. Given current political economy this implies that workers must stop producing period! In other words, class is only abolished through not working—a general strike. Through the general withdrawal of labor might the megamachine be ground to a halt and left to rust!

Historically, unions had responded to technological changes and increases to productivity with demands for a shortened workday and work week so that such gains might be deployed to benefit workers and their families by lightening the burden of work and freeing up time for activities in the home and community. Indeed the rich history of workers' struggles to shorten the working day enjoyed important successes, even in periods of economic decline and crisis when productivity has been weakened. As Walker (2002) notes, it was during the Great Depression, a period of mass unemployment, that organized workers won the basic eight-hour workday. Even more, demands for thirty hours work for forty hours pay became increasingly strong throughout the 1930s, partly as a way to give more people employment without impacting the pay of those workers who already had jobs.

At the same time it is clear that union leaders have generally abandoned such appeals for work reductions throughout North American unions. The expansion of overtime and the growth of the working day has been a feature of work life over the last two decades. As Walker notes: "Since the 1980s the eight-hour day for millions of workers, unionized and not, has been replaced with longer shifts, split shifts and weekend shifts. At the same time millions of families have been forced to seek multiple incomes just to protect, not raise their living standards" (2002, 8). Neoliberal governments have set about changing employment legislation to extend the working day legally so that employers can get workers to put in longer hours before they can claim even overtime pay. In Ontario the neoliberal Conservative government replaced the legal work week of forty-four hours with a sixty-eight-hour week and also cut legislated vacation time so workers can claim less time away from work.

Despite that, however, Rifkin (1995, 64) reports that the union officials with whom he has spoken are "universally reluctant to deal with the notion that mass labour, the very basis of trade unionism, will continue to decline and may even disappear altogether." Mainstream unionists have been incapable of any radical rethinking of their politics that might address the crucial transformations in jobs. Such failures to adapt, or even to remember their own radical histories, speak to the difficulties facing workers within traditional unions in the contemporary context and highlight the importance of the work of green syndicalists to once again bring such struggles forward within working-class movements.

Fortunately, as Walker notes, the desire for a shorter work week is not dead, even if unions leaders are unwilling to address it. For Walker a renewal of struggles for a shortened work week might serve to bridge the gap between older and younger workers, serving to further unite workers and possibly reorient and revitalize the labor movement. In his view: "Moreover, the work day concessions that labor unions have accepted—often without a fight—hurt younger workers the most. Younger workers' elan and idealism, the basis of youthful militancy, can be the dynamo that drives a fight for jobs and environmental projects to a deserved victory" (2002, 8).

Rifkin (1995), while not discussing specifically the ecological significance of a shortened work week, recognizes that such a shortening could serve as a rallying point for a powerful convergence of social struggles. Rifkin's analysis remains productivist (among other things undesirable), however, even arguing that a shortened work week could be beneficial for capital in allowing for a doubling or tripling of productivity! Rifkin never questions the legitimacy or the desirability of capitalist relations. Indeed a major reason for concern over "vanishing jobs" is that the transformation threatens a capitalist collapse through a weakening of consumer demand. Rifkin's main desire is to see an increase in the "purchasing power" of workers so that "[e]mployers, workers, the economy, and the government all benefit" (64).

Like the "structural-functionalist" sociologists of old, Rifkin's primary concern is with the possibility of "strain" in the system and the alleviation of any such strain. Rifkin worries that the decline of jobs could threaten the foundations of the modern state, something that does not concern green syndicalists who would actually encourage such a threat, through the destabilizing impact upon social relations that previously rested upon a shared valuing of labor, what he calls the heart of the social contract. Rifkin (1995, 60) even fears that the crisis in jobs will open the door to renewed militancy and to extralegal expressions of politics.

In like fashion, the optimism of Bridges (1995) over possibilities for the transformation of jobs speaks only to the strata of well-skilled, well-paid workers in an increasingly polarized workforce. The conclusions drawn by Bridges never question the hegemony of capital in structuring possible responses to the "death of the job," leaving the "employee" as an intact category facing such unsatisfactory and increasingly tenuous options as freelance work, part-time work, or piecework. The decline of the job simply comes to mean that those who are working have more work to do. Even limited concerns over what is being produced, how, by whom, and for what purpose, never appear on the horizon of Bridges's schema. Neither do questions regarding what happens to those newly "liberated"—the jobless.

Among abolitionists the "end of work" suggests much more intriguing and truly liberating possibilities. Far from being irrational responses to serious social transformations, workplace rebellion and workers' self-determination become ever more reasonable responses to the uncertainty and contingency of emerging conditions of (un)employment. They offer worker and community self-determination as alternatives to neoliberal perspectives on unemployment. Such alternatives provide an articulation of the end of work, which emphasizes workers actively overcoming their own workerness, against pessimistic or cynical responses such as mass retraining, which simply reinforce dependence upon elites.

An objection might well be raised that abolitionism need not imply a transformation of capitalism; after all, the "abolition of work" is a reference also employed by some neoliberal postindustrial theorists. There, however, the abolition of work is understood as completely realizable under capitalism. The possible end of work is conceptualized as coming from the application of innovative technological resources within capitalist relations, not as a destruction of those relations. At it most dramatic it implies a leisure society enabled through the development of artificial intelligence and robotics.

These are not acceptable alternatives. It is not conceivable how any ecological lifestyles could be constituted otherwise than with the outright cessation of capitalist production. Only the end of production for profit at the expense of real human needs can necessarily imply the end of nuclearism, weapons production, clear-cutting, toxic waste products—the varieties of harmful applications to which nature is commonly subjected. (Again, Black states this most effectively.) Among the prerequisites for ecological change is a reduction both in the amount of work being done and in the character of what is done. Much of work, involving massive appropriation of natural elements, is useless. That includes the defense and reproduction of work relations in political (ownership and control) and economic (circulation and consumption) forms.

Abolitionists envision work being performed through democratic, participatory means within which work is conceived more as craft or as play. Growing concerns over the regimentation and alienation of working conditions along with the fatal ecological consequences have contributed to the emergence of anti-technology/anti-civilization (anti-tech/anti-civ) discourses arguing quite persuasively that humans must abandon not only industry and technology, but civilization itself.

Abolitionist visions are raised against the undermining influences of work in contemporary conditions of globalism. They offer but one, though perhaps the most interesting, contribution to the problem of jobs and to the refusal of authoritarian and coercive social relations.

For theorists of green syndicalism (Kaufmann and Ditz 1992; Purchase 1994, 1997a, 1997b; Shantz and Adam 1999; Jakopovich 2007), an even more radical change is perceived as being required to transform the nature of what work might remain toward ecological ends such as recovery, repair, and reconstruction. Furthermore, the processes of transforming existing work involve those who perform and are most familiar with the tasks under question.

Production, within a green syndicalist vision (Kaufmann and Ditz 1992; Purchase 1994, 1997a, 1997b), may include the provision of ecologically sensitive foods, transportation, or energy. Work, newly organized along decentralized, local, democratic lines might allow for the introduction of materials and practices with diminished impact upon the bioregion in which each is employed. Green syndicalist discourses are raised against the undermining influences of work in contemporary conditions of globalism. Far from being irrational responses to serious social transformations, workplace democratization and workers' self-determination become ever more reasonable responses to the uncertainty and contingency of emerging conditions of (un)employment. Green syndicalists emphasize workers' empowerment and self-emancipation against pessimistic or cynical responses such as mass retraining, which simply reinforce dependence upon elites. They offer but one initiative toward the overcoming of work and a movement toward community-based economics and productive decision making.

5

Green Syndicalism
and Mainstream Unions

Flying Squads and Rank-and-File Organizing

The decreased demand for labor, within cybernetized capital relations, means that corporations are less compelled to deal with mainstream trade unions as under the Keynesian arrangement.[1] If unions
are to have any influence, it can only come through active efforts
to disrupt the labor process. These disruptive efforts may include
increased militancy within workplace relations. Evidence for a rebellion among workers has been reflected typically in such activities as
sabotage, slowdowns, and absences. IWW activists explicitly agitate
for "deliberate inefficiency" as a means to encourage the desecration
of work relations. For green syndicalists the desired tactics against corporate-sponsored destruction of the environment include such direct,
nonbureaucratic forms of action as shop-floor sabotage, boycotts,

---

1. Montgomery (1974) suggests that workers' struggles generally belong to
two types: control struggles and wage struggles. Employers spend much energy
trying to prevent the convergence of the two currents. Unions have, since 1945,
been preoccupied typically with wage struggles, while control struggles have been
traded for wages and benefits or diverted through limited participation schemes, as
exemplified in recent approaches to management, or in "commitments to quality."
The challenge again confronting organized labor is precisely to revitalize control
struggles. This challenge also faces "new movement" activists in their attempts to
engage with labor.

green bans, and the formation of extra-union solidarity outside of the workplace, within workers' home communities.

Of course, the strike, the power to halt production, is unmatched in its capacity to confront corporate greed. Environmentalists can stop production for a few hours or a few days. There is no more effective counterforce to capital accumulation and the pursuit of profit than the power of workers to stop work to achieve their demands. Ecological protection, as with work conditions, benefits, or wages, must be fought for. Where workers are involved that means they must be struck for.

The use of this power, however, requires that workers' develop a position of strength. That, in turn, means organizing workers so that they no longer face the prospects of "jobs versus environment" blackmail. In order for this to occur, nonunionized workers must be mobilized. (Otherwise they are mobilized by capital—as scabs.) Recognizing this need, the IWW gives a great deal of attention to organizing the traditionally unorganized.

A green syndicalist conception of workers' organization rejects the hierarchical, centralized, bureaucratic structures of mainstream unionism. Economistic union organizations and bureaucrats who have worked to convince workers that environmentalists are responsible for job loss point up the need for syndicalist unions organized around ecologically sensitive practices.

Green syndicalists generally reject the perspective of Fosterism the practice, as advocated by William Z. Foster in the 1910s, of "boring from within" the mainstream unions.[2] Examples abound of the difficulties of trying to build ecological perspectives, committees, and work within mainstream unions. Laurie Adkin (1998) provides detailed accounts of the obstacles faced by activists in the Canadian Auto Workers (CAW), supposedly the most progressive social union

---

2. For a discussion of the debates around Fosterism, see Bekken (2001). Recently, Wobblies in Edmonton, Canada, attempted to revive Fosterism within the IWW, a proposal that was overwhelmingly rejected.

in Canada, when they attempted to build rank-and-file environmental committees. There the National Executive worked against rank-and-file activists to contain environmental initiatives within the confines of bargaining, in a limited and marginalized way. Ontario's Green Work Alliance (GWA) provides another instance in which rank-and-file workers were thwarted by union bureaucrats in their efforts to establish green union perspectives. In that case union support for Ontario's ruling social democratic party, the New Democratic Party (NDP), interfered with the GWA criticisms of NDP environmental policies. Recent divisions between the "Teamsters and Turtles" alliance of the Seattle anti–World Trade Organization (WTO) protests, especially over labor support for President Bush's plan for oil drilling in the Alaska National Wildlife Refuge, emphasize the serious obstacles that remain in forging alliances with business unions (see Buss 2001).

It is not true to say that strong environmental policies cannot come from mainstream unions. Mainstream unions can and do at times take up specific policies and practices of syndicalism, but the lack of overall vision and participatory structures means that such policies and practices are not part of overall strategy and are often vulnerable to leadership control or the limitations of bargaining with employers.

While not a syndicalist union, the Builders Labourers Federation (BLF) in Australia did adopt a number of policies that are hallmarks of syndicalism, most notably openness, radical democracy, and participation. It must be stressed that these structural changes were essential for the development of the BLF's environmental perspective (Burgmann and Burgmann 1998). Job site autonomy was encouraged, officials' wages were linked to industry wages, and officials were not paid during strikes. The union also established a "limited tenure of office," and executive meetings were opened to all members (Burgmann and Burgmann 1998). The BLF also showed the expansive vision of working-class solidarity, which is a strength of syndicalism. For example, the union banned work at Macquarie University in Sydney after a gay student was expelled. The BLF also offered strong support for aboriginal land rights and squatters. The union also banned work on the construction of a $1 million maximum-security prison block.

Unfortunately the BLF was betrayed by the same authoritarian forces that have haunted the syndicalists. Maoists and Stalinists within the national union offices conspired with bosses to impose federal control over the union, expel leading militants, and end the bans.

Neither is it true to say that green syndicalists refuse to act in solidarity with workers in mainstream unions. Indeed, Local 1 worked in support of workers in Pulp and Paper Workers Local 49, and Judi Bari points out that many actions would have been impossible without inside information provided by workers in that local. Green syndicalists do work with rank-and-file members of mainstream unions, and many are themselves "two-carders"—simultaneously members of mainstream and syndicalist unions. In this chapter I examine attempts by green syndicalists to develop rank-and-file power within mainstream unions.

Developing Workers Autonomy: Green Syndicalists, Flying Squads, and Rank-and-File Groups

Indeed, despite its significance, the work of rank-and-file syndicalists and anarchists within mainstream unions has largely been overlooked. Ironically it is in rank-and-file labor struggles that contemporary green syndicalists have really been innovators, doing things that are quite atypical for many North American anarchist organizations. Unlike Left groups that have focused their energies on running opposition slates in union elections or forming opposition caucuses, green syndicalists in mainstream unions work to develop rank-and-file organization and militancy. They take the position that regardless of the union leadership, until there is a militant and mobilized rank-and-file movement across locals and workplaces, the real power of organized labor will remain unrealized.

Recently much interest and discussion has been generated by the emergence of union flying squads. Flying squads—rapid-response networks of workers that can be mobilized for strike support, demonstrations, direct action, and working-class defense of immigrants, poor people, and unemployed workers—present a potentially significant development in revitalizing organized labor activism and rank-and-file militancy. For many anarchist union activists they present a significant possibility for organizing rank-and-file power within the workplace. The flying squad is autonomous from all official union structures and is open to rank-and-file workers who hold no union position or to workers in unorganized workplaces or who are unemployed. The flying squad supports direct action against bosses of all types.

While these are not strictly anarchist or syndicalist organizations, involving as they do a cross-section of workers, they are areas in which contemporary anarchist unionists have focused their energies. It is within such rank-and-file initiatives that many green syndicalists have found the best possibilities for militant workplace organizing. Based on these examples, anarchists in Peterborough and Montreal have recently taken part in developing flying-squad networks in their cities. In Toronto, the anarchist collective Punching Out was active in forming an autonomous flying squad to coordinate strike support and help build workers' self-organization and solidarity, bringing together unionized and nonunionized workers along with unemployed members. The Precarious Workers Network coalescing in Montreal is primarily organizing among unorganized and unemployed workers. The Downtown Workers Union in Montpelier, Vermont, which organized service workers citywide, also developed a flying squad.

Militant anticapitalists of various stripes, recognizing the crucial roles played by workers within production relations, have viewed the flying squads as important in the development of workers' organization against capitalist authority and discipline. Anarchists and syndicalists, maintaining the necessity of working-class self-organization and autonomy from bureaucratic structures, have been encouraged by the possible emergence of active networks of rank-and-file workers bringing collective resources to defend broad working-class interests. Here are organizations with rank-and-file participation working to build solidarity across unions and locals and alongside community groups, engaging in direct action while striving to democratize their own unions. No wonder then that the reappearance of flying squads, particularly in Ontario, Canada, in a context of halting resistance to a vicious neoliberal attack, notably among some sectors of the labor movement, has been cause for much excitement among green syndicalists.

The flying squad is a rapid-response group of members who are ready to mobilize on short notice to provide direct support for pickets or direct actions. It is not necessarily an officially recognized body of the local. The flying squad structure may consist of little more than phone lists and meetings but, significantly, should maintain its autonomy from the local and national union executives. Generally flying squads should be open only to rank-and-file members because they must be free to initiate and take actions that the leadership may not approve. Some flying squads refuse even a budget line item so that they are in no way dependent upon leadership. In Canada, flying squads have offered crucial support to direct actions around immigration defense, tenant protection, squatters rights, and welfare support by mobilizing sizeable numbers of unionists who are prepared for actions without regard to legality. Flying squads take direct action to interfere with bosses' abilities to make profits. Not limited in their scope of action by specific collective agreements or workplaces, flying squads mobilize for community as well as workplace defense (Shantz 2005).

Working groups are generally recognized bodies that are established to deal with specific areas of need. They step beyond the limitations of traditional unionism to assist both members and nonmembers. Rank-and-file and community alliances offer examples of how to make the connections that are crucial to developing militant working-class solidarity. They can bring anticapitalist activists, community members, and unionists together to work on a day-to-day basis.

Rank-and-file committees and flying squads can become important parts of struggles over a broad spectrum of issues affecting working-class community life, including those the mainstream unions ignore, such as housing and unemployment. They can offer spaces for building bridges between workers, across unions and industries, and between union and community groups. Autonomous from traditional union structures and organized around militant nonhierarchical practices, rank-and-file working groups and flying squads can provide real opposition to conservatism within the unions as well. They provide a better approach than the more common model of the "left caucus," which tries to reform union policy, usually, again, through resolutions at conventions (Clarke 2002). The rank-and-file committees actively and directly challenge the leadership within their own locals and across locals.

Flying squads of various types have long been an important part of labor militancy internationally. In Britain, community flying pickets successfully mobilized to defend hospitals in working-class neighborhoods against closure in the 1970s. In India several farmers' unions recently formed flying squads to confront officials at purchase centers to ensure that their demands for proper payment for their crops were satisfied. Members of the Carpenters Union in southern California, who were primarily immigrants, many of them undocumented, used flying squads and direct action effectively during the framers' strike of 1995.

While some type of rank-and-file organizing, along the lines of what we now call flying squads, has been a constant in labor movements, the contemporary flying squads in Ontario are inspired by the flying pickets that emerged during the CIO strikes of the 1930s. Flying squads played an important part in the 1945 UAW strike against Ford in Windsor. That strike, which won the rights associated with the Rand Formula (union recognition, dues check-off, and closed shop) for workers in Canada, turned when strikers organized an incredible vehicle picket in which the entire Ford plant was surrounded and shut down by several rows of vehicles. Flying squads were used effectively to mobilize people for actions throughout the strike and to spread information throughout the community. By focusing on building flying squads, anarchists are thus drawing upon traditions and practices that have long played a part in working-class organizing, while attempting to radicalize them.

Not coincidentally, the contemporary flying squads in Ontario made their reappearance in several CAW locals in Windsor during the mid-1990s as a mobilization force for actions against the newly elected neoliberal provincial government (see Levant 2003, 20). The network within the CAW spread during organizing of the Ontario Days of Action, rotating, city-by-city one-day mass strikes against the Tories. In the midst of a lengthy strike against Falconbridge mining, during which picketers were subjected to ongoing violence by company goons and security thugs, members of CAW Local 598 initiated a regional Northern Flying Squad to reinforce and defend the lines and step up the struggle against the company. They helped to organize a solidarity weekend that brought flying squads from across Ontario for militant actions against Falconbridge, actions that many consider to have been the high point of the strike.

On different occasions the Ontario Coalition Against Poverty (OCAP) along with the CUPE 3903 (Canadian Union of Public Employees) flying squad have gone directly to Pearson International Airport to demand an end to threats of deportation against families. Leaflets are given to passengers alerting them to the situation, and visits are paid to the Immigration Canada deportation office in the basement of Terminal One. After demanding and receiving a meeting with the airport's Immigration management the combined efforts of OCAP and the flying squad have caused management to issue stays of removal with the deportations eventually canceled. This unusual result, in which the removal dates were canceled prior to a federal court challenge, is a testament to the powers of direct action (Shantz 2005).

It must also be stressed that the presence of flying squads has been crucial in the success of these and other actions. Clearly government officials, security, and cops respond differently when confronted with a room packed with workers holding union flags and banners than when confronted with a smaller numbers of people whom they are willing to dismiss as activists. Through such actions, the flying squad demonstrates how organizations of rank-and-file workers can step out of traditional concerns with the workplace to act in a broadened defense of working-class interests. The expansion of union flying squads, with autonomy from union bureaucracies, could provide a substantial response to the state's efforts to isolate immigrants and refugees from the larger community. The emboldened aggressiveness of Immigration Canada after September 11 makes such actions in defense of working-class people absolutely crucial.

In addition 3903 is home to vital working groups with real links to community struggles. In November 2001, 3903 provided an office and resources for OCAP to work along with members of the 3903 Anti-Poverty Working Group. The working group moves beyond the limitations of traditional unionism to assist people (members and non-members) experiencing problems with collection agencies, landlords, bosses, and police and to help anyone having difficulties with welfare or other government bureaucracies. The office provides a possibly significant example of a rank-and-file initiative that forges community alliances while fighting the local implementation of the global neoliberal agenda. This type of alliance offers one example of how to make the connections that are crucial to growing our movements. Indeed, it brings antiglobalization activists, antipoverty organizers, and unions together to work on a day-to-day basis.

Rank-and-File Committees

Another area of organizing work undertaken by green syndicalists has been within solidarity unionism and support for rank-and-file committees. Anarchist unionists have been actively involved in building and/or supporting alternative rank-and-file networks within and between unions and workplaces. In some cases this has meant supporting rank-and-file union members whose unions have refused to fight effectively for members' needs and concerns. One such case involves the Metropolitan Hotel Workers Committee (MHWC) in Toronto.

The hotel industry is the largest employer of immigrants, women of color, and single parents. It is generally acknowledged that hotel workers across the industry face horrible working conditions with rampant health and safety problems. Long hours of work are matched with low pay and unsafe working conditions. Workers deal with hazardous chemicals, often without adequate training, proper ventilation, or necessary safety equipment. Too often these conditions are also matched with an inactive and compliant union leadership that views these problems as "part of the business." That has been the case for workers at Toronto's Metropolitan Hotel, where conditions are so miserable that workers accurately refer to it as a "five-star sweatshop." Unfortunately, as is all too common, when the Met workers turned to their union, the Hotel Employees and Restaurant Employees International Union (HERE), for support, their concerns were ignored, minimized, or dismissed.

Faced with an ongoing situation of brutally racist management, awful working conditions, and a union that could only be described as passive, rank-and-file workers at the Metropolitan decided in 2005 to get organized to take care of things themselves. To begin, several workers came together to form the Metropolitan Hotel Workers Committee, a committee made up strictly of rank-and-file members, to share information and strategize effective actions and campaigns to improve working conditions and put an end to harsh management practices. Within months, more than one-quarter of the Metropolitan's workers had joined the committee. Efforts to challenge management at the hotel became a crucial struggle for rank-and-file workers, most of whom are immigrant women. Of the approximately two hundred workers at the Met, more than two-thirds are women, most of Filipino, Chinese, Southeast and South Asian, and West Indian backgrounds.

Green syndicalists, including some within the Ontario Coalition Against Poverty and CUPE Local 3903 played active parts in assisting the MHWC in its development. They helped organize and mobilize people for rallies, took part in skill-sharing to address issues within the workplace, and challenged the union leadership to support the committee. The quick growth of the committee spoke both to the seriousness of the problems facing Met workers and the long-standing need for effective action to deal with the issues, given the union's unresponsiveness.

Confronted by ongoing inaction, obstruction, and outright hostility from their local's leadership, the Met Workers decided to take things into their own hands. A true rank-and-file movement has come together to take on the boss in a manner that is direct and effective. Despite the hostility of local leadership, the committee has already made some important gains. Grievances have been satisfactorily resolved and committee members have done skill-sharing with each other to teach themselves how to take grievances forward. This is do-it-yourself solidarity unionism where members look after each other, share resources, and determine their course of action collectively—a real model for anarchism at work. Within weeks of forming the MHWC, workers were able to have a particularly nasty manager removed—after repeated requests to local reps to do something about this manager had left the situation unchanged. Owing to the efforts of the Met Workers Committee a conference scheduled to bring three hundred people to the Met was canceled, a move that stunned management. Through a series of direct actions and rallies the committee has confronted the hotel management directly with demands that management rehire, with compensation, all victimized workers who have been forced from their jobs and stop the practice of harassing and firing injured workers.

While the union leadership bemoaned the lack of translators, without explaining why a union would hire staff who do not speak the same language as large proportions of the membership, the Met Workers Committee members shared skills with each other to teach themselves how to pursue grievances and work refusals. While the union's top-down authoritarian structure prevents it from drawing on the skills and talents, including multilingualism, of members, the Met workers have provided translations skills that have allowed OCAP to expand its own antipoverty casework to people it otherwise could not have assisted.

All along the MHWC has maintained that they identify not only as members of a particular union or as part of a specific workplace, but on a broad working-class basis. Thus they have reached out to poor and unemployed workers in community groups like OCAP as well as making alliances with rank-and-file members of other unions, such as the Anti-Poverty Working Group of CUPE 3903. With support from these groups the MHWC organized several direct actions and rallies at the workplace. In addition the committee broadened its efforts to take the boss on in the community as well as in the workplace. Met Workers worked with the CUPE 3903 Anti-Poverty Working Group to press York University to remove the Met's owner, Henry Wu, from the board of the York Foundation. This class-based organizing is significant not just in terms of bringing greater resources to bear on the situation, but also in helping to break down the sectoralism that often keeps working-class folks divided by workplace, union, or employment status.

As the committee grew and enjoyed some successes they were approached by workers from other hotels about starting similar committees in more workplaces. These are crucial steps in building a vital network among rank-and-file activists geared toward autonomy and self-activity. Significantly the MHWC focused its efforts on building an informed and active rank-and-file base rather than on putting together a reform slate for infrequently held executive elections. These efforts will do more than any Left-led reform movements, leadership slates, or caucuses to establish the basis for a revitalized and militant workers' movement. That the MHWC has had difficulty standing up under the pressures of hostility and lack of support from its own union leadership shows also the obstacles and challenges that such rank-and-file networks face.

Green Syndicalism and Greenpeace

One of the areas in which green syndicalists have mobilized flying squads and rank-and-file committees again illustrates quite sharply the pressing need for green syndicalist analysis within environmental movements. Ironically it involved Greenpeace canvassers. Greenpeace door canvassers are used to pounding the pavements. Every evening, they walk kilometers to spread the Greenpeace message of environmental care. However, the organization's canvass workers never expected to be pounding the pavement in a picket outside the Greenpeace office in Toronto. The workers, members of Office and Professional Employees International Union (OPIEU) local 343, were forced to do just that in Toronto through the cold winter of 2003 after they were locked out with a year left on their contract.

The contract negotiated between the workers and Greenpeace Canada was due to expire on December 31, 2003. However, in early July, Greenpeace management illegally tried to renegotiate the contract, with the threat that its canvassing operation would close without a new deal. When the workers refused to accept management's unfavorable new terms of employment, Greenpeace carried out its threat on October 15. As a result, thirteen canvassers were illegally locked out. The workers had shown their commitment to Greenpeace by working in the high-turnover job for up to eight years. One of the locked-out workers was still facing court charges after being arrested for taking part in a Greenpeace protest action.

Canvassers have been the grassroots face of Greenpeace for fourteen years. In Canada, many canvassers pull off the direct actions—without pay—that are so much a part of Greenpeace's image and reputation. Canvassers have raised millions of dollars for Greenpeace over the years. Despite this, most canvassers are poorly paid, making little more than the minimum wage. They also put in many unpaid hours. Many do the work because they have a real concern for the environment and a commitment to social change. That makes Greenpeace's actions even more disturbing.

During the lockout Greenpeace Canada refused to communicate with the OPIEU. Greenpeace Canada's then executive director Peter Tabuns said that the door-to-door canvass workers had been offered jobs in a call center. However, this was unacceptable given that call-center work in no way resembles the job that the workers were contracted to do. In addition, the new jobs would result in a cut in pay.

Carrying signs reading "Greenpeace clearcuts jobs" and "Protection for the environment and for workers," the locked-out canvassers picketed the Toronto Greenpeace office for several hours each day for months. While many social justice groups avoided supporting the canvassers in order to avoid criticizing Greenpeace, green syndicalists in Toronto organized regular support pickets, media work, and solidarity visits to other unions and labor councils to build support for the locked-out workers. Thus support developed among some social justice, environmental, and antiracist groups, and by unions such as the Canadian Union of Public Employees and United Steelworkers of America.

Recognizing the importance of fending off this blatant attempt at union busting, green syndicalists formed a broader Workers Solidarity Club to provide support to the canvassers. It organized a series of "solidarity days" to bring labor and social justice groups to the picket line to show Greenpeace that workers' rights are central to building a green society. Indeed it was only with the support of green syndicalists, and the efforts and resources they shared, that the locked-out Greenpeace workers were able finally to reach a settlement.

Struggles Over the Flying Squads

The national and local executives of some unions in which flying squads and rank-and-file committees have emerged have clearly shown concern about these developments, as the case of the MHWC and its struggles with HERE illustrate. It has played out particularly badly within the CAW.

During the summer of 2001, people in cities, reserves, and towns throughout Ontario were gearing up for a campaign of economic disruption that would directly confront and interfere with the political programs and economic practices of the government and their corporate backers. This effort suffered something of a setback when the CAW leadership decided in June to withdraw support from the campaign. The decision came following a mock eviction of the finance minister from his constituency office by OCAP, students, and members of CAW and CUPE flying squads. Then national president of the CAW, Buzz Hargrove, was so upset by the action that he agreed to meet with the labor minister to discuss union support of OCAP. In an inexplicable act of collaboration, Hargrove sat down to establish union policy with the man who only months before had introduced legislation gutting the Employment Standards Act and extending the legal workweek from forty-four to sixty-two hours.

Significantly, not only did Hargrove cut OCAP's largest source of funding, but he also clamped down on the CAW flying squads, which were only beginning to grow. CAW flying squads were brought under control of the National by requiring approval of the National or of local presidents prior to any action. The National even tried to prohibit use of CAW shirts, hats, and banners at actions not sanctioned by the National. Thus the CAW leadership cynically used the excuse of the eviction to clamp down on a rank-and-file movement that it saw as a possible threat to its authority. The strangling of the flying squads may be one of the sharpest blows rank-and-file activists have suffered recently and deeply hurt fight-back efforts in Ontario.

These actions effectively derailed actions in major industrial centers like Windsor, where activists, recognizing the vulnerability of just-in-time production in Windsor and Detroit, had initially planned to blockade the Ambassador Bridge, the main US-Canada node in the NAFTA superhighway. Stopping traffic on the bridge for even a short period of time would have caused millions of dollars in damages because of the reliance on just-in-time production in the factories on both sides of the border. This possibility was not lost on Hargrove, who let it slip during a meeting with representatives of OCAP allies when he angrily voiced his concern that in Windsor some members were talking about shutting down production at "our plants."

Right now the CAW bureaucracy's clampdown on the flying squads is complete. At a panel discussion on creative tactics that I took part in at a Labor Notes conference, Michelle Dubiel, a CAW "Ontario Chapter" flying squad representative, stated approvingly that marshals had finally been instituted in the CAW flying squads. Dubiel noted that there had been much discussion and some resistance to it, but she was reassured that members were eventually brought to see the necessity of marshals. The impact of this takeover of the flying squads has been lethal in some areas. A flying squad member in Sudbury told me that the northern flying squads were virtually extinct. Similarly the rank-and-file, cross-local flying squad in Windsor was shut down before it really got started.

Beyond Union Reformism
and Flying Squads as Left Opposition

Some union activists have viewed the flying squads primarily as a means of union reform, a companion piece of the left caucus's loyal opposition to the union leadership. A prime example of this approach is expressed by Alex Levant (who has put much work into building my former union's flying squad and served as a vice president in the local), in an article in *New Socialist* magazine (March/April 2003). Levant poses the problem for rank-and-file activism largely as one of "conservative leaders who practice 'business unionism'" (Levant 2003, 22). Levant suggests that flying squads "pose a threat to such union leaders' positions by fostering membership activism, which bolsters left opposition currents in these unions" (22). Business unionism, far from being a preference of specific leaders, however, is a structured relationship, legally and organizationally, within unions and between unions and bosses. Levant is correct to suggest that such locals "contribute to the crisis of working-class self-organization by discouraging members' self-activity" (22), but this crisis will not be overcome by replacing conservative leaders with leftist ones. Nor should we accept that social unionism is not still a form of business unionism (Shantz 2009a), which is shown clearly in the case of the CAW, which has long practiced "social unionism."

Taking the left opposition perspective, Levant is unable or unwilling to criticize leadership in the CAW openly or directly for their ongoing efforts to control that union's flying squads. In his article, Levant quotes CAW representative Steve Watson approvingly while making no mention of his role in the CAW National breaking of the rank-and-file aspects of the flying squads. Notably, at the above-mentioned antideportation action at the airport, it was Watson who intervened at the last minute to keep CAW flying squads from participating, even though many workers at the airport are CAW members and could have played an important part in stopping the deportation.

I do agree with Levant that the flying squads have a tremendous potential in building rank-and-file militancy and self-organization. However, that potential can only be met if autonomy from the leadership is established and defended with vigilance. Flying squads do *not* "work best" when they "respect" the roles of the leadership as Levant advocates. Flying squads work best when they understand the roles the leadership plays, including the role of taming and reining in members' self-organizing initiatives at various points.

Notes on Bureaucracy

For all of their potential power, the trade unions are restricted by a leadership that cannot allow decisive force to be unleashed. To understand the difficulties facing rank-and-file resistance, we must understand the roles and structures of leadership beyond a focus on conservative or progressive union leaders. In Ontario, during the 1930s and 1940s waves of union organizing, wildcat strikes and occupations pressed a tactical retreat on the bosses and their state, leading to the extension of new rights to workers' organizations.

In place of open class war, a process of limited and uneven concession granting was established. This truce had the effect of regulating and compartmentalizing workplace struggles to keep them below the level of serious disruption. Each industry, workplace, or section of workers was viewed as having its own issues to attend to or, indeed, to bargain over. A new layer of union functionaries emerged to broker and execute this deal. These union executives needed to placate membership with regulated contract gains, simultaneously ensuring labor force stability and an environment conducive to accumulation for the bosses. Negotiation is presented as a reasonable and effective solution to most problems. Bureaucrats strive to get the best possible deal for labor power rather than attack or end the overall system of exploitation. Emphasis is placed on bargaining power within the capitalist labor market.

Strike action became a last resort to be deployed only under very limited and legally defined conditions. Wildcat strikes and varieties of worker-initiated shop-floor actions are negotiated away and prohibited within contracts. Workers who engage in such actions are open to sanction, a point the union leadership often reinforces within the membership.

Although limited outbursts were permitted, leaders were obliged to police the deal and restore order in the ranks of the workers when the bosses deemed it necessary. Bosses are not going to negotiate with people who can't or won't deliver what is agreed to. The bureaucracy developed centralized structures and methods of control and direction that fit its role and function. In times of mobilization the union leaders, rather than helping to overcome hesitation, view those who are mobilizing as a threat to be isolated or stopped entirely. Critically, all of this is related to structural pressures on the union leadership based on their role within capitalist relations of production rather than on personal characteristics or perspectives as the Left reformists would have it.

At times leadership will call on the services of Left militants when a show of strength is tactically advantageous, only to abandon, isolate, or purge them when things have gone as far as the leadership deems necessary. This is a crucial lesson that must be kept in mind when we consider flying squads with marshals under the direction of national and local executives. For anarchists, militant activists must reject the role of "left critics" of the bureaucracy, refuse the terms of the compromise with the bosses, and directly challenge those who seek to enforce it. It is necessary to build a rank-and-file rebellion in the unions that actually works to break the hold of the bureaucracy.

Which Side Are You on Again?

The crucial challenges facing movements for positive social change, as in the broad mobilizations opposing the 2010 G20 meetings in Toronto, involves the relationship between unions and community-based social movements. The form of alliances, coalitions, and organizations involving unions and community-based groups (antipoverty activists, no-borders activists, and anarchists) will determine the scope of opposition to states and capital and the real potential of evolving opposition to neoliberal politics. Perhaps the key point on which this challenge pivots is the question of direct action and civil disobedience, the relationship of social movements to violations of law and property destruction. These are questions of strategy and tactics to be sure, but even more they are questions of how we understand the character of the state within liberal democratic capitalist societies like Canada. These questions have been ongoing, intensifying in the period of neoliberal globalization and the emergence of alternative globalization movements and demonstrations against institutions of global state-capital, such as the G8/G20.

In events like the G20 protests and clampdown there emerge real opportunities for recognition and understanding that are not always so readily available behind the screen of "business as usual." The learning curve shifts and some things become much clearer.

One of the interesting revelations of the G20 fallout is the extent to which many in the union leadership are governed by the morals, values, and prejudices of the dominant classes. This has been expressed in the numerous calls for repression of the black bloc by would-be spokespeople of the labor movement in Canada. A rather stunning case in point has been the number of open statements of support for, indeed appeals for, the state capitalist rule of law. For some the rule of law should have held against the black bloc. Others turn to the rule of law as a statist security blanket providing the basis for—the very conditions of—their "peaceful protests," which the black bloc supposedly infringed upon. One of the most striking examples comes in the form of an incredible statement from CUPE-Ontario, my former union federation:

> Property was damaged, publically-owned [sic] police vehicles were burned, and innocent people were attacked and detained as a result of taking part in protests. All of this is wrong. What we have witnessed is nothing short of the abandonment of the rule of law, both by a small group who took part in the protests, and by a massive and heavily armed police force who were charged with overseeing them.

Having equated the black bloc with the police in their scorn, the statement goes on to say:

> And it's a sad day when some of those, who feel powerless to change the direction of their elected leaders, find in that feeling of powerlessness an excuse to break the law and vandalize the property of their fellow citizens and who, in so doing, silence the legitimate voices of so many others whose commitment to protest and dissent is matched by their rejection of violence and vandalism.

Suggesting that the black bloc is an expression of powerlessness rather than confidence is one thing, but suggesting that breaking the law renders any activists or organizers illegitimate, as the statement does, is incredible. It is the logic of the bosses and the state (who set the property laws and benefit from them in the first place). And why should we view capital as our "fellow citizens anyway?" (This is not about CUPE-O; the statement expresses sentiments that have been put forward by many in leadership positions within unions in Ontario).

The CUPE-O denunciation of direct action was echoed by the officialdom of the Ontario Federation of Labour (OFL), the provincial union federation. OFL president Sid Ryan, former CUPE-O head, boasted that OFL leadership "liaised with the Toronto Police and cooperated at every turn" during the large-scale June 26 protest. He then went further, denouncing other activists, organizers, and indeed union members: "Shamefully, a small number of hooligans used the cloak of our peaceful and lawful demonstration to commit petty acts of vandalism in the streets of Toronto." Once again the publicly stated commitment of leadership was to state capitalist order, the restricted terrain of capitalist legality that serves such an important role in neoliberal legitimation of anti-working-class policies (which are if nothing else legal).

Incredibly the Canadian Labour Congress, the national union federation, felt the need to add its voice to the chorus attacking activists: "The Canadian Labour Congress abhors the behaviour of a small group of people who have committed vandalism and destroyed property in activities related to the G20 summit in Toronto." They also felt it important to make note of their collaboration with police: "We cooperated with police in choosing the route and had hundreds of parade marshals to maintain order." How such assertions are helpful in building movements that might actually halt neoliberal capitalist regimes is not clear. What is clear is that many rank-and-file union members were troubled by these public displays of deference to the very authorities who were still holding activists and organizers, including union members.

That the CUPE-O and OFL pronouncements did not express a consensus view among union members is reflected in the rank-and-file statement released on July 5, 2010. The open letter to the Canadian Labour Congress was signed by more than 250 rank-and-file unionists. The hundreds who signed the letter included members of a variety of union locals, including CUPE, the Public Service Alliance of Canada, the British Columbia General Employees Union, United Steel Workers, Canadian Union of Postal workers, Ontario Secondary School Teachers Association, the Ontario Public Service Employees Union, and the Canadian Auto Workers. Their letter starts:

> We are labour activists, many of whom were involved in organizing against the G20 Summit in Toronto and solidarity actions across the country. After the "Peoples First" march, many of us remained on the streets throughout the weekend contesting the unprecedented militarization of our city and the G20 neoliberal agenda.
>
> We are disturbed and concerned to read the statement by Ken Georgetti, President of the Canadian Labour Congress, issued during the G20 summit. The CLC issued a statement condemning "vandalism" and declaring their commitment to working with the police throughout the summit; however, the CLC's statement is shockingly silent about the violence perpetrated by the state and police, aimed at rendering the right of people to assemble, organize and resist obsolete, brutalizing our sisters, brothers and children.

The statement then outlines the problems created by open appeals to state authority and criminalization of activists by union leadership:

The focus on vandalism and attacks on private property espoused by the CLC statement and some mainstream media outlets, expels from the debate the legitimate concerns and lived injustices of many within the labour movement who turned out to protest the G8/G20. By commission or omission this limited focus legitimizes the suspension of rights and liberties in this city, including the right to assembly and the right to political protest.

In conclusion, the rank-and-file members point ahead to the many tasks facing working-class movements more broadly:

> We as a labour movement must commit to organize social movements along with our allies in social justice, environmental justice, grass-roots, anti-poverty, anti-racist, feminist, non-status, Indigenous, Queer and international movements to challenge and resist neoliberal capitalist governments' ruthless assaults on the working people in Canada and globally. We will not and cannot win the struggle we face against the violent onslaught of neoliberalism by abandoning our allies and our communities in the wake of a massive crackdown on dissent.

In response Georgetti showed a barely restrained contempt for this broad range of members from diverse locals. He referred to their statement as fiction and addressed them as "whoever you are." Even more troubling, those who signed the letter were dismissed as activists and "retirees" (as if that's some sort of insult). Unfortunately, this response reflects long-standing defensiveness and dismissive attitudes toward critics of leadership, even when those critics are longtime, committed union members.

Georgetti also drops the hammer that is often used by labor officials against other movements and groups—the financial contributions of unions. In his words: "We expended the lion's share of staff and financial resources for the huge civil, peaceful protest on Saturday involving an estimated crowd of 40,000 people. Most all of them were there to demand the world's leaders focus on the issues of jobs, maternal health, peace, the environment, the list goes on."

In addition the CLC chair's statement makes a rather broad, though typical, assumption that most people were there to make demands on world leaders rather than, say, to show their collective power and opposition to those very leaders. Referring again to some protesters, including union members, as thugs, Georgetti goes on to lecture people on respect for state capitalist laws: "The CLC does not and will not condone that kind of behaviour or tactics perpetrated by a few and must disassociate itself from it when it appears to be part of our action. People and groups who loot and steal and vandalise are not those whom we want as allies." Never mind that these are the same sorts of accusations that are routinely used against workers during labor disputes and on picket lines.

In the current period these institutional pressures and habits have constrained working-class responses to structural transformations of neoliberalism and economic crises. Unions have sought to limit losses rather than make gains. The approach has been to negotiate severance deals that limit the harm done to former employees (and members) rather than contest the rights of employers and governments to determine the future of workplaces and workers' livelihoods.

These arrangements have also engendered a certain faith in or reliance upon the system among the working classes. Rather than seeking new relations, a new society, the institutions of the working class presented and replayed the message that working-class desires and needs could not only be met within capitalist society, but, even more, depended upon capitalism for their realization.

Such a notion played into the "trickle down" fantasies of neoliberal Reaganomics, which insisted that policies and practices that benefited business should be pursued as some of the gains made by capital would eventually find their way to the working class and the poor. Such was the justification for the massive multi-million-dollar bailouts handed to corporations as part of the economic crisis of 2008 and 2009.

This fatal position is reflected in the CLC statement around the G20: "We were exercising a democratic right to tell G20 leaders that there can be no recovery from the economic crisis unless they place a priority on the creation of good jobs." Again the demonstrations are posed simply as a request that capital try to keep workers in mind. There is no analysis here of exploitation and no recognition that neo-liberal advances for capital have been underlined by lousy jobs. Even more troubling is this incredible passage in the statement: "We are urging the leaders not to move too quickly to austerity measures and warning them not to chop public services." Urging political and economic leaders *not to move too quickly to austerity measures?* The problem is not austerity, but the timeline in which it is imposed? Austerity is all right if it is portioned out over time? No sign of fight-back, resistance, or alternatives?

The problem is not simply one of the unions, however. Community organizers have too often avoided real engagement with labor institutions or have avoided forums in which they might meet and discuss matters with rank-and-file union members. Sometimes younger activists have little sense of the tenor and rhythm of workplace organizing. While I was involved in antipoverty organizing I helped to establish a phone tree for members interesting in doing worker solidarity. A crew of younger members came forward to say that they did not know what "rank and file" meant.

Too often the measure of labor involvement in coalitions in Ontario has been the amount of money given to a campaign, the forcefulness of rhetoric from high profile leaders, or the winning of a motion at this or that convention. The only way that any sort of credible resistance movement is going to be forged in Ontario, however, is through a redoubling of efforts to make connections between grassroots community groups and rank-and-file workers.

It is crucial to stress that during the G20 actions, as in previous protests like the June 15, 2000, riot at Queen's Park and the Quebec City protests against the Free Trade Area of the Americas in 2001, there were rank-and-file union members who chose to go to the front to challenge the police lines, fences, and weapons that are the material expressions of the rule of law. Many refused simply to march to hear empty speeches or uphold the fetishization of "peaceful protest" regardless of actual effectiveness. After Quebec City, in fact, rank-and-file unionists, angry with the defeatist call of leadership to march away from the fences and into an empty field miles away from the meeting site, demanded direct action training in their locals when they returned home. Many of those who called for and those who gave direct action workshops were CUPE members.

Indeed direct action workshops are something anarchist and syndicalist activists can and should offer. They should also be ready to provide picket support, help build flying squads or industrial unions among unorganized workers as the Industrial Workers of the World (IWW) have done among squeegee workers in Vancouver, and involve themselves in the creation of joint union-community antiracism and antipoverty working groups. Activist workers must play an active part in building true rank-and-file flying squads and working groups whether in a union, in unorganized workplaces, or unemployed.

Community activists should attend labor council meetings and make themselves familiar to union activists. They should also attend picket lines and organize support for striking workers. One project I helped initiate in Toronto was an autonomous flying squad of community members organized specifically for strike solidarity actions. Another activity I have helped to organize, while doing antipoverty work, has been plant-gate discussions to talk with workers and distribute literature during shift changes. My experience as an auto assembly worker taught me that people will readily take a range of reading material to have on hand for breaks.

Other Developments

In order to move beyond the union/community activist, direct action/ mass action dichotomies it is important to learn from real efforts by union members to develop militant action in solidarity with community organizers. Happily there have been important developments that have emerged in working-class political practice in Ontario over the last few years. Unfortunately, these developments have been overlooked and too little remarked upon in recent debates and discussions over the G20 protests.

One of the most interesting developments to emerge in Toronto, suggesting an incipient syndicalism, and one that has increased its profile since the G20 protests is the Greater Toronto Workers' Assembly (GTWA). Initiated partly in response to the economic crisis, the Assembly participants sought to address the constraints of existing movements, including the labor movement, and bridge the gaps that keep elements of the working class divided along lines of race, class, gender, sexuality, but also job sector, workplace, employment, and citizenship status. The GTWA's aim is solidarity among the working class, defined in the broadest possible terms. Members are involved in many of the community groups that helped organize the militant G20 opposition, including OCAP and No One Is Illegal. As well, union members who have contributed to, and participated in, direct actions, have been active members of the GTWA. The Assembly provides an organizational space to get past the gap that exists locally between broad anticapitalist politics and the very specific, particular focus of many community-based groups and unions (Upping the Anti 2010).

One of the primary concerns expressed within the Workers' Assemblies has been the isolation of the labor movement and its seemingly growing insulation from the concerns of larger sections of the working class. As Rosenfeld and Fanelli (2010) recall:

> As well, we were struck by the unwillingness of the organized labour movement to ally with increasingly isolated and impoverished sectors of the working-class, to link up with community movements, and to address larger social issues. The trade unions were, and still are, mired in concessions, wage freezes, and other kinds of compromises with employers, and a politics of tailing after the social democratic NDP, which was going nowhere—hence the lack of a real fight-back against the crisis.

The First Assembly was held in October 2009, following a series of broad *consultas* involving participants from a range of unions and social-movement groups in Ontario. Crucially, the Assembly decided at the initial gathering that membership would be based on individual membership rather than by group. This decision has helped to overcome some of the tokenism of alliances and coalitions. It was also decided that membership would be regional, rather than casting a net for support from outside the Toronto area, which would allow for real face-to-face involvement and discourage symbolic membership. As of this writing, one assembly had been held in 2011 with another scheduled.

In the lead-up to the G20, ahead of the Fourth Assembly, the GTWA joined a range of community advocacy groups to host several events to mobilize opposition to the G20. The GTWA stressed the need to build for the protests with an eye toward longer-term organizing that might challenge political and economic elites on a more durable basis (that would not dissipate after the big event was over, as has too often been the case). GTWA members state their goals as follows:

> To bring together activists within the broad working class movement, to explore the experiences and approaches to struggle that both unite and divide us as a starting point for overcoming divisions and building greater collaboration, exchange, strategic discussion and action amongst us.
>
> To share our understanding of the problems created by capitalism and the current economic crisis and the need to develop alternative visions that challenge the logic and power of private corporations, and the states that back them, over our lives.
>
> To identify and develop concrete strategies and organizational forms of struggle which defend working-class people's immediate needs and lay the groundwork for an equitable and democratic alternative to our present economic and political system. (Greater Toronto Workers' Assembly)

The GTWA currently involves over 250 members and almost 300 supporters (who maintain varying levels of activity). Members come from about forty community organizing groups and approximately twenty unions or locals. The GTWA has formed committees or caucuses around a range of organizing issues, including campaigns; membership, finance, and outreach; internal political development and education; publications and external political education; culture; labor; and G20 solidarity (Rosenfeld and Fanelli 2010). The early goals have been regular city-wide assemblies, and discussions have occurred over mutual aid and shared resources such as publications, a website, and eventually a space. Educational forums and discussion series have already progressed and happen regularly, on a range of topics, including movement publishing and analysis of the crisis.

Participants in the GTWA have been clear from the outset that contemporary movements in Canada, labor and otherwise, pose an inadequate challenge to state capitalist political, economic, and social systems. While movements have been inspiring, and at times impressive, their capacities for struggle have come up short against powerful opponents. The GTWA stands as one attempt to address, and move beyond, those shortcomings. It makes an appeal for a new politics, with new organizational structures and infrastructures. As Rosenfeld and Fanelli (2010) suggest:

> Seeking to move beyond coalition and network politics the Assembly is an organization that individuals belong to without giving up their membership and allegiances to community organizations, unions and left groups. We are committed to developing our understanding of what we're up against, who our potential allies are, and to organize and act in new ways that will take us from a politics of resistance to emancipatory alternatives.

The GTWA is attempting to transcend the divide between mass action and direct action, between labor movements and militance. Members seek a renewed labor movement that is democratic and participatory and that does nor eschew practices that challenge state capitalist terms of legitimacy and illegitimacy. Still, the usual challenge, and the big question, remains: "If the assembly process is to give birth to an organizational force capable of challenging the hegemony of capital, however, it must surmount the impasse of the old politics of networks and coalitions, as well as business-as-usual unionism" (Rosenfeld and Fanelli 2010). Interestingly, the GTWA has seen labor activists working alongside and in productive harmony with direct-action anarchists, including groups like Common Cause, which have long supported, in an outspoken but critical manner, direct actions during alternative globalization protests. Here is an example of labor and anarchy complementing each other rather than posing opposite ends of a stark dichotomy.

Significantly, the politics and practices of the GTWA have resonated powerfully with working-class activists in locales elsewhere in Canada, notably Vancouver, Ottawa, Montreal, and London, Ontario. There is then the possibility for a new form of labor organization that is connected throughout the country. This new politics and new organizing could hint at a new national labor politics beyond the legal structures of collective bargaining, contracts, and craft or trade divisiveness. Participants are attempting to shift the focus from protest to alternatives.

Conclusion: Rank-and-File Autonomy

For anarchists, rank-and-file autonomy means being prepared and willing to fight independent of the leadership and against it when required. As syndicalists and anarchists they are upfront, open, and direct about confronting the conservatives within their unions. No gloss should be put on efforts to contain rank-and-file militancy or excuse it for any reason. Anarchists contest reformist approaches to rank-and-file movements, which would position them as little more than conscientious pressure groups.

None of this is meant to imply that the leadership is holding back an otherwise radical membership. That is, of course, romantic silliness. Rather, the point is that developing militancy within union movements requires a clear recognition of the necessity for developing experiences of effective struggle that go beyond what the bosses or governments would permit and, at the same time, viewing honestly how the current unions' leadership impedes this effort.

Rank-and-file movements offer a space for radicalizing workers to come together and focus members' energies. When people engage in struggles, whether strikes or demonstrations against neoliberalism, they develop at least some sense of collective power, confidence, and an experience of doing things differently. This experience can encourage an openness to more radical ideas and practices with which to address the problems we find ourselves facing. Mainstream unions, even where some resources are given to political education, are generally not going to present and develop openly radical alternatives. Certainly the leadership of mainstream unions cannot be expected to do so. As workers, this area is one in which anarchists can and should be active. Putting forward radical alternatives, agitating for those alternatives, and working to make them real should be part of the work that is done within rank-and-file networks.

These are merely first steps in a long process of building rank-and-file opposition, though it is encouraging that green syndicalist efforts have been well received in various contexts. They are initiatives for working-class self-activity that should not be limited to being a democratic complement to the bureaucracy. Anarchists and syndicalists try to think beyond this stage to see something more in the emergence and growth of autonomous rank-and-file networks. The need to build a resistance that includes rank-and-file unionists, nonorganized workers, nonstatus workers, and migrants is critical.

The capitalist offensives of the last decades have broken down working-class organization and infrastructures of resistance. Dismantling employment standards, freezing the minimum wage, eliminating rent controls, and deepening cuts to social assistance for unemployed workers have made life more precarious for broadening sections of the working class. "This situation is not just a matter for deep humanitarian concern but a serious warning to the workers' movement. If the working class is reaching such a level of polarization and a section of it is experiencing such misery and privation, we are in a profoundly dangerous situation" (Clarke 2002, 1).

Many workers are becoming tired of engaging in struggle only to find themselves under attack not only by the boss, but by the officials of their own unions. The questionable actions of the Ontario Federation of Labour, especially during a recent Conservative Party convention in Ontario, when the OFL organized a separate action and then left the scene when activists were attacked by police, have convinced some grassroots activists and rank-and-file workers of the need to make end runs around the unions officialdom and develop real alliances. Certainly this is a healthy development, one which anarchists must take seriously. This means meeting with fellow rank-and-file workers and having serious discussions about what sort of assistance anti-capitalist movements can offer in their struggles against conservative leadership, policies and structures in their own unions. This is something to which even anarchists who are less comfortable with workplace organizing can contribute.

For green syndicalists, anarchist ideas are not the responsibility of a vanguard or intellectual elite of "advanced workers." Anarchist militants should not attempt to push movements into proclaiming an "anarchist" position but should instead work to preserve their anarchist thrust, that is, their natural tendency to be self-organized and to fight militantly for their own interests. This approach assumes the perspective that social movements will reach their own logic of creating revolution not when they as a whole necessarily reach the point of being self-identified "anarchists," but when as a whole (or at least an overwhelming majority) they reach the consciousness of their own power and exercise this power in their daily lives, in a way consciously adopting the ideas of anarchism.

The green syndicalist organizer does play an ideological part within social movements, for anarchists, in actively contesting and opposing the opportunistic elements that emerge to shift the movement toward the dead ends of electoralism or vanguardism (Weaver 2005). Anarchists and syndicalists also play a part in opposing the reactionary elements that emerge within movements that seek to limit the movement from within or make concessions to opponents in the state and capital.

As an active minority within the working class, green syndicalists work to provide a rallying point, through example and ideas, in struggles against capital and the state as well as standing against authoritarian ideologies or practices in working-class organizations. For the most part they remain small though growing. They certainly have no illusions about "leading" the anarchist movement, let alone the working class more broadly. Instead they try to maintain relationships of solidarity and mutual aid with anarchists who take different strategic and tactical approaches while disagreeing honestly with them. Given the marginalized position of syndicalist, anarchist and communist ideas alike within the working class in North America at this point in time, much work is still spent in getting green syndicalist perspectives out there.

There are many important lessons from anarcho-syndicalist history that need to be learned, revived, and shared. At the same time, the work contemporary anarchists have put into building rank-and-file workers' committees, flying squads, and precarious workers' networks shows that, despite their numbers, they can make real material contributions to building the capacities of working people for struggle. These interventions are not made in a vanguardist way to build our organization or recruit members but in a principled way to help build class-wide resources and win material gains.

If alliances, coalitions, and organizations are to develop and thrive on a more durable basis, it is important not to paper over differences and divergences and instead to have honest, open, and critical analysis of challenges and obstacles to building movements that might be capable not of criticizing or complaining about neoliberal regimes but of stopping them.

In expressing fidelity to the "rule of law," what is really being affirmed is fidelity to the state and to the bosses. Any union that expresses fidelity to the rule of law must be responsive to questions. To do so is to negate the rich history of the working class and labor movements. For much of its history, right up to the present, the union movement has been "against the law," its actions criminalized, its organizers arrested and worse. Anyone who's been on a picket line when it really mattered should know how to take the "rule of law." Would CUPE-O have sided with the rule of law against the sit-down strikers of the 1930s, against the Windsor strikers of 1945, the Mine Mill strikers of 2000–2001, against the various general strikes? What about the recent factory occupations? Siding with the rule of law really does make clear "which side you are on," to answer one of labor's ancient questions. Unions that uphold the "rule of law" in the face of employers who steadfastly and routinely do not are accepting conditions of capitulation and defeat. Nothing less.

Indeed it was through the UAW's 1945 strike against Ford that unions won what would become crucial features of collective bargaining in Canada, including the closed shop and dues check-off. Notably the strike against Ford climaxed with a direct action in which workers surrounded the plant with vehicles creating a barricade of the facility, several cars deep, that prevented any attempt by the company to access the plant and its materials while preventing the police from reaching workers. It was a show of creative militance, in which union flying squads played a significant part, that remains a compelling testimony to struggles beyond the confines of legal bargaining.

Mass actions are, of course, desirable and necessary. Unfortunately organizers in mainstream unions often draw a false dichotomy between mass action and direct action. What is necessary is mass direct action. And, while numbers are important, they are not sufficient. Large scale rallies that do little to challenge economic and political power holders, or give them cause to change course, must be viewed critically. At some point economic and political disruption, imposing a real cost on the political and economic elites who would impose harmful social, political, and economic policies upon us, is required. This is one of the things that the history of the labor movement, and strike action, teaches. So the question is really about how to show the *social power* of the working class, not simply a portion of its numerical strength. Even large-scale protests can be ignored if they do not demonstrate a real capacity to effect social change, as numerous demonstrations against various neoliberal governments in Ontario has shown. This is a lesson that should certainly have been learned by the longtime organizers who crafted the CUPE-O statement.

Even more, union organizers are wrong to assume that rank-and-file members will not engage in direct action, or even prefer it. The frustration expressed by rank-and-file members after actions from Quebec City to Toronto over the lack of preparation for more militant action during mass demos, and calls for greater preparation next time, offer ongoing testimony to this fact.

As P. J. Lilley and I have suggested elsewhere: "If anarchists are to seize the opportunities presented by recent upsurges in anarchist activity and build anarchism in movements that have resonance in wider struggles, then we must face seriously the challenges of organization, of combining and coordinating our efforts effectively. We will be aided in this by drawing upon the lessons of past experiences and avoiding, as much as possible, past errors." It is clearly a mistake to approach movements either as recruitment grounds (as more formal organizations often do) or as social clubs (as is more typical for informal groups). For contemporary anarchist communists the key is to be involved in a principled way that prioritizes building working-class strength in their communities, neighborhoods, and workplaces rather than in building their specific organizations. Developing particular anarchist organizations is worthwhile only in as much as it contributes to that larger goal.

Conclusion

Beyond Leftism: A Nonproductivist Radicalism

Through an engagement with green syndicalism there emerge certain points of similarity between anarcho-syndicalism and ecology. These include, but are by no means limited to: decentralization; regionalism; direct action/sabotage; autonomy; and pluralism and diversity. Syndicalists, however, can no longer disregard—as some Marxists (see Raskin and Bernow 1991; Blackie 1990; Burkett 2006) are wont to do—the linkages between industrialism, hierarchy, and ecological destruction. The mass-production techniques of industrialism cannot be reconciled with ecological sustenance, regardless of whether bosses or sturdy proletarians control them; that is a lingering illusion from a more innocent, progressive time. In this regard the utopians have surely been more insightful.

Ending capitalist relations of production remains necessary for a radical transformation of the social world because these relations encompass many positions of subordination. However, this is only one aspect of a neoradical project. As Laclau and Mouffe (1985) and Aronowitz (1990) argue, to be anticapitalist does not have to imply being pro-ecology. The often ugly histories of socialist movements with respect to nature provide us with ample evidence of that. Again, neither does it suggest that a unity between the discourses is impossible. It just means that any connection will only result from an articulation.

For this very reason, when one speaks of socialization of the means of production as one element in the strategy for a radical and plural

164

democracy, one must insist that this cannot mean only workers' self-management, as what is at stake is true participation by all subjects in decisions about what is to be produced, how it is to be produced, and the forms in which the product is to be distributed. Only in such conditions can there be *social appropriation* of production. To reduce the issue to a problem of workers' self-management is to ignore the fact that the workers' "interests" can be constructed in such a way that they do not take account of ecological demands or demands of other groups which, without being producers, are affected by decisions taken in the field of production. (Laclau and Mouffe 1985, 178)

This is especially important when one remembers the positions occupied by déclassé elements within radical ecology and their exclusion from the production process. Furthermore, green syndicalists reject the workerist premises of "old-style" leftists who argue that issues such as ecology are external to questions of production and only serve to distract from the essential task of organizing workers, at the point of production, toward emancipation. Within green syndicalist discourses ecological concerns cannot, with any reason, be divorced from questions of production or economics. Rather than being represented as strictly separate discursive universes, nature, production, economics, or workplace become understood as endlessly contested topographical features in an always shifting terrain.

The workplace is but one of the sites for extension of a democratic imaginary. Given the prominent position of the workplace under capitalism, as a realm of capitalist discipline and hegemony, activists must come to appreciate the significance of locating struggles within everyday workplace relations. Within a green syndicalist perspective workplaces are understood as sites of solidarity, innovation, cultural diversity, and personal interactions expressed in informal networks and through multiple antagonisms. In turn, those social realms that are typically counterposed to the factory within radical ecology discourses—Bookchin's "community"—should be recognized as influenced by matters of accumulation, profit, and class. The character of either realm is not unaffected by workplace antagonisms.

This "steel cage" appears inescapable only because it remains isolated, practically and conceptually, from a host of important social,
cultural, and political-economic dynamics operating inside and out
of workplaces proper. Critical to any discussion, work organizations
must be seen as series of settings and situations providing choices
that are constrained, but not immutably, by the broader fabric of
the society into which they are woven. (Guarasci and Peck 1987, 72)

Radical ecology must now come to recognize that expressions of
working-class radicalism are conditioned by multiple engagements,
of capital, labor, ecology, and so forth, across various social spheres.
Emergent conditions for an end to nature, the outcome of a multiplicity of battles over economics and production, have simultaneously
made possible the "end of work"—a state of affairs once desired by
radical working-class activists. If organizing is to occur at all, at least
in the counterexploitative sense of organizing toward emancipation, it
enters an articulatory arena in which ownership, production, distribution, consumption, or elimination—as moments in the humanization
of nature—are already constituted as ecological.

As envisaged within green syndicalist discourses, human relations
within nature occupy the grounds upon which the most significant of
transformations must occur. The transformations in question make
recognizable moments of exploitation within the presently given constituting of both "nature" and "human." Furthermore these interpenetrations of exploitative relations contradict any univocality in the
articulation of responses. Thus a moving away from workerist assumptions, as always tentative and unsure, is undertaken for green syndicalism through the emphasized mutuality of what had been—for political
action—prior separates, that is, nature, culture, workers. Significantly,
it is expressed in a manner that excludes the merely sequential linkages
of socialist discourse.

We are not trying to overthrow capitalism for the benefit of the proletariat. In fact, the society we envision is not spoken to in any leftist
theory that I've ever heard of. Those theories deal only with how

to redistribute the spoils of exploiting the Earth to benefit a different class of humans. We need to build a society that is not based on the exploitation of Earth at all—a society whose goal is to achieve a stable state with nature for the benefit of all species. (Bari 1994, 57)

Green syndicalism calls for the replacement of profit-driven capitalist production with socially necessary production through means that are ecologically sensible (Purchase 1994). Production would be organized around human and ecological considerations rather than the rapacious requirements of accumulation and expansion characterizing capitalist organization. Syndicalists suggest that if production and distribution are to be carried out in a dark-green manner workers must stop producing for capitalist elites according to the whims of the market. Syndicalists are interested neither in profit nor in growth, and their conception of industry has nothing to do with the consumerism of advanced capitalism. Finally, green syndicalist discourses express a realization that overcoming ecological devastation depends upon shared responsibilities for developing convivial ways of living wherein respectful relations, both within our own species and with other species, are nurtured.

Wobbly demands for a shortened work week are derived from a belief that little time would be necessary for social production once it is freed from the consumerist demands of an expansionist, growth-oriented, capitalist megamachine. Within this perspective it is held that industrialism as a system or mode of power—not individual productive processes—compels the slavery of the workplace and regimentation of everyday living, that is, the systemic rationalization of labor and extensions of control.

There is some sense that the reintegration of production with consumption, organized in an egalitarian and democratic fashion—such that members of a community contribute to social production—will allow for a break with consumerism. People might consume only that which they have had a hand in producing; people might use free time for creative endeavors rather than tedious, unnecessary production of luxuries; and individual consumption might be regulated by the capacities of individual production, like personal creativity, not from the hysterics of mass advertising. Syndicalism might be freed thusly from requirements of growth or mass consumption characterizing industrialism as "social relations" (Purchase 1994). Green syndicalism, as opposed to Marxism or even anarcho-syndicalism, opposes large-scale, centralized, mass production. Green syndicalism does not hold to a socialist optimism of the liberatory potential of industrialism.

Ecological calls for a complete, immediate break with industrialism, however, contradict radical eco-philosophical emphases upon interconnectedness, mutualism, and continuity. Simple calls for a return to nature reveal the lingering fundamentalisms afflicting much ecological discourse. The idea of an immediate return to small, village-centered living as espoused by some deep ecologists and anarchists is not only utopian, it also ignores questions concerning the impacts that the toxic remains of industry would continue to inflict upon their surroundings. The specter of industrialism will still—and must inevitably—haunt efforts at transformation, especially in decisions concerning the mess that industry has left behind. How can we disconnect society from nature, given the mass interpenetrations of social encroachments upon nature, such as global warming or depletion of the ozone layer? This interference may be understood as the process of civilization itself—the socialization of nature. Where do you put toxic wastes? What of the abandoned factories? How will decommissioning occur? One cannot just walk away from all of that. Without romanticizing the role played by workers, green syndicalists are aware that workers may offer certain insights into these problems.

Green syndicalism is concerned with the possibilities for reconstructed spaces for living that might be better integrated with the local ecology, rather than a simple return to a wilderness that no longer exists (Purchase 1994). The wounds caused by industrialism will require much care. Even acts of ecological recovery are social acts, the results of articulatory practices not accessible simply by referring to nature. A break must be made but it cannot, given the existence of enormous industrial structures and relations, be immediate.

In responding to this dilemma, green syndicalists (Kaufmann and Ditz 1992; Purchase 1994; Jakopovich 2007; Shantz 2010) have tried to ask the crucial question of where those who are currently producers might belong in the multiple tasks of transformation—cultural as well as ecological. They have argued that radical discourses in ecology can no longer leave out producers. Given the ongoing character of articulation, they will either be allies or enemies. Green syndicalism, almost alone among radical ecology, suggest that peoples' identities as producers, rather than representing fixed entities, may be articulated against industrialism. The processes of engaging this articulation, wherein workers understand an interest in changing rather than upholding current conditions, present the perplexing task that has as yet foiled ecology.

For their part theorists of green syndicalism envision the association of workers toward the dismantling of the factory system, its work, hierarchies, regimentation (Kaufmann and Ditz 1992; Purchase 1994; Jakopovich 2007; Shantz 2010). This work may involve a literal destruction as factories may be dismantled or perhaps converted to "soft" forms of localized production. Likewise, productive activity can be conceived in terms of restoration, including research into a region's natural history. Reconstruction might be understood in terms of food and energy provision or recovery monitoring. These are acts in which all members might be active, indeed will need to be active in some regard. These shifting priorities—toward nonindustrial relations generally—express the novelty of green syndicalism as both green and syndicalist. It is no longer simply a discourse of industrial control, with the factory as the training ground of social reconstruction.

Of course, these matters are to be decided democratically by those involved, not handed down from theory. Green syndicalists consider it important that ecology engage with workers in raising the possibilities for resisting, challenging, and even abandoning the megamachine. However, certain industrial workshops and processes may be necessary (how would bikes or windmills be produced, for example), a point that is recognized within green syndicalism (see Purchase, 1994). The failure to develop democratic workers' associations would then seem to render even the most well-considered ecology scenarios untenable. Not engaging such possibilities restricts radicalism to mere utopia building (Purchase 1994; Shantz and Adam 1999; Jakopovich 2007; Williams 2009a).

Dismantling industrial capital, the radical approach to industrialism, would still require the participation of industrial workers, provided it is not to be carried out as part of an authoritarian articulation. Any radical articulation, assuming it be democratic, implies the participation of industrial workers in decision-making processes. Of course, as has already been stated, the democratic character of any articulation cannot be assumed; the possibility for reaction, to the exclusion of workers (see Foreman 1991; Watson 1994; Zerzan 2008a, 2008b), is ever-present. One need only be reminded of certain discourses discussed above to imagine the articulation of ecology as part of an authoritarian problematic. One sees this in ecological fundamentalism, articulated as pure separation, or within certain manifestations of strengthened corporatist alliances pitting labor/capital against ecology. In the absence of a grassroots articulation with workers, any manner of authoritarian, elite articulation, even ones that include radical ecology (see Foreman 1991; Watson 2005; Jensen 2006), might be envisioned.

There has been recognition among green syndicalists (Purchase 1994; Kaufmann and Ditz 1992; Shantz and Adam 1999; Jakopovich 2007; Williams 2009a) that excluding workers implies a totalitarian response to ecological destruction, usually taking the form of a centralized and bureaucratic enforcement of regulations. A contradiction again emerges against ecological imperatives of mutualism, connectedness, democracy, decentralization, and participation. Constituting an ecological "*Gestalt* switch" among workers implies that radical ecology engage in tasks of organizing with workers. This is suggestive of a communicative, democratic, dialogic approach opposing the closure of authoritarian fundamentalist approaches.

Anarcho-syndicalism reveals an affinity with ecological discourses in traditional calls to replace state and capital with decentralized federations of bioregional communities (Purchase 1994). Green syndicalists argue for the construction of "place" around the contours of geographical regions, in opposition to the boundaries of nation-states that show only contempt for ecological boundaries as marked by topography, climate, species distribution, or drainage. Affinity with bioregionalist themes is recognized in green syndicalist appeals for a replacement of nation-states with bioregional communities. For green syndicalism such communities might constitute social relations in an articulation with local ecological requirements to the exclusion the bureaucratic, hierarchical interference of distant corporatist bodies.

Local community becomes the context of social/ecological identification. Green syndicalism encourages knowledge deepening as a remedy to the anonymous, detached, knowledge broadening that is endemic to the conditions of postmodernity. This does not mean complete isolation or insularity, however. Rather it speaks to social relations, either local or federated, organized in a decentralized, grassroots manner. Likewise any federative associations, if it is assumed they be democratic, would be voluntary.

Bari (1994) notes the difficulties environmentalists face by virtue of being "outsiders," not part of the community. There is a lingering need for local involvement to overcome the "Greenpeace phenomenon" of entering an area and "hijacking" a local campaign without building alliances or leaving any roots. One aspect of a green syndicalist theoretic, thus, involves ecology activists helping workers to educate themselves about regional, community-based ways of living (Bari 1994; Purchase 1994). A green syndicalist perspective encourages people to broaden and unite the individual actions, such as saving a park or cleaning up a river, in which they are already involved toward regional efforts of self-determination protecting local ecosystems (Purchase 1994; Williams 2009b). It might be argued that only through such concerted community-based ecological defense against the excesses of corporate plunder might change occur.

Eco-defense, then, should begin at local levels: in homes, workplaces, and neighborhoods. It cannot be overlooked that this new radicalism lives largely outside of the state and is organized toward self-reliance. Indeed, the "neighborhood" reappears as the context in which a particularist politics can be expected to thrive. Thus, green syndicalist discourses urge that people identify with the ecosystems of their locality and region and work to defend those areas through industrial and agricultural practices that are developed and adapted to specific ecological characteristics. Green reconstruction around interconnected regionalism is envisioned as nonhierarchical, for no region can claim predominance over others on ecological grounds (Purchase 1994; Jakopovich 2007).

The point here, however, has not been (nor is it for theorists of green syndicalism generally) to draw plans for the green syndicalist future; to do so would be to succumb to utopianism. Specific questions about the status of cities, organization of labor, means of production, or methods of distribution cannot here be answered. They are the outcome of active articulation. Most likely there will be many varieties of experimental living; some are already here, like Temporary Autonomous Zones (TAZ), Permanent Autonomous Zones (PAZ), squats, and co-ops. These are the new politics of "organizing" (Shantz 2009b).

I have simply tried to address the outlines of an ecological syndicalism and points that inspire activism. In order to accomplish this I have identified emerging themes that I have drawn from green syndicalist praxis and offered my interpretations of those themes.

An ecological mythopoetic that articulates notions of personal and collective responsibilities through characteristic themes of the inviolability of life, preservation of species, and long-range consequences might yet transcend individual social divisions or conflicting interests. There is, however, no intrinsic, determinate relation between nature and human cultural manifestations. Articulation disrupts the knowledge/control nexus; reality is no longer independent of forms of knowledge applied to capture it. Rather, reality may be said to exist as that knowledge; it is influenced by that knowledge. Ethics, environmental or otherwise, appears at the nexus of human interference and the dissolution of nature. Decisions are no longer fixed or given permanence by a natural order (nature has disappeared). We are compelled to construct them—but out of what? Traditional touchstones have shattered under the wheels of modernity. New fundamentalisms emerge while past "truths" are undermined. Any eco-myth—wherein ecology becomes a nodal point for convergence—might be one of unity in diversity, and cooperation rather than Watson's desired *submission* to an organic system or natural order.

The articulatory nature/human conjoining is not necessarily anti-authoritarian. IWW activists, in conflicts against misanthropic expressions within Earth First!, are well aware of that. "Not taking up ecological issues leaves these issues open for a green fascism and a situation where the cost of repairing the damage is taken out of the working class instead of the boss class" (Kauffman and Ditz 1992, 42). Given the construction of workers and stated aims not to change social structures, deep ecology remains especially susceptible to such articulations. As Laclau (1990) reminds us, there always remains the possibility for degeneration into reaction. Thus green syndicalism represents a simultaneous two-fold articulation; both "against" and "for" radical ecology.

Concerns over EF!, and especially over deep ecology philosophies, have emerged within Wobbly circles and could further threaten relations. Indeed, the various misanthropic statements made by EarthFirst!ers have already led to some Wobblies dissociating themselves from EF!

As Laclau and Mouffe (1985, 190) assert, "without the possibility of negating an order beyond the point that we are able to threaten it, there is no possibility at all of the constitution of a radical imaginary— whether democratic or of any other type." However, if green syndicalism fails to offer visions for a positivity of the social, that is, proposals for positive social relations, it will remain unsuited to serve as a nodal point in the reconstitution of social relations. In other words, green syndicalism cannot provide a radical alternative by operating strictly as negativity, by asserting antisystemic demands alone. That belongs to the realm of oppositional rather than transformative politics. Negativity remains important in its effects of destabilizing each established system of differences, but it is not sufficient for the construction of a popular pole of social transformation. As Laclau and Mouffe (1985, 189) argue: "If the demands of a subordinated group are presented purely as negative demands subversive of a certain order, without being linked to any viable project for the reconstruction of specific areas of society, their capacity to act hegemonically will be excluded from the outset."

The analysis offered in this book suggests that green syndicalism is presently preoccupied with the politics of opposition, the assertion of antisystemic demands. The bulk of efforts are engaged in the negation, through tactics of *scission, detournement,* and mockery and calls to abolish work, of the industrial social order (the "megamachine"). The general lack, with some limited exceptions, of strategies through which novel, positive reconstructions of social relations might be constituted probably accounts, at least partly, for the relegation of green syndicalism to a condition of marginality.

Of Marginality and Experiments Against Alienated Labor

Harter (2004) notes that much of "official" or recognized environmental activism, in particular Greenpeace, comes from the so-called "new middle class" or new managerial classes of upwardly mobile, educated professionals. This in part accounts for the distance that has persisted between environmental groups and blue-collar workers, the poor and unemployed. Conversely, green syndicalism, in addition to expressing working-class concerns and developing within blue-collar circles, has been, in part, a discourse of marginal workers—those who reject the alienating character of labor and capitalist relations generally. "And when it comes to liberating their desires, some Wobblies are in the forefront of that as well; many members have chosen to drop-out [*sic*] (of the wage system) rather than work as a slave" (Meyers 1995, 73). Certainly many themes constituting radical ecology suggest the supposedly premodern, irrational themes of marginals, who have no interest in the amassed shit of consumerism. Taken together, marginality might be understood as a movement (or more properly as movements)-of-the-day against both state and capital.

It should be noted that a major source of environmental movement activists has long been those whom I have here termed (respectfully) the "marginals," that is, the "neo-proletariat" of Gorz (1982), the "decommodified" of Offe (1985), and the "déclassé" of Bookchin (1987). The marginals are those who exist primarily outside of the labor market and may include students, the unemployed, the underemployed, injured workers, retirees, or street persons. Ongoing evidence (Rifkin 1995; Aronowitz and DiFazio 1995; Aronowitz and Cutler 1998) suggests that the part-time or temporary workers, those working illegally, the unemployed, welfare recipients, the scholastically supported, and volunteers have supplanted the regular, permanent wage worker. To these groups we might add the clandestine self-sustainers, those who support themselves through such creative, and sometimes illegal, activities as squatting or "dumpster-diving." Current indications suggest that globalist transformations of the labor market will ensure that the marginal "class" continues to grow. Significantly, it is this very grouping that was excluded (except as negativity) from the Keynesian compromise. They represent those whose "labor," because it is truly independent from capital, is deemed illegitimate, unworthy, or even nonexistent. As environmental activists, their predominance is to be found, conversely, as direct actionists or "eco-warriors," often engaging in singular feats of bravery, and as low-profile "foot soldiers" performing mundane and anonymous, though usually necessary, tasks such as canvassing or distributing information.

This most complex of groupings, however, is vastly underrepresented in works of sociology and is vastly undertheorized. When one speaks of the distance separating sociology theorists from movement activists, this critique is most acute where it specifically regards members of the déclassé strata.

Considered most broadly the environmental movement activists who have received the overwhelming burden of attention sociologically are those belonging to the "new (middle) class." This "new class," about which there has been much recent theorizing, includes those who are relatively well educated and with backgrounds in the public sector or human services professions (Aronowitz and Cutler 1998). Offe (1985) argues that these constituents are most likely, given their experiences, to be aware of the threats posed by further modernization in the varied realms of politics and economy. They typically occupy high-profile, relatively powerful decision-making positions, (i.e., campaigner, lobbyist, researcher, director), within the various, especially mainstream, environmental organizations. Within his analysis Offe expects a radicalized Left-ecology formation to be encouraged predominantly by elements of the new middle class within environmentalism.

Environmentalists have also drawn participants from among the old middle class—farmers, shopkeepers, or artisans—looking to protect their always tenuous positions against the threatening transformations wrought through globalization. Within such manifestations as organic farming, cooperative agriculture, green craftwork, or health food co-ops have been articulated a mutualism of concern and resistance against the multiple eroding of traditional territories and lifeways. Some (Cotgrove and Duff 1980; Offe 1985) have addressed the old middle class presence to theorize the environmental movement as a defensive or conservative reaction to conditions of modernity.

The organizing and direct action practices of marginals (and even of the old middle classes) have been largely overlooked because of academic sociology's misplaced preoccupation or infatuation with its new class cousins. As the new class impetus has typically been not to radicalize, this preoccupation has necessarily meant that academic sociology has tended to overemphasize activism of mainstream varieties.

To his credit, Offe recognizes that the emergence of a counterhegemonic articulation involving labor also depends largely upon a willingness among traditional organizations of the Left to develop positive relations with those among the decommodified. His schema allows for an opening of avenues by which the limits of the industrial proletariat might be transcended in both directions (Offe 1985, 864). However, Offe remains relatively silent about participation by members of decommodified groupings and focuses almost all of his theorizing upon new middle-class elements. Offe maintains his assumption that a counterhegemonic articulation of ecology will most likely come through the dominant efforts of the new class members. However, he mistakenly downplays, in making this assumption, the possible articulations with "old class" or "peripherals" which might take very different shapes.

Members of decommodified groupings may well provide the most likely point of alliance with workers. There are a number of characteristics of déclassé members that support this claim: many are themselves ex-workers, now unemployed but with friends still working; many have been through the labor market and have developed much contempt for the demeaning aspects of that process; many are themselves poor or of working-class backgrounds; and, significantly, their praxis arises from confrontation with state and capital (permitting a transparency of power relations at that level). Recently unemployed people often bring an ecological understanding developed through direct workplace experiences; some have witnessed chemical contamination, while others are injured workers.

Members of déclassé groupings have long offered highly original, creative resistance to corporatist articulations. Such creativity, largely missed by sociologists, is expressed in the squats, co-ops, alternative organizations, Temporary Autonomous Zones (TAZs) and Permanent Autonomous Zones (PAZs), "rags" and "zines," and "do-it-yourself" experimentalism. These activities—of which green syndicalism seems one expression—reveal emergent spontaneous reformulations of communitarian, as opposed to corporatist relations.

Within the environmental movement—I would argue—it is among the marginals that the loudest voices for radicalization are raised. From among this grouping an improbable though highly interesting articulation with labor is emerging, one that deserves, nay demands, further sociological attention.

The conservator lifestyles of déclassé constituents, consumptive minimalism, solidarities, sharing, reusing, have much to teach us. This includes—perhaps most crucially—the rejection of disembedded, detached and alienating work.

It is my view that green syndicalism suggests a "marginals/working-class" articulation expressed around themes of the control or even the abolition of work and the rejection of extensions of workplace discipline and control into wider social realms. It might even be argued that presently this articulation offers the main vocalization of radicalized relations between ecology and labor. It may also offer some explanation as to the limited nature of radicalization. To understand green syndicalism means that we must understand the ways in which it has expressed déclassé or marginal themes.

As for any articulatory manifestation, this particular articulation may always remain small—especially given the traditional distrust of marginals by the working classes (Offe 1985; Adkin 1992b). This point is especially pertinent given that the distrust seems to have hardened with the ravages and concomitant fears attending globalist transformations. The tactics of direct action and the mocking of production and "jobs" may continue to alienate many workers who still dream of "making it" or of securing the "good life" promised by capitalism. I would suggest that this is a highly complex and potentially rich area requiring further research and analysis.

Future manifestations of radical articulation may be expected to emerge from among marginal realms. Such spheres of activism may, at least, offer the more radical of expressions. However, given the indeterminacy of articulation, a radicalization could emerge from among the new class as Offe (1985) suggests, or even, though less expected, from elements of the old class. There may emerge, at various locations, certain limits (see Offe 1985; Adkin 1992b; Zerzan 2008a, 2008b), but there remains the possibility for articulation beyond those limits—possibly through the renovation of radical labor themes.

Green Syndicalism and Radical Ecology: "Talking Nature Blues"

Through the present discussion I hope to have illustrated that human relations with nature do not exist independent of discursive structures. The materiality of the world is presented to us as discourse. These discourses do not belong to nature itself. Rather the elements of nature "exist" within the discourses constituting them. They are provided for and maintained by specific means of production, which are in turn always discursive (Laclau 1990). What matters is the way in which nature is variously constructed within contestatory languages, that is, how we talk about "nature." As Laclau (1990, 218) reminds us, "nature is also as discursive as a poem by Mallarme, and the pressure it exerts on us always takes place in a discursive field." While nature does not exist for us outside of all discursive contexts, that is not the same as saying that nature has no existence independent of such contexts.

Rather, we may distinguish between a "real" nature and constructions of ecological values, keeping in mind that there is no necessary relationship between them (Daly 1994; see also Laclau 1990). This brings up a distinction between epistemological and political projects and returns us, once more, to the distinction that Sorel (1941) has drawn between *nature naturelle* and *nature artificielle*. In similar fashion, Daly (1994, 176) reminds us of the distinction that Rorty makes "between the unobjectionable realist claim that 'the world is out there'—i.e. that the world exists independently of human language/mind/history—and the claim that 'truth is also out there.'" Nature does not give voice to a set of truths which need only be discovered. As Daly (1994, 176) argues, nature can be described only within specific discourses and is, therefore, always susceptible to competing depictions. This susceptibility raises the possibility for alternatives, such as a new nature, to emerge:

> For example, environmental and animal-rights campaigners are also, at some level, involved in a process of grammatical subversion in which the articulation of their demands transcends the traditional human/non-human distinction in an alternative construction of political identity which attempts to establish a new semantic authority over the idea of a 'we' and 'global belonging', etc. (Daly 194, 199)

To speak of values inherent to nature, as the deep ecologists are wont to do, is to speak a historically contextualized language. The qualities of nature are themselves open to redescription or rejection. Thus the character of these "inherent" qualities of nature are represented differently depending upon the social practices through which we encounter nature, or upon such contextual matters as region or era. Nature is always articulated from the struggle of competing discourses or language games with which we describe the world. Nature is fixed within a vocabulary that allows us to make some sense of it. Categories such as "wilderness," "environment," "jobs," or "worker," rather than signifying objectivities, emerge from specific articulatory practices (Daly 1994).

As I have attempted to illustrate, nature can be articulated in widely ranging interpretations and discourses and can be deployed for vastly different purposes. This articulation reflects the instability of nature as nodal point. Nature as pure possibility remains undefined—indeed it is undefinable—in any absolutist sense, which provides for the strength of nature as a realm of freedom but paradoxically leaves it open to discourses of unfreedom. Green syndicalism, therefore, cannot be precise, given nature's "silence."

Much of the impediment to radicalized green articulation derives from the location of ecological devastation within an anthropocentric discursive hierarchy, society, which accepts it as necessary, thereby inhibiting its constitution as antagonism. This "common sense" perspective operates around a society/nature duality, a hierarchical opposition in which the first term is provided a position of superiority (associated with a machine myth, i.e., progress, efficiency, stability etc.). This opposition serves to shape social practice as it enters institutions such as unions and is extended in consumer culture. Green syndicalism seeks to displace this oppositional hierarchy, opening spaces of difference and autonomy.

As noted earlier, a site of antagonism is constituted when a relation of subordination comes to be articulated as a relation of oppression. Relations of subordination, in themselves, only establish differential positions between social actors, and, as Laclau and Mouffe (1985, 153) contend, they only suggests oppression if we assume a "unified nature" or an "essential subject," such that every deviation from it becomes an oppression. "It is only to the extent that the positive differential character of the subordinated subject position is subverted that the antagonism can emerge" (Laclau and Mouffe 1985, 154).

Relations of subordination only become defined as relations of oppression through articulatory practices.

Within the discursive space of mainstream environmentalism and eco-socialism, relations of subordination between nature and humanity are contained as legitimate positions of difference. Terms such as "resources" or "environment" serve as markers for a system of differential positivity, in which case they do not designate positions of antagonism. Viewed in this light, a "jobs versus environment" discourse might be understood as a stabilization attempt; ecological devastation is simply the price we pay for a high living standard (eco-socialist "jobs and environment" discourses just represent a lowering of the price).

Subversion of the differential positivity signaled by these categories requires the intervention of a different discursive formation, for example "inherent rights of nature," "web of life" or "imbeddedness within nature"—the varied elements of an ecomyth, or mobilizing imagery. Green syndicalism calls an end to the construction of "environment" as object, wherein "nature" and "human" become ideological separates. Rather than limiting their efforts within existing political configurations green syndicalists have engaged a process of political reconstruction. These subversive strands emerge from various radical discourses, anarchist, libertarian, socialist and conservative, and are not strictly democratic discourses (Laclau and Mouffe might suggest that each reflects a specific articulation within the equivalent logic of the democratic revolution). Ecology has no essence in itself, it depends upon clusters of relations around it. And only if ecological struggle is articulated with the struggles of workers, women, minorities, or the poor does it express a nonauthoritarian (a large part of what I have termed radical) struggle. The necessity of articulation raises, of course, the question of solidarity.

According to Daly (1994, 179), a conviction to act in solidarity results from continuing political attempts to make competing descriptions "compatible with people's wider descriptions (cultural, social, religious, etc.) of themselves and the world." It may thus be inferred that peoples' views about nature have nothing to do with the uncovering of a truth. Were that the case, green syndicalism might be freed of many of the difficulties it now faces. Rather, depictions of the "natural world" come to be accepted because of their compatibility with other discursive universes—such as those in which hopes and desires are carried:

> This perspective also recognizes the attempts by ecological groups to extend humanist-type rights to animals and the environment, thus not only breaking with the tradition of fixing the identity of right-holders in advance, but also modifying the identity of right-holders in regard to the construction of a more integrated type of planetary belonging. (Daly 1994, 196n9)

Daly argues that deciding among values (humanist, ecologist, etc.) occurs through historical and political struggles over identification, not through progressive revelatory discoveries of what, for example, the human or the ecological, really are. "What it is to be a human being, and the nature of personhood, cannot finally be determined. These will always depend upon the social practices we share and the frontiers of social exclusion: in short, politics" (Daly 1994, 196n9). We may speak of nonhuman nature in the same manner when looking to the political constitution of ecological identities among humans. It is important to recognize that ecological mobilizations are largely engaged in struggles over the desecration of ancient dogmas or prejudices about the "natural" position of nature (as resource, as environment, as wilderness, etc.). Green syndicalism offers new languages for speaking about nature that restrict the frontiers of exclusion in favor of developing a more inclusive or encompassing tradition of nature (and the human). What is at stake is nothing less than a reconfiguration of what it means "to be" as a human—the construction of new human beings.

Across the Great Divide: Wilderness and Workplace

The machine/nature chasm is perhaps best reflected in radical conceptions of wilderness (the anti-machine). Wilderness only comes into being (as in certain deep ecology discourses and among specific campaigns of Earth First!) at its moment of nullification. Wilderness—or environment for that matter—is the map by which we locate nature's loss in civilization. According to Melucci (1992, 65) "the planetarization of the world system means that there is no longer an 'outside world': territories and cultures exist only as internal dimensions of the same system." Contemporary theorizing, thus, stands at "the end of nature," wherein nature can be understood as any relations outside of or independent of human penetration and interference. Nature is, for green syndicalism, not an externalized objectivity in need of rescue—marked by its designation as "environment" (or as "wilderness," which becomes much the same thing).

Preservation presumes, though many deep ecologists seem to miss the point, radical social transformation and raises for us the question of how we might organize social relations. Recognition of this critical relationship has emerged within green syndicalism. "'We want to expand our horizons from dealing strictly with wilderness issues to dealing with systematic change,' observes Darryl Cherney. 'We have to change the way corporations do business in the world. That's the way to save rain forests and to aid natives who are displaced when the forests are logged'" (Short 1991, 184). Radical questions regarding how we might live are implicit in ecology and raise both ethical and practical concerns within a context of radical unfixity in which nothing, including nature, can any more be taken for granted.

Human relations with nature still pose crucial and difficult questions for radicalism. Those relations, under capitalism, have taken the form of "jobs" where nature and labor both become commodified. Indeed nature as "resources" and work as "jobs" provide the twin commodity forms that have always been necessary for the expansion of the market (see Polanyi 1944). Thus the capitalist regimes are still aspects of radical contention; accumulation, growth, and commodification remain crucial concerns for ecological politics. Questions concerning the organizing of life are still radical questions, though what might constitute acceptable answers has changed. One might ask: "What does work—intervention in nature—mean for ecology?" Or as Bari has asked with respect to Earth First! radicalism: "Should our slogan be No Compromise in Defense of Mother Earth on Public Land Only, and Only If We Don't Have to Confront the Corporate Power Structure?" (Bari 1994, 105). The time has come for radicals to answer with their actions. Attentiveness to ecology means that entire realms of work, leisure (work's accomplice), sustenance, need—what might be called production—must be brought into question.

⩔

Throughout the present analysis certain themes have been explored. At a broad level there emerges a question concerning the extent to which the language games of green syndicalism might express the problematic and uncertain constitution of ecology as nodal point in an emergent anti-hegemonic formation or, in Sorelian terms, the forging of social myth. Recognizing this requires identification and understanding of the sustaining worldviews of green syndicalism. Within the praxis of green syndicalism one sees evidence of "deep-green" perspectives by which are expressed new conceptions of relations with nature and with work. Analysis suggests tentative formulations of nonanthropocentrism, workers' radicalism, and possibilities for some synthesis that unites yet transcends each.

The examination of the language games and the practices of syndical ecology disclose the immanent (de)constructions of categories—"worker," "nature" and "class"—suffusing radical ecology projects. One sees the transformation of communicative tools among syndicalist (re)constructions of ecological vocabulary. In their demands to transform discourse, certain green syndicalists (Kaufmann and Ditz 1992; Bari 1994; Purchase 1994) have engaged in the desecration and tentative reconstitution of previously given notions of class, class struggles, and nature. Where ecology exhibits a specifically "class" character it does so necessarily as part of an anthropocentric problematic. The sustaining of class is only possible through the humanization and appropriation of nature through production. Indeed, it must finally be admitted that class serves as little more than a marker for one's position with regard to the social appropriation of nature.

Class as a totalizing category has become obfuscatory. But we should not mourn its loss; if we can no longer speak of class, we can finally speak of workers.

Green syndicalist alternatives impel a critical reconceptualizing of the aims of production and forms of consumption as currently constituted; they may challenge the very meanings of work and time in a bourgeois context. Such efforts may open spaces for a (re)constitution of the "commons" by denying the right of any single totalizing discourse, be it one of culture, gender, theory, or class, to assert privilege over, to enclose, all other discourses. Rather than return to foundational assertions, green syndicalism may instead emphasize social and political consequences and situational considerations. These pragmatic concerns, by which we address the political (or ecological) implications of constructed knowledge, provide us with the discourses to justify forms of knowledge according to purpose or impact.

The visions offered within radical ecology may sometimes appear unrealistic or even impossible (Lange 1990). It remains to be seen if these developments are suggestive of any durable and broadening synthesis of ecology and labor beyond established categories. However, that is a question that cannot here be answered; and anyway, it will only be answered in the doing. My concern has been with a detailed interpretation of a particular articulation. The motive for the present research is to develop a theoretical perspective that may be used to better understand the specificity of ecology movement activism. Theory requires a more sophisticated understanding of those struggles that allow for the reproduction of categories, inhibit or encourage the forging of unity, and prevent alternatives from emerging. The emergence of the green syndicalist voice is important in the possibilities it raises; there is always the chance that they will stay possibilities only. This possibility derives partly from a rejection of legitimizing mechanisms or externally imposed definitions. However, studies of social movements have undertheorized the place and significance of nonrational aspects of movement rhetoric. Thus, the present analysis offers an attempted understanding of nonrational discursive strategies—beyond critiques of applicability or "realism."

Marginal struggles open spaces for experimentation in liberty. Through the construction of "futures in the present" they nurture possibilities that cannot be measured in immediate terms of success or failure, realism or unrealism. For example, we may see interesting paths toward radicalized articulations between ecology and labor in the theoretics of subterranean radicalisms that receive scant attention even from the Left. When analyzing the discourses of marginal actors we must remember that their significance emerges as part of an ongoing dialogue within the context of the broader movements in which they are articulated. The worldview offered within green syndicalism differs not only from that of mainstream environmentalism but also, and importantly, from that of other radicals (see especially Watson 1994). "Interests and groups defined as marginal because they have become 'disturbances' in the system of social integration are precisely the struggles that may be the *most* significant from the point of view of historical emancipation from social hierarchy and domination" (Aronowitz 1990, 111). I hope that *Green Syndicalism* draws some attention to marginalized but novel ways of living in the present that attempt to refuse and transcend work and other forms of domination and control that are interwoven with ecological destruction.

References ⤓ *Index*

References

Abbey, Edward. 1976. *The Monkey Wrench Gang*. New York: Avon Books.

———. 1986. "Letter to the Editor." *Bloomsbury Review*. April–May.

———. 1988. *One Life at a Time Please*. New York: Henry Holt.

Adam, Barry D. 1993. "Post-Marxism and the New Social Movements." *Canadian Review of Sociology and Anthropology* 30, no. 3:316–33.

Adkin, Laurie E. 1992a. "Counter-Hegemony and Environmental Politics in Canada." In *Organizing Dissent*, edited by William K. Carroll, 137–56. Toronto: Garamond Press.

———. 1992b. "Ecology and Labour: Towards a New Societal Paradigm." In *Culture and Social Change*, edited by Colin Leys and Marguerite Mendell, 75–94. Montreal: Black Rose Books.

———. 1998. *The Politics of Sustainable Development: Citizens, Unions, and the Corporations*. Montreal: Black Rose Books.

Adkin, Laurie, E., and Catherine Alpaugh. 1988. "Labour, Ecology, and the Politics of Convergence." In *Social Movements/Social Change: The Politics and Practices of Organizing*, edited by Frank Cunningham, Sue Findlay, Marlene Kadar, Alan Lennon, and Ed Silva, 48–73. Toronto: Between the Lines.

Anderson, K., and J. M. Jacobs. 1999. "Geographies of Publicity and Privacy: Residential Activism in Sydney in the 1970s." *Environment and Planning A* 31, no. 6:1017–30.

Arblaster, Anthony. 1991. "Thomas Paine: At the Limits of Bourgeois Radicalism." In *Socialism and the Limits of Liberalism*, edited by Peter Osborne, 51–72. London: Verso.

Aronowitz, Stanley. 1990. *The Crisis in Historical Materialism*. Minneapolis: Univ. of Minnesota Press.

———. 1996. "Towards Radicalism: The Death and Rebirth of the American Left." In *Radical Democracy: Identity, Citizenship, and the State*, edited by David Trend, 81–101. London: Routledge.

Aronowitz, Stanley, and Jonathan Cutler. 1998. *Post-Work: The Wages of Cyber-Nation.* New York: Routledge.

Aronowitz, Stanley, and William DiFazio. 1995. *The Jobless Future: Sci-Tech and the Dogma of Work.* Minneapolis: Univ. of Minnesota Press.

Bahro, Rudolf. 1982. *Socialism and Survival.* London: Verso.

————. 1984. *From Red to Green.* London: Verso.

Bari, Judi. 1990. "Expand Earth First!" *Earth First!* September 22, 5.

————. 1991. "Why I Am Not a Misanthrope." *Earth First!* February 2, 25.

————. 1994. *Timber Wars.* Monroe: Common Courage Press.

————. 2001. "Revolutionary Ecology." *Hodgepodge* 7:35–38.

Barker-Benfield, Ben. 1973. "The Spermatic Economy: A Nineteenth Century View of Sexuality." In *The American Family in Socio-Historical Perspective,* edited by Michael Gordon, 336–72. New York: St. Martin's Press.

Barnes, Robby, and Sylvie Kashdan. 2002. "Summing Up the Kaiser Strike and Lockout, 1998–2002." http://flag.blackened.net/revolt/inter /seattle/kaiser.html.

Barol, B. 1990. "Eco-Activist Summer: Earth First! vs. the Loggers in California." *Newsweek,* July 2, 60.

Bekken, Jon. 2001. "The Tragedy of Fosterism." *Anarcho-Syndicalist Review* 31:13–22, 36–37.

Berg, John. C. 2002. *Teamsters and Turtles?: U.S. Progressive Political Movements in the 21st Century.* New York: Rowman and Littlefield.

Biehl, Janet. 1989. "Ecofeminism and Deep Ecology: Unresolvable Conflict?" In *The Anarchist Papers 2,* edited by D. I. Roussopoulos, 19–31. Montreal: Black Rose Books.

————. 1991. *Finding Our Way: Rethinking Ecofeminist Politics.* Montreal: Black Rose Books.

————. 1995. "'Ecology' and the Modernization of Fascism in the German Ultra-Right." In *Ecofascism: Lessons From the German Experience,* edited by Janet Biehl and Peter Staudenmaier, 32–73. Edinburgh: AK Press.

Black, Bob. 1985. *The Abolition of Work and Other Essays.* New York: Autonomedia.

————. 1995. *Beneath the Underground.* Port Townshend, WA: Feral House.

————. 1997. *Anarchy After Leftism.* San Francisco: C.A.L. Press.

Blackie, Duncan. 1990. *Environment in Crisis.* London: S.W.P.

Boggs, Carl. 1986. *Social Movements and Political Power: Emerging Forms of Radicalism in the West.* Philadelphia: Temple Univ. Press.

Bookchin, Murray. 1978. "Beyond Neo-Marxism." *Telos* 36:5–28.

———. 1980. *Toward an Ecological Society.* Montreal: Black Rose Books.

———. 1982. *The Ecology of Freedom.* Montreal: Black Rose Books.

———. 1986. *Post-Scarcity Anarchism.* Montreal: Black Rose Books.

———. 1987. *The Modern Crisis.* Montreal: Black Rose Books.

———. 1989. *Remaking Society.* Montreal: Black Rose Books.

———. 1990. *The Philosophy of Social Ecology.* Montreal: Black Rose Books.

———. 1993. "The Ghost of Anarcho-Syndicalism." *Anarchist Studies* 1, no. 1:3–24.

———. 1995. *Social Anarchism or Lifestyle Anarchism: An Unbridgeable Chasm.* Edinburgh: AK Press.

———. 1997. "Deep Ecology, Anarchosyndicalism and the Future of Anarchist Thought." In *Deep Ecology and Anarchism: A Polemic,* edited by Freedom Press, 47–58. London: Freedom Press.

Bookchin, Murray, and Dave Foreman. 1991. *Defending the Earth.* Edited by Steve Chase. Boston: South End Press.

Bourdieu, Pierre. 1987. "What Makes a Social Class? On the Theoretical and Practical Existence of Groups." *Berkeley Journal of Sociology* 32:1–18.

Bowles, Samuel, and Herbert Gintis. 1987. *Democracy and Capitalism.* New York: Basic Books.

Braverman, Harry. 1974. *Labor and Monopoly Capital: The Degradation of Work in the Twentieth Century.* New York: Monthly Review.

Brecher, Jeremy. 1972. *Strike!* San Francisco: Straight Arrow Books.

Bridges, William. 1995. "The Death of the Job." *The National Times,* September, 44–48.

Brym, Robert. 1998. "Social Movements and Politics." In *New Society: Sociology for the 21st Century,* 461–75. Toronto: Harcourt Brace.

Bullard, Robert, D. 1990. *Dumping in Dixie: Race, Class and Environmental Quality.* Boulder: Westview Press.

Bullard, Robert D. (ed.). 1993. *Confronting Environmental Racism: Voices From the Grassroots.* Boston: South End Press.

Bullard, Robert D., and Beverly Hendrix Wright. 1986–87. "Blacks and the Environment." *Humboldt Journal of Social Relations* 14, nos. 1–2:165–84.

———. 1987. "Environmentalism and the Politics of Equity: Emergent Trends in the Black Community." *Mid-American Review of Sociology* 12, no. 2:21–38.

Burgmann, Meredith, and Verity Burgmann. 1998. *Red Union: Environmental Activism and the New South Wales Builders' Labourers' Federation.* Sydney: UNSW Press.

Burgmann, Verity. 2000. "The Social Responsibility of Labour versus the Environmental Impact of Property Capital: The Australian Green Bans Movement." *Environmental Politics* 9, no. 2:78–101.

Burkett, Paul. 2006. *Marxism and Ecological Economics.* Amsterdam: Brill.

Buss, Alexis. 2001. "What Happened to Teamsters and Turtles?: Arctic Drilling, the Labor Movement, and the Environment." *Industrial Worker* 98, no. 8:1, 5.

Callinicos, Alex. 1990. *Against Postmodernism.* Cambridge: Polity.

Campbell, Jim. 1994. "The Litton Bombing: 10 Years Later." In *Canadas,* edited by Jordan Zinovich, 177–82. New York/Peterborough: Semiotext(e)/Marginal Editions.

Carr, Barry. 1996. "A New Era for Labor Internationalism? The Experience of NAFTA 1994–1996 in Historical Perspective." American Sociological Association paper. New York, August 16–20.

Carroll, William K., and Robert S. Ratner. 1996. "Master Frames and Counter-Hegemony: Political Sensibilities in Contemporary Social Movements." *Canadian Review of Sociology and Anthropology.* 33, no 4:407–35.

Carty, Anthony. 2008. "Marxism and International Law: Perspectives for the American (Twenty-First) Century?" In *International Law on the Left: Re-examining Marxist Legacies,* edited by Susan Marks, 169–98. Cambridge: Cambridge Univ. Press.

Cassio, Jim, and Alice Rush. 2009. *Green Careers: Choosing Work for a Sustainable Future.* Gabriola: New Society Publishers.

Castells, Manuel, Shujiro Yazawa, and Emma Kiselyova. 1996. "Insurgents Against the Global Order: A Comparative Analysis of the Zapatistas in Mexico, the American Militia, and Japan's AUM Shinrikyo." *Berkeley Journal of Sociology* 40:21–59.

Chase, Steve. 1991. "Whither the Radical Ecology Movement." In *Defending the Earth,* edited by Steve Chase, 7–26. Boston: South End Press.

Clarke, John. 2002. The Labor Bureaucracy and the Fight Against the Ontario Tories. Unpublished manuscript.

Cleaver, Harry. 2000. *Reading Capital Politically.* Edinburgh/Leeds: AK Press/Anti/Theses.

Clow, Michael. 1986. "Marxism and the 'Environmental Question': An Assessment of Bahro." *Studies in Political Economy* 20 (Summer): 171–86.

Cohen, Jean 1985. "Strategy or Identity: New Theoretical Paradigms and Contemporary Social Movements." Social Research 53, no. 1:663–716.

Cotgrove, Stephen, and Andrew Duff. 1980. "Environmentalism, Middle-Class Radicalism, and Politics." *Sociological Review* 28, no. 2:333–51.

Daly, Glyn. 1994. "Post-Metaphysical Culture and Politics: Richard Rorty and Laclau and Mouffe." *Economy and Society* 23, no. 2:173–200.

Darnovsky, Marcy. 1995. "Introduction." In *Cultural Politics and Social Movements,* edited by Marcy Darnovsky, Barbara Epstein, and Richard Flacks, vii–xvii. Philadelphia: Temple Univ. Press.

Day, Richard J. F. 2005. *Gramsci Is Dead: Anarchist Currents in the Newest Social Movements.* Toronto: Between the Lines.

DeCaux, Len. 1978. *The Living Spirit of the Wobblies.* New York: International Publishers.

Deitche, Scott M. 2010. *Green Collar Jobs: Environmental Careers for the 21st Century.* Santa Barbara: Praeger.

Deutsch, Steven, and Donald Van Houten. 1974. "Environmental Sociology and the American Working Class." *Humboldt Journal of Social Relations* 2, no. 1:22–26.

Devall, Bill. 1979. "Reformist Environmentalism," *Humboldt Journal of Social Relations* 6:129–58.

————. 1988. *Simple in Means, Rich in Ends: Practicing Deep Ecology.* Salt Lake City: Peregrine Smith Books.

Devall, Bill, and George Sessions. 1985. *Deep Ecology: Living As If Nature Mattered.* Salt Lake City: Peregrine Smith Books.

Dobson, Andrew. 1990. *Green Political Thought: An Introduction.* London/Boston: Unwin Hyman.

Douthwaite, Richard. 1999. *The Growth Illusion: How Economic Growth Has Enriched the Few, Impoverished the Many, and Endangered the Planet.* Gabriola: New Society Publishers.

Dubofsky, Melvyn. 1969. *We Shall Be All.* Chicago: Quadrangle Books.

Early, Steve. 2009. *Embedded With Organized Labor: Journalistic Reflections on the Class War at Home.* New York: Monthly Review.

Eckersley, Robyn. 1989. "Green Politics and the New Class: Selfishness or Virtue. *Political Studies* 37, no. 2 (June): 205–23.

Eder, Klaus. 1990. "The Rise of Counter-Culture Movements Against Modernity: Nature as a New Field of Class Struggle." *Theory, Culture and Society* 7:21–47.

Engler, Mark. 2008. *How to Rule the World: The Coming Battle Over the Global Economy.* New York: Nation Books.

Epstein, Barbara. 1996. "Radical Democracy and Cultural Politics: What About Class? What About Political Power?" In *Radical Democracy: Identity, Citizenship, and the State,* edited by David Trend, 127–39. London: Routledge.

Faber, Daniel, and James O'Connor. 1993. "Capitalism and the Crisis of Environmentalism." In *Toxic Struggles: The Theory and Practice of Environmental Justice,* edited by Richard Hofrichter, 12–24. Philadelphia: New Society Publishers.

Fellner, Kim. 2008. *Wrestling with Starbucks: Conscience, Capital, Cappuccino.* New Brunswick: Rutgers Univ. Press.

Foreman, Dave. 1989. *Ecodefense: A Field Guide to Monkeywrenching.* Tucson: Ned Ludd Books.

———. 1991. *Confessions of an Eco-Warrior.* New York: Harmony Books.

Foster, John Bellamy. 2000. *Marx's Ecology: Materialism and Nature.* New York: Monthly Review.

———. 2002. *Ecology Against Capitalism.* New York: Monthly Review.

Foster, John Bellamy, Brett Clark, and Richard York. 2011. *The Ecological Rift: Capitalism's War on the Planet.* New York: Monthly Review Press.

Frankel, Boris. 1987. *The Post-Industrial Utopians.* Cambridge: Polity Press.

Ghimire, Kléber. 2011. *Organization Theory and Transnational Social Movements: Organizational Life and Internal Dynamics of Power Exercise Within the Alternative Globalization Movement.* Lanham, MD: Lexington.

Gorz, Andre. 1980. *Ecology as Politics.* Boston: South End.

———. 1982. *Farewell to the Working Class.* London: Pluto Press.

Gramsci, Antonio. 1971. *Selections From Prison Notebooks.* New York: International Publishers.

Gray, Elizabeth Dodson. 1993. "We Must Re-Myth Genesis." In *Radical Environmentalism: Philosophy and Tactics,* edited by Peter C. List, 55–69. Belmont: Wadsworth.

Green, James R. 1974. "Comments on the Montgomery Paper." *Journal of Social History* 7, no. 4:530–35.

Grundmann, Reiner. 1991. "The Ecological Challenge to Marxism." *New Left Review* 187 (May–June): 103–20.

Guarasci, Richard and Gary Peck. 1987. "Beyond the Syndicalism of Workplace Democracy." *The Insurgent Sociologist* 14, no. 2 (Summer): 49–76.

Guattari, Felix and Toni Negri. 1990. *Communists Like Us.* New York: Semiotext(e).

Gusfield, Joseph, R. 1992. "Nature's Body and the Metaphor of Food." In *Cultivating Differences: Symbolic Boundaries and the Making of Inequality,* edited by Michèle Lamont and Marcel Fournier, 75–1030. Chicago: Univ. of Chicago Press.

Halfmann, Jorst. 1988. "Risk Avoidance and Sovereignty: New Social Movements in the United States and West Germany." *Praxis International* 8, no. 1:14–25.

Hall, Stuart. 1988. "The Toad in the Garden: Thatcherism Among the Theorists." In *Marxism and the Interpretation of Culture,* edited by Cary Nelson and Lawrence Grossberg, 35–74. Urbana and Chicago: Univ. of Illinois Press.

Hardt, Michael, and Antonio Negri. 2000. *Empire.* Cambridge, MA: Harvard Univ. Press.

———. 2001. *Empire.* Cambridge, Mass.: Harvard Univ. Press.

———. 2004. *Multitude: War and Democracy in the Age of Empire.* New York: Penguin.

Hargis, Mike. 2001. "Birth of an International Libertarian Network: A Libertarian Manifesto for the 21st Century." *Anarcho-Syndicalist Review* 32:11–16.

Harter, John-Henry. 2004. "Environmental Justice for Whom? Class, New Social Movements and the Environment: A Case Study of Greenpeace Canada, 1971–2000." *Labour/Le Travail* 54:83–120.

Harvey, David. 2007. *Limits to Capital.* London: Verso.

Heider, Ulrike. 1994. *Anarchism: Left, Right, and Green.* San Francisco: City Lights.

Hirst, Paul Q. 1986. *Law, Socialism, and Democracy.* London: Allen and Unwin.

Hobsbawm, E. J. 1979. "Inside Every Worker There Is a Syndicalist Trying to Get Out." *New Society* 48, no. 861:8–10.

Holton, R. J. 1980. "Syndicalist Theories of the State." *Sociological Review* 28, no. 1 (February): 5–21.

Jakopovich, Dan. 2007. "Green Unionism in Theory and Practice." *Synthesis/Regeneration* 43:16–20.

Jennings, Jeremy. 1991. "Syndicalism and the French Revolution." *Journal of Contemporary History* 26:71–96.

Jensen, Derrick. 2006. *Endgame, Volume 1: The Problem of Civilization*. New York: Seven Stories Press.

Jezer, Marty. 1977. "The Socialist Potential of the No-Nuke Movement." *Radical America* 11, no. 5:63–71.

Johnson, L. E. 1991. *A Morally Deep World*. Cambridge: Cambridge Univ. Press.

Kaufmann, Mark, and Jeff Ditz. 1992. "Green Syndicalism." *Libertarian Labor Review* 13 (Summer): 41–42.

Kivisto, Peter. 1986. "What's New About the 'New Social Movements'? Continuities and Discontinuities With the Socialist Project." *Mid-American Review of Sociology* 11, no. 2:29–44.

Kornblugh, Joyce L. 1964. *Rebel Voices: An IWW Anthology*. Ann Arbor: Univ. of Michigan Press.

Kornegger, Peggy. 1996. "Anarchism: The Feminist Connection." In *Reinventing Anarchy, Again*, edited by Howard J. Ehrlich, 156–68. Edinburgh: AK Press.

Kropotkin, Peter. 1955. *Mutual Aid*. Boston: Extending Horizons Books.

———. 1994. *Fields, Factories, and Workshops*. Montreal: Black Rose Books.

Laclau, Ernesto. 1988. "Metaphor and Social Antagonisms." In *Marxism and the Interpretation of Culture*, edited by Cary Nelson and Lawrence Grossberg, 249–57. Urbana and Chicago: Univ. of Illinois Press.

———. 1990. *New Reflections on the Revolution of Our Time*. London: Verso.

———. 1991. "The Impossibility of Society." *Canadian Journal of Political and Social Theory* 15, no. 1–3:24–27.

———. 2005. *On Populist Reason*. London: Verso.

———. 2007. *Elusive Universality*. New York: Routledge.

Laclau, Ernesto, and Chantal Mouffe. 1985. *Hegemony and Socialist Strategy*. London: Verso.

Lange, Jonathan, I. 1990. "Refusal to Compromise: The Case of Earth First!" *Western Journal of Speech Communication* 54 (Fall): 473–94.

Levant, Alex. 2003. "Flying Squads and the Crisis of Workers' Self-Organization." *New Socialist* 39:20–22.

List, Peter C. 1993. "Introduction." In *Radical Environmentalism: Philosophy and Tactics,* edited by Peter C. List, 1–14. Belmont: Wadsworth.

Llewellyn, A. Bronwyn. 2008. *Green Jobs: A Guide to Eco-Friendly Employment.* Avon, MA: Adams Media.

Loeb, Paul. 2004. *The Impossible Will Take a Little While: A Citizens' Guide to Hope in a Time of Fear.* New York: Basic Books.

Lowe, Graham. 2000. *The Quality of Work: A People-Centred Agenda.* Toronto: Oxford Univ. Press.

Lyons, Dan. 1979. "Are Luddites Confused?" *Inquiry* 22:381–403.

Manes, Christopher. 1990. *Green Rage: Radical Environmentalism and the Unmaking of Civilization.* Boston: Little Brown.

Martel, Larry. 1997. "Loggers vs. Greenpeace: Corporate Blackmail." *Canadian Dimension* 31, no. 5:33–34.

Marshall, Peter. 1993. *Demanding the Impossible: A History of Anarchism.* London: Fontana Press.

Masterson-Allen, S., and P. Brown, P. 1990. "Public Reaction to Toxic Waste Contamination: Analysis of a Social Movement." *International Journal of Health Services* 20, no. 3:485–500.

Meisel, James H. 1962. *The Myth of the Ruling Class: Gaetano Mosca and the Elite.* Ann Arbor: Univ. of Michigan Press.

Melucci, Alberto. 1989. *Nomads of the Present: Social Movements and Individual Needs in Contemporary Society.* Philadelphia: Temple Univ. Press.

———. 1992. "Liberation or Meaning? Social Movements, Culture, and Democracy." *Development and Change* 23, no. 3:43–77.

Merchant, Carolyn. 1993. "Ecofeminism and Feminist Theory." In *Radical Environmentalism: Philosophy and Tactics,*" edited by Peter C. List, 49–54. Belmont: Wadsworth.

Meyers, Bill. 1995. "Kicks Boss Butt?!?" *Anarchy* 41 (Winter): 73.

Miller, Arthur J. 1993. "Don't Trash the IWW." *Anarchy* 37 (Summer): 55–56.

Miss Ann Thropy. 1987. "Population and AIDS." *Earth First!* May 1, 32.

Montgomery, David. 1974. "The 'New Unionism' and the Transformation of Workers' Consciousness in America, 1909–22." *Journal of Social History* 7, no. 4 (Summer): 509–29.

Moore, Donald. 1996. "Marxism, Culture, and Political Ecology: Environmental Struggles in Zimbabwe's Eastern Highlands." In *Liberation*

Ecologies: Environment, Development, Social Movements, edited by R. Peet and M. Watts, 125–47. London: Routledge.

Mouffe, Chantal. 1988. "Hegemony and New Political Subjects: Toward a New Concept of Democracy." In *Marxism and the Interpretation of Culture,* edited by Cary Nelson and Lawrence Grossberg, 89–101. Urbana and Chicago: Univ. of Illinois Press.

———. 2005. *On the Political.* New York: Routledge.

Nash, Roderick Fraser. 1989. *The Rights of Nature.* Madison: Univ. of Wisconsin Press.

Negri, Antonio. 1984. *Marx Beyond Marx: Lessons on the Grundrisse.* New York: Autonomedia.

———. 1989. *The Politics of Subversion: A Manifesto for the Twenty-First Century.* Cambridge: Polity.

O'Connor, James. 1998. *Natural Causes: Essays in Ecological Marxism.* New York: Guilford.

Offe, Claus. 1985. "New Social Movements: Challenging the Boundaries of Institutional Politics." *Social Research* 52, no. 4 (Winter): 817–68.

Olofsson, Gunnar. 1988. "After the Working-Class Movement? An Essay on What's 'New' and What's 'Social' in the New Social Movements." *Acta Sociologica* 31, no. 1:15–34.

Omi, Michael, and Howard Winant. 1996. "Imagine There's No Heaven: Radical Politics in an Age of Reaction." In *Radical Democracy: Identity, Citizenship, and the State,* edited by David Trend, 157–64. London: Routledge.

Peet, Richard, and Michael Watts. 1996. "Liberation Ecology: Development, Sustainability, and Environment in an Age of Market Triumphalism." In *Liberation Ecologies: Environment, Development, Social Movements,* edited by Richard Peet and Michael Watts, 1–45. London: Routledge.

Pepper, David. 1993. *Eco-Socialism: From Deep Ecology to Social Justice.* London: Routledge.

Pickett, Karen. 1993. "Redwood Summer Retrospective." In *Radical Environmentalism: Philosophy and Tactics,* edited by Peter C. List, 207–12. Belmont: Wadsworth.

Polanyi, Karl. 1944. *The Great Transformation.* Boston: Beacon Press.

Purchase, Graham. 1994. *Anarchism and Environmental Survival.* Tucson: See Sharp Press.

———. 1997a. *Anarchism and Ecology.* Montreal: Black Rose Books.

———. 1997b. "Social Ecology, Anarchism, and Trades Unionism." In *Deep Ecology and Anarchism: A Polemic,* edited by Freedom Press, 23–35. London: Freedom Press.

Raskin, P., and S. Bernow. 1991. "Ecology and Marxism: Are Green and Red Complementary?" *Rethinking Marxism* 4, no. 1 (Spring): 87–103.

Rifkin, Jeremy. 1995. *The End of Work: The Decline of the Global Labor Force and the Dawn of the Post-Market Era.* New York: Putnam

Rohrschneider, R. 1990. "The Roots of Public Opinion Toward New Social Movements: An Empirical Test of Competing Explanations." *American Journal of Political Science* 34, no. 1:1–30.

Rosemont, Franklin. 1997a. "Introduction to the Life and Ravings of Slim Brundage." In *From Bughouse Square to the Beat Generation: Selected Ravings of Slim Brundage,* edited by Franklin Rosemont, 11–45. Chicago: Charles H. Kerr.

———. 1997b. "Mysteries of a Hobo's Life." In *Juice Is Stranger than Friction: Selected Writings of T-Bone Slim,* edited by Franklin Rosemont, 7–33. Chicago: Charles H. Kerr.

Rosenfeld, Herman, and Carlo Fanelli. 2010. "A New Type of Political Organization." *The Bullet,* August 6.

Ross, Andrew. 1996. "The Lonely Hour of Scarcity." *Capitalism Nature Socialism* 7, no. 3:3–26.

Roussopolous, Dimitrios. 1991. *Green Politics: Agenda for a Free Society.* Montreal: Black Rose Books.

Routledge, Paul, and Andrew Cumbers. 2010. *Global Justice Networks: Geographies of Transnational Solidarity.* Manchester: Manchester Univ. Press.

Rudig, Wolfgang. 1985–86. "Eco-Socialism: Left Environmentalism in West Germany." *New Political Science* 14 (Winter): 3–37.

Rustin, Michael. 1988. "Absolute Voluntarism: Critique of a Post-Marxist Concept of Hegemony." *New German Critique* 43 (Winter): 146–73.

Salerno, Salvatore. 1989. *Red November, Black November: Culture and Community in the Industrial Workers of the World.* Albany: State Univ. of New York Press.

Sandilands, Kate. 1992. "Ecology as Politics: The Promise and Problems of the Ontario Greens." In *Organizing Dissent,* edited by William K. Carroll, 157–73. Toronto: Garamond Press.

Scarce, Rik. 1990. *Eco-Warriors.* Chicago: The Noble Press.

Schrecker, Ted. 1975. "Labour and Environment: Alternatives Conference Report." *Alternatives* 4:34–43.

Scott, Alan. 1990. *Ideology and the New Social Movements*. London: Unwin Hyman.

Seidman, Steven. 1994. "Introduction." In *The Postmodern Turn: New Perspectives on Social Theory*, edited by Steven Seidman, 1–26. Cambridge: Cambridge Univ. Press.

Selbin, Eric. 2010. *Revolution, Rebellion, Resistance: The Power of Story*. London: Zed Books.

Sessions, George. 1988. "Deep Ecology." *Communities* 75 (Summer): 30–32.

Shantz, Jeff. 1999a. "Beyond Productivism: Syndicalism and Ecology." *Anarcho-Syndicalist Review* 25:20–23.

———. 1999b. "Searching for Peace in the 'Timber Wars': A Report on Nonviolence and Coalition Building During the Redwood Summer." *Peace Research* 31, no. 3:1–12.

———. 2003. "The Criminalization of Dissent." *Social Anarchism* 34:5–11

———. 2005. "No One Is Illegal: Organizing Beyond Left Nationalism in Fortress North America." *Socialism and Democracy* 19, no. 2:1–7.

———. 2009a. "The Limits of Social Unionism in Canada." *Working USA* 12, no. 1:113–29.

———. 2009b. *Living Anarchy: Theory and Practice in Anarchist Movements*. Academica: Bethesda/Palo Alto.

———. 2010. "Workplace Occupations in Ontario, Canada: Re-building Infrastructures of Resistance." *WorkingUSA: The Journal of Labor and Society* 13, no. 3:133–51.

———. 2011. *Against All Authority: Anarchism and the Literary Imagination*. Exeter: Imprint Academic.

Shantz, Jeff, and Barry D. Adam. 1999. "Ecology and Class: The Green Syndicalism of IWW/Earth First Local 1." *International Journal of Sociology and Social Policy* 19, nos. 7–8:43–72.

Shantz, Jeff, and P. J. Lilley. 2003. "The Platform: It's Not Just For Platformists Anymore." http://www.nefac.net/node/243.

Shapiro, Stewart. 1979. "Environmental Protection for Whom?" *Social Policy* 10, no. 1:24–28.

Short, Brant. 1991. "Earth First! and the Rhetoric of Moral Confrontation." *Communication Studies* 42, no. 2 (Summer): 172–88.

Sills, David, L. 1975. "The Environmental Movement and its Critics." *Human Ecology* 3, no. 1:1–41.

Simms, Andrew. 2005. *Ecological Debt: The Health of the Planet and the Wealth of Nations.* London: Pluto.

Sklair, Leslie. 1995. "Social Movements and Global Capitalism." *Sociology* 29, no. 3:495–512.

Smith, Mick. 2001. *An Ethics of Place: Radical Ecology, Postmodernity, and Social Theory.* Albany: SUNY Press.

———. 2006. "Environmental Risks and Ethical Responsibilities: Arendt, Beck, and the Politics of Acting into Nature." *Environmental Ethics* 28, no. 3:227–46.

———. 2007. "Wild Life: Anarchy, Ecology and Ethics." *Environmental Politics* 16, no. 3:470–87.

Smith, Sharon. 1994. "Mistaken Identity—Or Can Identity Politics Liberate the Oppressed." *International Socialism* 62:3–50.

Sorel, Georges. 1941. *Reflections on Violence.* New York: Peter Smith.

———. 1984. *Social Foundations of Contemporary Economics.* New Brunswick: Transaction Books.

Spitzer, A. 1963. "Anarchy and Culture: Fernand Pelloutier and the Dilemma of Revolutionary Syndicalism." *International Review of Social History* 8:379–88.

Sprouse, Martin. 1992. *Sabotage in the American Workplace.* San Francisco: Pressure Drop Press/AK Press.

Starn, Orin. 1997. "Villagers at Arms: War and Counterrevolution in Peru's Andes." In *Between Resistance and Revolution: Cultural Politics and Social Protest,* edited by Richard G. Fox and Orin Starn, 223–50. New Brunswick: Rutgers Univ. Press.

Stentz, Zack. 1993. "Osprey Grove Falls." In *Radical Environmentalism: Philosophy and Tactics,* edited by Peter C. List, 203–6. Belmont: Wadsworth.

Tarrow, Sidney. 1994. *Power in Movement: Social Movements, Collective Action, and Politics.* Cambridge: Cambridge Univ. Press.

Telò, Mario. 1982. "The Factory Councils." In *Approaches to Gramsci,* edited by Anne Showstack Sassoon, 200–210. London: Writers and Readers.

Thompson, E. P. 1963. *The Making of the English Working Class.* London: Victor Gollancz.

Thompson, Fred W., and Patrick Murfin. 1976. *The I.W.W.: Its First Seventy Years*. Chicago: I.W.W.

Touraine, Alain. 1981. *The Voice and the Eye: An Analysis of Social Movements*. New York: Cambridge Univ. Press.

Tucker, Kenneth. 1991. "How New Are the New Social Movements?" *Theory, Culture and Society* 8, no. 2:75–98.

Upping the Anti. 2010. "With Eyes Wide Open: Notes on Crisis and Resistance Today." *Upping the Anti* 10.

Walker, Charles. 2002. "Jobs of Environment?: A False Choice." *Industrial Worker* 99, no. 6:1,8.

Walker, R. B. J. 1994. "Social Movements/World Politics." *Millenium: Journal of International Studies* 23, no. 3:669–700.

Watson, Captain Paul. 1994. "In Defense of Tree-Spiking." In *Canadas,* edited by Jordan Zinovich, 125–27. New York/Peterborough: Semiotext(e)/Marginal Editions.

———. 2002. *Seal Wars: Twenty-five Years on the Front Lines with the Harp Seals*. Toronto: Key Porter.

———. 2005. "Report on the Death of Environmentalism Is Merely Wishful Thinking." http://lowbagger.org/watson.html. Accessed September 21, 2008.

Weaver, Adam. 2005. "Especifismo: The Anarchist Praxis of Building Popular Movements and Revolutionary Organization in South America." http://www.nefac.net/node/2081.

Williams, Chris. 2010. *Ecology and Socialism: Solutions to Capitalist Ecological Crisis*. Chicago: Haymarket.

Williams, Dana M. 2009a. "Anarchists and Labor Unions: An Analysis Using New Social Movement Theories." *WorkingUSA: The Journal of Labor and Society* 12, no. 3:337–54.

———. 2009b. "Red vs. Green: Regional Variation of Anarchist Ideology in the United States." *Journal of Political Ideologies* 14, no. 2:189–210.

———. 2011. "Why Revolution Ain't Easy: Violating Norms, Re-Socializing Society." *Contemporary Justice Review* 14, no. 2:167–87.

Witheford, Nick. 1994. "Autonomist Marxism and the Information Society." *Capital and Class* 52 (Spring): 85–125.

Wood, E. M. 1986. *The Retreat from Class*. London: Verso.

Worster, Donald. 1979. *Nature's Economy: The Roots of Ecology*. Garden City: Anchor Books.

Zerzan, John. 2005. *Against Civilization: Readings and Reflections*. Port Townshend, WA: Feral House.

———. 2008a. *Running on Emptiness: The Pathology of Civilization*. Port Townshend, WA: Feral House.

2008b. *Twilight of the Machines*. Port Townshend, WA: Feral House.

Zimpel, Lloyd, ed. 1974. *Man Against Work*. Grand Rapids: Eerdmans.

Index

Abbey, Edward: *The Monkey Wrench Gang,* 59; racist statements, 34
AFL-CIO (American Federation of Labor and Congress of Industrial Organizations), xxxiii, lvi, lvii
Alaskan Wildlife Refuge: oil drilling plan (ANWAR), xxxiii, lvi, 132
American Federation of Labor and Congress of Industrial Organizations (AFL-CIO), xxxiii, lvi, lvii
anarchism: Bari's integration with labor and ecology, 77, 86–87; Biehl and Bookchin's libertarian munici-palism and, 85–86; syndicalist, libertarian influences on, lii, 52
anarchists: affinity groups in anarcho-syndicalist unions, 88; as militants within labor, social movements, 158–60, 161
anarcho-syndicalism: and affinity with decentralized bioregional-ism, 170–72; Judi Bari, IWW, and, 58, 64; bioregionalism and, 170–72; Bookchin's critiques of, 41–44, 103–6; in building labor-environmentalist alliances, li, liv, lviii, 86–88, 102; and class struggle as broader than workplace, 43–44, 106–8; ecology and, 164; old influences in new movements,

xlvii–xlix, 161; Spanish, French (old influences in new movements), xlviii–xlix, 88; women, workers' equality and independence, 87
anthropocentrism, xxxix; rejections of dualism including, 92–94
anticapitalist struggle, role of workers in, 12, 160, 165–68
antihegemonic formations, 165, 184
antipoverty: union working groups on, 138, 140–41, 154. *See also* marginality; precarity
austerity measures, 32
Australia: Builders Labourers Federa-tion (BLF), li–lii, 132–33; green bans movement, li–lii
authoritarianism: necessity of constant opposition to, 170, 173
autonomous: Marxism, 82; zones, 172
autonomy: importance of, 81–82, 158–59. *See also* workers' control; workplace democratization
auto workers, xxxiii, 136. *See also* CAW; UAW

Bahro, Rudolf, xxxvi, 39–40, 77
bans. *See* green "bans"
bargaining, collective, xxxiv, 162

Bari, Judi: bombing of, 68–71; community alliances/roots and, 171; criticisms of Marxism, 86; direct action in Earth First!, 82; feminism of, 70, 72n14, 82–92; feminization of Earth First!, 72; IWW and, liv–lv, 58, 64; against misanthropy and anthropocentrism, 75, 91–93; Redwood Summer, 67–74; timber workers' organizing, 64–67, 77. *See also* ecofeminism; Local 1

Biehl, Janet: on anthropocentrism, xxxix, 60, 92–93; on ecofeminism and deep ecology, 89–90, 91n25; missing workers, class analysis, 85–86, 92–93

biocentrism, 89–92; criticisms of, 34–35, 40–41; as against property, 76; revolutionary implications of, 92; of syndicalist Local 1, 35, 83. *See also* deep ecology

bioregionalism, 129, 170–72

Black, Bob, 124, 128

black bloc, xiv, 148–52

blockades: of highway construction, xiii–xiv; as IWW/EF! tactic, xv, liv, 59, 65, 67, 119; as strike, direct action tactic, 144, 162

blue-collar workers, 174

Bookchin, Murray: "classless class," cultural rebellion, 14, 21; "community" discourses, 165; criticisms of factory system, 41; criticisms of Left preoccupation with "working class," 22; critique of his antisyndicalism, 103–6; on libertarian municipalism, 85n19; limitations of "community" analysis, and anticlass perspectives, 40–44; post-scarcity, 50;

regionalism and syndicalism, 88; *Remaking Society*, 55; social division of blame, xxxix

Builders Labourers Federation (BLF, Australia), li–lii, 132–33

Bush, George W.: homeland security legislation, 98; plan for oil drilling in Alaska, xxxiii, 132

business unionism, 132, 145, 158

Canadian Auto Workers. *See* CAW

Canadian Union of Public Employees. *See* CUPE

capitalism: harm to workers, xxiv; neoliberal, 1–2; relations of production as, 164–67. *See also* anticapitalist struggle

CAW (Canadian Auto Workers): eco-social alliances, 47; flying squads, 136–37, 143–45; Local 598 strike against Falconbridge, 137; rank-and-file environmental committees within, 132

CGT (Confederación General de Trabajadores, Spain), li, lii

Cherney, Darryl: bombing, FBI civil suit, 96–101; *Earth First! Journal* and, 74; need for systematic change, 183; Northern California Earth First!, 61; *Potter Valley Mill* (1990 song), 65; Redwood Summer actions, 73; Redwood Summer bombing, 68–71

class: consciousness, 63; ideological dimensions of, 42–43; as non-deterministic, 16, 105; "radical" versus "fundamentalist" ecology and, 21–23; and social appropriation of nature, 184; tensions,

conflicts, contradictions of, 15, 43.
  See also Bookchin, Murray
class environmentalism, xlvii. *See also*
  eco-socialism; red/green alliances
class struggle: ethical, cultural (and
  economic) rebellions, 43–44. *See
  also* anticapitalist struggle; work,
  abolitionism
CLC (Canadian Labour Congress),
  149–52
CNT. *See* Confederación Nacional
  del Trabajo, Spain; Confédération
  Nationale du Travail, France
COINTELPRO (Counter Intelligence
  Programs, FBI, US), 98–100
commodification, processes of, xxx
Common Cause, 158
commons: (re)constitution of, 106,
  185
communism: principles of, xxiv–xxv
community: base building over individual heroism, 118–19
Confederación Nacional del Trabajo,
  Spain, green syndicalism in, li;
  green syndicalists and, lvi; Libertarian International Solidarity
  network of, lii; Spanish Revolution,
  xlix
Confédération Nationale du Travail,
  France: green syndicalism in, li;
  Libertarian International Solidarity
  network of, lii
consumerism, 4, 31, 167–68; green,
  26, 27
corporatism. *See* green corporatism
CUPE (Canadian Union of Public
  Employees): CUPE 3903 (York
  University), 137, 139, 140–41;
  CUPE-Ontario, denunciation of
  black bloc, 148–50, 161–62

dark green ecology, xxxiv, xxxviii, 26
déclassé groupings, 165, 175–78. *See
  also* marginality
decomposition, labor movement:
  1980s to present, xxxi–xxxii
deep ecology: Judi Bari and ecofeminism, 89–92; and hostility to class
  struggle analyses, xxxviii, 173;
  misanthropy and, 75n17, 92, 173;
  philosophy of, 30, 59; as radical,
  rooted, 28; syndicalist, deep-green,
  184. *See also* fundamentalist ecology
deskilling, 115
dialectics, 21
direct action: "mass," disruptive, 162;
  practices of marginals, 176–78;
  as strategy (versus statist, "legitimate"), xxxiv; syndicalist tactics,
  working-class, l; vehicle picket
  around Ford plant (1945), 136,
  162; workshops on, 154
duality: community/workplace, 105–
  6; overcoming essentialist, xxxvii,
  10, 15–16, 92; society/nature, 9,
  24, 106, 180. *See also* jobs versus
  environment

Earth First!: deep ecology of, 59; early
  alliance with IWW, liv–lv; emergence of, 58; philosophy, tactics,
  59; wilderness fundamentalism,
  59–61. *See also* Local 1
*Ecodefense: A Field Guide to Monkey-
  wrenching* (Foreman), 66
ecofeminism, 82, 89–93. *See also* Bari,
  Judi, feminism of
ecology, radical: fundamentalism
  within, 21–22; humans embedded
  in nature, mutuality, 27–29;

ecology, radical (*cont.*): relationships to state, social movements, 26–27. *See also* fundamentalist ecology

eco-socialism: commitment to productivism, 48; "light green," limitations of, xlv–xlvi, 44–46; Marxian influences, xlvii, 48–49. *See also* red/green alliances

ecotage, 116–20. *See also* sabotage; tree-spiking

EF! *See* Earth First!

Electrical Trades Union: green bans of, lii

emancipation, 129, 165, 166, 186

endangered species, lii, 50

environmental movements: multiplicity, complexity of, 25

essentialism, 10

essentialist duality: Judi Bari's rejection of, 92

factories, factory system: decommissioning, dismantling of, 168–69

fascism: green, 29, 37, 173; Spanish resistance to, xlix

FBI (Federal Bureau of Investigations, US): lawsuit over Redwood Summer bombing, 96–98; Redwood Summer bombing, 68–71. *See also* COINTELPRO

feminism: anarchist influences in second wave, 88; anarcho-syndicalist organization and radical, 87; Judi Bari and, 89–92; "housewife" analogy of working class struggle, 40. *See also* ecofeminism

flying squad(s): CAW national clampdown on, 143–45; of CUPE 3903 (York University) against deportations, 137; formation, structure of, 133–37; and Greenpeace workers lock-out, 141; importance of autonomy in, 147, 154; international, 134, 136; mock eviction of finance minister, 143; origins in CIO 1930s strikes, 136; strike against Falconbridge mining, 137; structure, 133, 135; support for hotel workers, 139, 140–41

Ford: 1945 strike against, 136, 162

Foreman, Dave: Bookchin's criticisms of, 106; neo-Malthusianism of, 34, 60; on workers, 23

Fosterism (in unionism, boring from within), 131

fundamentalism, wilderness, 59–61; anti-labor narratives in, 35–37; moralism of, 33–34, 37–39; racism and misanthropy in, 34; as utopian, simplistic, 168. *See also* deep ecology; neo-Malthusianism

fundamentalist ecology, 29, 33–35, 39

"futures in the present," 186

G8/G20 meetings, Toronto (2010): opposition to, 147–56

Georgetti, Ken, 150–52

German Green Party, 39–40

Gestalt switch, 170

globalization: alternative, xxxiii, 1, 7–8, 148

global warming: differing perspectives based on control of production, xlii; industrialism as "socialization of nature," 168

Greater Toronto Workers' Assembly (GTWA), 155–58

green "bans," li–lii, 116, 131
green corporatism, xxxiii, 25
"green jobs" strategy: failures of, xxvi
Green Party: German, 39–40
Greenpeace: acceptance of existing structural relations, xxxvii; author's membership in, x, xiii; Judi Bari bombing investigation, 71; boat corralled by loggers, xxxv; canvasser's lockout (Toronto, 2003), 141–43; "hijacking" local campaigns, 171; social composition, upwardly mobile, x–xi, 174
green socialism. *See* eco-socialism
green syndicalism: no totalizing discourse of, 184–85; rejection of hierarchical, centralized, bureaucratic structures, 131; against vanguardism, 160–61; workplace control and, 113–14
GTWA. *See* Greater Toronto Workers' Assembly
Guarasci, Richard and Gary Peck: community/workplace integration, 105–6; liberative shop-floor political culture, 113, 114–16, 166

Hargrove, Buzz, 143–44
Headwaters Forest, 73
health and safety: workplace democracy, 114–15
hegemony, discourses of: consumerism, growth, resourceism, 26–28
hierarchies: confronting/breaking down, 92
highway blockades, xiii, 144
hotel workers: autonomous organizing, 138–41

Hurwitz, Charles, xxviii, lv. *See also* Maxxam Corporation

industrialism: difficulties recovering from, 46, 122, 167, 168–71
Industrial Workers of the World. *See* IWW
IWW (Industrial Workers of the World): abolition of class system via general strike, 125; class war and, 80; depiction of bosses as eco-terrorists, 79; four-hour day, shorter work week demands, 124, 167; greened preamble adopted, liii; history, basis of unity, organizational principles, xlix–l, 87, 131; squeegee workers in Vancouver, 154; strike tactics, disruption of work hierarchies, 108–9, 116; women, feminism, and, 87. *See also* Earth First!; Local 1

jobs versus environment: discourses of, xxiv, xxxvi, xlv, 57, 102, 106, 131, 181, 183

Kaiser Aluminum, strike against (1998–2000), xxviii, lv
Keynesianism: as labor's postwar compromise, xxix, xlii, xlvi, 30, 32, 40, 130, 175. *See also* welfare state
Kornegger, Peggy, 88

labor council: solidarity alliances, xii, 142–43, 154. *See also* Greater Toronto Workers' Assembly

Laclau, Ernesto: antagonism in capital-
    ist relations of production, 12–13
Laclau, Ernesto and Chantal Mouffe:
    beyond orthodox Marxian dualism,
    totality, 7, 15–17; social appropria-
    tion of production, 13–14, 165;
    on subversion, 80, 173–74, 180;
    welfare state capitalism, xxxi
law: rule of, 153; state capitalist, favors
    employers, 148, 161–62
liberalism: ecological personal conver-
    sion, xlii
libertarianism, 49; and Judi Bari's
    unionism, 86–88; liberty, 186;
    municipalist, 85n19; solidarity
    network formed (2001), lii. See also
    emancipation
libertarian socialism, xxvii, 49. See also
    anarcho-syndicalism; red/green
    alliances, 102
Local 1 (IWW and Earth First! alli-
    ance), xxxviii–xxxix, 61, 63–65;
    alliance building, 93–96; femini-
    zation of, 86; formation of, 58,
    76–77; politics of, 77–80, 86, 173;
    tree-spiking and, 116–18. See also
    Redwood Summer
Luddites, 119

Malthus, Thomas, 60. See also
    neo-Malthusianism
Manes, Chris, 75, 91
marginality: organizing and direct
    action practices in, 49, 94, 174–78,
    186; social scarcity, austerity, and, 32
Marx, Karl: analysis of capitalism, xxiv
Marxism: autonomous, 82; ecology
    and, xliv–xlvii; as overly "total-
    izing," economistic, 7, 14–17; as

reductionist, 10; working class as
    agent of social transformation,
    8–10. See also eco-socialism
Maxxam Corporation (logging), lv,
    62, 72, 78
Metropolitan Hotel Workers Commit-
    tee (MHWC), 138–41
migrants: defense of, 137–38, 145;
    and 1995 framers' strike, 136;
    poor working conditions of, 138-
    39; racism against, 34, 139
misanthropy: Judi Bari's article
    against, 75, 91–92; of deep ecolo-
    gists, 34–35, 173
misogyny, 70, 75
Miss Ann Thropy, 61. See also Manes,
    Chris
Monkey Wrench Gang, The (Abbey),
    59n1
monkeywrenching, 59, 66, 117. See
    also sabotage
moralism, 36–39; rejection of, 83,
    107, 148
Mouffe, Chantal: on commodification
    of social life, 30; critique of class
    interests, 11–12, See also Laclau,
    Ernesto and Chantal Mouffe
mutual aid, mutuality, xxvii, 48, 53,
    85, 157, 168, 170
myth: social conceptions of, xli, l,
    125, 184. See also Sorel, Georges
mythopoetics, 24–25, 172–73; eco-
    tage as disruptive, 116

NAFTA (North American Free Trade
    Agreement), xxxii, 144
nature: contextualization, compet-
    ing discourses of, 38, 178–84;
    dualism with humans/society, 9,

24, 92; with "environment" as its brand name, 31; fundamentalism, hard primitivism of, 37–39; global warming as "socialization" of, 168; social appropriation of, 184–85; unfixed, as site of antagonisms, 25–27. *See also* scarcity

neighborhoods. *See* regionalism

neoliberalism: austerity, social scarcity, 32

neo-Malthusianism, xxxix, 34–35, 60–61

New Democratic Party (NDP) (Canada), 132

new social movements: class, social transformative potential in, 2–8; Marxist economism, criticisms of, 8–11; postmodernist skepticism of unity, xxxv–xxxvi; problems of convergence and solidarity in, 14–18; similarities with twentieth-century French revolutionary syndicalism, xlviii; theories and practices of, 6, 48–49, 158

9/11. *See* September 11, 2001

North American Free Trade Agreement (NAFTA), xxxii, 144

Oakland police: lawsuit against, 73n15, 96–100; Redwood summer bombing, 69–71. *See also* COINTELPRO

OCAP (Ontario Coalition Against Poverty), 140, 143, 144

OFL (Ontario Federation of Labour), 149–50, 160

oil industry: public subsidies toward, xiv, xxxiii. *See also* Alaskan Wildlife Refuge

One Big Union, 87. *See also* IWW

Ontario Days of Action (1990s), 137

Ontario Federation of Labour (OFL), 149–50, 160

oppression: relations of, 25

overpopulation, 75, 91n25

parody, irony, and satire, 80

Peck, Gary. *See* Guarasci, Richard and Gary Peck

Pelloutier, Fernand, 107

Pepper, David, xlvi, xlviii, li, 102

pipelines (oil, gas), xiii, lii

politics: nature of struggles, 182

post-scarcity, 50. *See also* scarcity

postwar accommodation, xxxi. *See also* Keynesianism

pranksterism: IWW-EF! use of mockery, 80–81

Precarious Workers Network, 134

precarity, xlix, 134, 159, 161, 174–75; marginality and blue-collar workers, 174–75. *See also* marginality

proletariat, 9; as abstraction, 105; neo-proletariat, 124, 175; overcoming divisions within, 87–88, 109

propaganda by deed, 120

property: destruction, 148; problems of private, 76

prostitutes union, 87n21

public/private separation, 76, 115

Purchase, Graham, 87n21, 88, 114, 168, 169, 172

racism, 34, 82, 139

radicalism: class and, 29, 39; ecological and political, 27–29, 49, 184

rank-and-file committees, 133–41;
autonomy crucial to, 158–59. *See
also* Greater Toronto Workers'
Assembly
red/green alliances, li, lv; anarcho-
syndicalist and libertarian socialist
origins of, xlvii–xlviii; tree-spiking
denounced within, 66. *See also*
eco-socialism
Redwood Summer, xxviii, 67–74
regionalism: local level eco-defense,
170–72
Remaking Society (Bookchin), 55

sabotage: Earth First! and IWW "ecotage," 116–20; Earth First! tactics
and, 59; IWW and guerilla tactics,
109; song about, 65; timber workers and Earth First!, 66
satire: IWW use of mockery, 80–81
scab labor, lv, 131
scarcity, 29; social versus natural, austerity measures, 29–32, 35, 55. *See
also* fundamentalist ecology
scission (ecologic, metaphorical), 81,
174
Seattle: 1999 demonstrations, xxviii
self-management. *See* workers' control
September 11, 2001, xxxiii, 99, 101,
138
Sessions, George, xxxviii
social ecology: "post-industrial values" and, 22; in practice, in Spain,
li. *See also* Bookchin, Murray
social myth. *See* myth
social relations: commodification of,
xxx; transforming, xxv– xxvi, 162,
164–67

social scarcity. *See* scarcity
social totality: criticisms of, 16
solidarity: across movements, xxviii,
xxxv, lv, 12, 58, 132; plurality,
14–18; rifts between labor and eco-
activists, xxiii, 23, 24, 63
solidarity unionism, 138, 140, 142,
153, 154. *See also* rank-and-file
committees
Sorel, Georges, xli, l, 107, 179, 184.
See also myth
South Fraser Perimetre Road, blockade during construction, xiii–xiv
Spain: ecology and CGT (Confederación General de Trabajadores), li;
CNT (Confederación Nacional del
Trabajo), xlix
species: threats to, lii, 50
squatting, 175
Steelworkers, xxviii, lv, 143
strike(s): capital, xlv, 96, 112; framers',
136; general, l, 83, 125, 137, 162;
importance of capacity to, 57, 102,
109, 131, 159; IWW and, xlix;
Kaiser, lv; support for, 133–34,
154; wildcat, 116, 146. *See also* flying squad(s); myth
Sugarloaf EF!: misanthropy and,
74–75
Sweeney, John (AFL-CIO president),
xxxiii
Sydney, Australia, li–lii, 132–33
syndicalism: anarchist or anarcho-syndicalism, xlix, 87–88, 102; Bookchin's antisyndicalism, 103–6;
CNT, Spanish, French, xlviii–xlix,
88; historical theories of, 106–9;
importance of autonomy to, 81–82;
origins of term "syndicalisme,"

xlviii; revolutionary, l. *See also*
anarcho-syndicalism; green syndicalism; IWW

Tabuns, Peter, 142
Teamsters and Turtles alliance: collapse, xxvii, xxxiii, xxxvii, lvi, 132;
formation, xxvii, xxviii, xxxii
timber workers, organizing, 52,
63–68, 77–78, 96, 117–19
trade unionism. *See* unionism
transformation: social/political tasks
of, 169, 173–74
tree-spiking: EF!/IWW debate over,
66, 75, 117–18

UAW (United Auto Workers): against
improved fuel efficiency, xxxiii;
strike against Ford (Windsor,
1945), 136, 162
underground movements: relationships with above-ground movements, 118–19. *See also* sabotage
unionism: business, 131–32, 145, 158;
hierarchical structures in, 87; two-
carders, 133. *See also* solidarity;
solidarity unionism
unionization: corporatism within,
xxxiii
unions: bureaucrats versus rank-and-
file responses to G20 meetings
in Toronto, 147–53; corporatism
within, xxxiii; debates at G20 over
property destruction, 147–53; insti-
tutionalization and co-optation by
capital, 30. *See also* Keynesianism
United Auto Workers. *See* UAW

United States: economy of, xxxvii
utopian ecology, xxxviii–xxxix, xl–xli
utopianism: dark green ecologically,
light green socially, xli; versus
industrial toxins, 168; restrictions
of, 170

vanguardism, xxxvii, 160, 161; as
dead end, 160; of despair, 37
voluntarism, 37–39

Watson, Paul, 60; anti-worker
commentary, x, 35–36; neo-
Malthusianism of, 60; on tree-
spiking, 117–18
Watson, Steve (CAW), 145
welfare state, xxxiv
wilderness fundamentalism. *See* fundamentalist ecology
wilderness: as anti-machine, 182–83.
See also nature
Windsor: CAW flying squads, 136,
144; Labour Council, Environmental Committee, xii, 47; UAW strike
against Ford (1945), 136, 162
Wobblies. *See* IWW
women: labor exploitation, 90. *See also*
Bari, Judi, feminization of Earth
First!; ecofeminism
work: abolitionism, 123–25, 127–28;
hierarchies and disruption of, 115–
16; refusal, 186; revolts against
long hours, 120–21, 124–26
workers' control, 111–15, 123;
Bookchin's critique of, 104; over
dismantling of factories, industrialism, 169–70

working class: as agents of change, 21; capitalist offensives against self-organization of, 159; against essentializing of, 10–18; as "housewife" to industrial capitalism, 40

workplace democratization, organization, 104–5, 113, 129, 130n1, 165; agitation for health and safety, 114–16; in dismantling industrial capital, 170